EMDR AND THE
ENERGY THERAPIES

www.emofree.com
www.energypsych.org
www.unsheesforsuccess.com
www.BeFreeFast.com

EMDR AND THE ENERGY THERAPIES

Psychoanalytic Perspectives

Phil Mollon

KARNAC

LONDON   NEW YORK

First published in 2005 by
H. Karnac (Books) Ltd.
6 Pembroke Buildings, London NW10 6RE

British Library Cataloguing in Publication Data

A C.I.P. for this book is available from the British Library

   ISBN 1 85575 376 6

Edited, designed and produced by The Studio Publishing Services Ltd, Exeter EX4 8JN

Printed by Hobbs the Printers Ltd, Southampton

10 9 8 7 6 5 4 3 2 1

www.karnacbooks.com

CONTENTS

For Hawkie,
... Bridging the worlds ...
the Shamanic and the Psychoanalytic

ABOUT THE AUTHOR

Phil Mollon is a member of the Independent Group within the British Psychoanalytical Society. He is also a clinical psychologist, and trained in psychotherapy at the Tavistock Clinic. In addition, he is an accredited practitioner of EMDR, an advanced practitioner of meridian energy therapies, and a licensed trainee of EmoTrance™. His interests have included Heinz Kohut and Self Psychology, trauma and traumatic memory, dissociative states of mind, shame, and disturbances in the experience of self. He is on the Advisory Board of the New York Institute for Psychoanalytic Self Psychology. He works primarily within the British National Health Service, in Hertfordshire.

ACKNOWLEDGEMENTS

In exploring new and unconventional psychological therapies, the support and encouragement provided by others who are venturing into relatively uncharted spaces are vital. I am full of admiration for pioneers, such as Francine Shapiro, John Diamond, Roger Callahan, Gary Craig, Fred Gallo, Silvia Hartmann, and many others who have brought us these new methods. Each, in their own way, brings a level of dedication and courage similar to that shown by Freud a century ago. More locally, I would like to express appreciation to my colleague, Sid Singer, for his work in developing EMDR in the UK. His enthusiasm has been an inspiration to many. I am also grateful to Richard Reeves and Baya Salmon-Hawk for contributing accounts of their personal experiences with EMDR and EFT respectively. Finally, I would like to thank Sandra Hillawi for training me in energy psychology methods, and for her lucid and well-grounded approach to teaching the magic of EFT.

The AMT online
http://theamt.com
site

PREFACE

Most people who enter psychoanalytic therapy find that it is somewhat helpful. It provides a space for thinking and feeling, an opportunity to reflect upon current and past emotional experiences, and a psychological theatre within which the conflicts of early attachment relationships can be played out—and to some extent resolved. The analysand becomes more aware of deeper sources of desire, hope and dread, while at the same time gaining a familiarity with the mysterious language of dreams and the unconscious mind.

This is all good. However, it would surely be fair to say that traditional talking therapies, whether they be psychoanalysis, cognitive therapy, or person-centred counselling, often do not deliver the results that one might hope for—and the gains that do occur come about rather slowly (Leuzinger-Bohleber & Target, 2002; Roth & Fonagy, 1996). Usually this failing is explained in terms of the inherent difficulty in bringing about deep psychological and psychodynamic change—and the inevitable time involved in the process of maturation of the personality. We can become so familiar with these assumptions that we fail to acknowledge the stark truth that talking therapies are not particularly effective or efficient in their stated task of resolving dysfunctional patterns of emotion, thought and behaviour. Psychoanalysis can result in much insight—but deep change in feeling and behaviour can be slow to catch up. The inertia of the therapeutic process means that analysts and therapists can debate at length on meanings of the client's verbal material, and speculate interminably on what is going on between client and therapist. However, without clearly discernible information regarding progress in resolving the client's problems, there may be little grounds on which to select one hypothesis in preference to another. Moreover, there are some common psychological disorders, involving severe distress, that are often not helped at all by either psychoanalysis, pure cognitive therapy, or person-centred counselling. One of these is post traumatic stress disorder.

A high proportion of patients attending NHS mental health services suffer from some degree of post traumatic stress. The stress may result from turbulent recent events, or from interpersonal trauma in childhood—and usually both (Allen, 2001; Mollon, 2002a). Trauma, in its various forms, is increasingly recognised as forming the basis of a new paradigm for understanding psychopathology, particularly in combination with advances in neuroscience and the study of early attachment (Schore, 1994; 2003a; 2003b; 2003c).

However, it is only since the late 1980s that we have begun to understand post traumatic stress disorder and to develop effective therapies. Partly this development was driven by the realization in the USA that there were many veterans of the Vietnam War who were failing to recover from severe mental health problems resulting from their traumatic experiences. Dr Charles Figley edited a book in 1978, detailing the psychological problems of Vietnam veterans. More recently, he commented: "Fifteen years later, after hundreds of research and treatment articles on helping war veterans recover from psychological effects of the war, no one talked about cures" (Figley, 1999, p vii). Frustrated by this lack of therapeutic success, he and colleagues established the "Active Ingredients Project" (Figley & Carbonell, 1995) in an endeavour to stimulate research on better and faster treatments for PTSD. They contacted thousands of clinicians worldwide, asking for submissions of potentially effective new treatments. Two of these were EMDR and a method within the new genre of Energy Psychology, called Thought Field Therapy. Both were found to be greatly more effective and faster than traditional talking therapies, and both make use of eye movements.

EMDR and approaches within the emerging field of energy psychology (Hartung & Galvin, 2003) combine very well and procedurally have much in common. They are also compatible with much of the original insights of Freudian psychoanalysis, as well as later perspectives from attachment studies (Cortina & Marrone, 2003). It is possible to use EMDR and methods from energy psychology in ways that are informed by psychoanalysis. They are not superficial treatments, but reach profoundly into the psychosomatic system. Moreover, with the concept of "reversal of the body morality", developed by Kleinian-influenced psychiatrist, John Diamond (1988), as well as similar observations by other energy psychologists, we gain glimpses into the deep bodily processes of perversion, certain aspects of physical illness, and the "death instinct".

However, these methods, and their therapeutic success also raise important questions about some of the trends within psychoanalysis since Freud. For example, how important is the transference as a central vehicle of cure? Since the transference is not central to EMDR and energy methods, is it possible that the extensive focus on "transference", in many variants of contemporary psychoanalysis, is actually unhelpful, impeding the necessary therapeutic process? Could an excessive focus on the here-and-now interaction in the consulting room function to take attention away from the required task of processing trauma and conflicts embedded and embodied in both explicit and implicit memory? Has something important been lost in the widespread jettisoning of Freud's libido theory—an energy model, preserved within Kohut's work but not really elsewhere within contemporary psychoanalysis? Is it possible that, for effective therapy, the lengthy, unstructured and free-associative nature of psychoanalytic enquiry needs to be combined with a more focused targeting and processing of crucial emotional issues? Alongside the verbal expression of emotion, is it important also to attend to the experience of this within the body, an area largely neglected within psychoanalysis since the pioneering explorations of Wilhelm Reich (1949)? Can we develop a more comprehensive model of the psychosomatic system and the various therapeutic interventions that are possible, outlining the hierarchical levels of energy body, cognition and emotion, neurobiology, and the physiology of the physical body (Furman & Gallo, 2000)? These are some of the questions explored in the following chapters, which are designed to be read in any order.

Cautions

There are some obvious cautions, readily appreciated by well-informed clinicians, in relation to the ideas discussed in this book. Although EMDR does evoke memories that a client may not have thought of for some time, it should not be assumed that EMDR forms the basis of a "recovered memory therapy". It is absolutely not intended for that purpose. Newly emerging memories should always be treated with caution with respect to their literal or veridical nature (Mollon, 2002a). Similar cautions apply in relation to "muscle testing", as used on occasion within the field of energy psychology. While there is research supporting the validity of the principles of this kind of muscle testing in kinesiology and energy psychology (see the Summary in Chapter Eleven), the method is inherently subjective and intuitive, depending a great deal on the skill of the tester. It can be a guide, but should never be viewed as an entirely reliable indicator, either of the nature of illness or of pathogenic experiences. Finally, clinicians should not apply the methods outlined in this book unless they are satisfied they are competent to do so and have a good understanding of the psychopathology of the particular patient.

Use of the term "EMDR"

The term "eye movement desensitisation and reprocessing (EMDR)" relates to a method of treatment, based on theory and research, originally and carefully developed by Francine Shapiro, who described a clear eight-stage protocol for clinical practice. Others, including the present author, have used some of the principles and methods in ways that are different from these well-established and researched techniques recommended by Shapiro. The present volume describes the work of a clinical psychologist who has also trained in psychoanalysis, EMDR, and energy psychology. While the author regards his adaptation of EMDR as being essentially psychoanalytic, it probably would not be regarded as such by most psychoanalysts. Similarly, much of the work would not be regarded as EMDR if this were defined by Shapiro's eight-stage protocols. It is not recommended that clinicians use the

EMDR-derived methods outlined here unless they are fully grounded in the method of EMDR as taught within an approved training. Readers wishing to be informed of the conventional, evidence-based, practice of EMDR should consult the comprehensive volume by Francine Shapiro (2001).

CHAPTER ONE

Eye movement desensitization and reprocessing (EMDR), emotional freedom techniques (EFT), and psychoanalysis

> "If the clinical use of EMDR has shown clinicians anything during the past decade, it is that PTSD [post traumatic stress disorder] is an excellent benchmark for the problems that underlie most pathologies. That is, dysfunctional physiological encoding of perceptions is not limited to the obvious trauma victims but is actually a contributor to most problems that bring clients into therapy"
>
> (Shapiro, 2002b, p. 8)

What is (EMDR)?

EMDR is a therapeutic method, incorporating eye movements and other "bilateral" or "dual attention" stimuli, and involving a free-associative exposure to anxiety-evoking or emotionally distressing memories, thoughts, and images. Clinicians who become skilled in its use tend to find that it is greatly more effective than purely verbally based forms of psychological therapy. The method has adherents from a wide range of therapeutic backgrounds, including psychoanalytic, cognitive, behavioural, systemic, and neurobiological (Shapiro, 2002a).

Shapiro's discovery of eye movements

EMDR was originally a method of desensitization for anxiety, used primarily in relation to post traumatic stress disorder. It was developed by a clinical psychologist, Francine Shapiro, after she noticed herself experiencing some relief following the spontaneous performance of side-to-side eye movements during a period of stress. She conducted a controlled study (1989a) and a case study (1989b), which supported her hypothesis that eye movements were related to desensitization of traumatic memories. From this observation, Shapiro developed a therapeutic protocol incorporating deliberate eye movements. This strategy, of deliberately undertaking actions that are often done spontaneously, is a recurrent feature of Shapiro's development of EMDR. In this way it builds upon the natural healing processes of the mind and brain. Eye movements turned out to be an extremely effective means of desensitization. It was taken up by Joseph Wolpe, one of the founders of behaviour therapy (Shapiro, 2002a, p. xix), and his report of therapeutic success with the method (Wolpe & Abrams, 1991) helped to attract wider interest. However, Shapiro discovered that EMDR also led to spontaneous change in the person's dysfunctional thoughts—their trauma-related cognitions. Rather astonishingly, eye movements appeared to bring about a radical reappraisal of the trauma and the person's view of self. As a result, Shapiro added the word "Reprocessing" to the name of the method—and thus placed it beyond the realm of a purely behavioural desensitization therapy. Later, Shapiro recognized that the method brings about a general accelerated processing of emotional information. She also discovered that the effect is not reliant upon eye movements, but can occur using any kind of bilateral stimulation, whereby the two sides of the body or sense organs are stimulated alternately— presumably thereby stimulating the two cerebral hemispheres. For these reasons she subsequently regretted the name she had given the method, preferring a term such as "adaptive information processing", but the original has stuck. Emotion processing, facilitated by bilateral stimulation, appears to bring about changes at a neurobiological level (Levin, Lazrove, & van der Kolk, 1999; Stickgold, 2002), revealing a profound healing of psychological trauma.

Emotions are bodily events

EMDR is, in part, a bodily-based form of therapy, recognizing that emotions are indeed bodily events.[1] The client is asked to notice bodily sensations—"just notice that . . ." being the facilitating comment. Somehow, the act of directing attention to the sensation, while continuing the eye movements or other bilateral stimulation, tends to bring about a bodily change, usually in the direction of reduction of physiological agitation. Some emotional states—such as severe anxiety or panic—are intensely physical in their manifestation, with pounding heart, sweating, shaking, breathing difficulties, dryness of the mouth, etc. These are notoriously difficult to alleviate through talking therapies alone. In the case of post traumatic stress disorder, psychoanalytic discourse may bring about understanding but the tendency to re-experience the disabling physiological symptoms of anxiety will remain unchanged. EMDR addresses these somatic imprints of trauma (van der Kolk, 2002).

"Mindfulness"

The EMDR procedure leads the client to an observant stance in relation to his or her mental contents and processes. He or she is advised just to notice the thoughts, feelings, and images that pass through consciousness. This is rather similar to Freud's "fundamental rule" of free association. It is also somewhat akin to the practice of "mindfulness", recently developed as a component of cognitive therapy (Segal, Williams, & Teasdale, 2002) and of dialectical behaviour therapy (Linehan, 1993).

Changes in self-related cognitions

The EMDR practitioner is alert to the significant thoughts that a person has developed in relation to the trauma. Those that are particularly important concern beliefs, judgements, or negative attributions about the self. As the traumatic experience is processed, these begin spontaneously to change. The shift in the "negative cognitions" can be facilitated by choosing an appropriate "positive cognition". The latter must be a realistic, yet positively-toned, appraisal of the self. With further processing, these become increasingly accepted as valid. On first encountering EMDR I was puzzled by its apparent capacity both to *remove* excessive emotional reactions (desensitization) and to *install* positive cognitions. The underlying principle appears to be that EMDR always moves emotional processing in a positive direction.

Chains of associated traumatic memories

EMDR leads to the emergence into consciousness of associatively linked memories of trauma or emotional pain. A present-day trauma may have evoked seemingly exceptional or prolonged stress reactions because it is associatively linked with an earlier experience, perhaps from childhood. The more recent trauma cannot be fully processed until the earlier event with which it resonates has been processed. Often these chains of associated experiences will emerge spontaneously during bilateral stimulation, but they may be elicited more rapidly by a simple question, such as, "When have you felt like this before?" The sequence of processing involving tracking back through chains of linked emotional memories, paying attention to the bodily aspects of these, is greatly resonant with features of Freud's original approach to hysteria (Breuer & Freud, 1895d).

Does EMDR involve insight?

Although EMDR was not originally designed as an insight-based form of psychotherapy, insights and understanding of psychodynamic conflicts and their origin do emerge. To a large extent these emerge spontaneously in response to bilateral stimulation, but they can be facilitated by content introduced by the therapist—the so-called "cognitive interweave"—that would include the psychoanalytic interpretation. Shapiro has noted that a frequent feature of EMDR is the progressive emergence of an adult perspective regarding a childhood trauma. The childhood feelings of powerlessness, confusion, lack of control, and sense of inadequacy, begin to give way and are replaced by the adult's more realistic view.

Is EMDR a "stand alone" therapy?

Shapiro did not design EMDR as an entire psychological therapy. She viewed it initially as a treatment for desensitizing traumatic memories and reducing the intensity of distressing emotions in post traumatic stress disorder, and its proven effectiveness has been most clearly demonstrated in this area. However, other practitioners have explored its use with a very wide range of mental health problems. It seems to have some applicability in almost every area of psychopathology, but particularly where trauma or anxiety plays a part. Nevertheless, its effective and safe use depends upon considerable skill and prior clinical experience of the therapist. It would normally be incorporated within another more traditional therapeutic framework. While EMDR treatment of a single traumatic experience, in the absence of significant prior psychopathology, is often easy and rapid, more complex problems inevitably require longer and more complex work. A person whose childhood was characterized by repeated interpersonal traumas, rejections, and humiliations by care-givers, will have developed a personality structured around traumatic experiences. His or her adult behaviour will feature deeply embedded reactions designed to ward off the danger of re-experiencing unbearable mental pain, combined with recurrent surges of overwhelmingly negative affect on encountering circumstances that act as associative triggers to early traumatic experience. EMDR may usefully form part of the therapeutic work, but a great deal of more traditional psychotherapeutic or psychoanalytic activity will also be required.

Is EMDR an exposure therapy?

EMDR evokes psychodynamic, cognitive, physiological, and neurobiological phenomena, bringing about change at all these levels. How does it do that and what is its crucial mechanism of change? Research has demonstrated beyond question that the changes brought about by EMDR are substantial and cannot be attributed to placebo or non-specific effects (Carlson, Chemtob, Rusnak, Hedlund, & Maraoka, 1998; Davidson & Parker, 2001; Marcus, Marquise, & Sakai, 1997; Scheck, Schaeffer, & Gillette, 1998; Van

Etten & Taylor, 1998) Some have argued that EMDR might be essentially an exposure therapy, similar to other standard behavioural treatments involving exposure to anxiety-eliciting stimuli in order to bring about extinction of response through the principles of classical conditioning (e.g. Lohr, Lilienfield, Tolin, & Herbert, 1999). However, it is usually assumed that in such treatments the exposure should be prolonged, continuous and uninterrupted, without shifting from the target scene or stimulus (Foa & McNally, 1996; Lyons & Keane, 1989; Marks, Lovell, Noshirvant, Livanou, & Thrasher, 1998). All of these apparently necessary conditions are violated in EMDR's protocol of brief, interrupted exposures, and elicitation of free-association. — or calling up of images of

Are eye movements necessary?

The role of eye movements in relation to emotion processing was known long before EMDR was developed (Antrobus, Antrobus, & Singer, 1964), and Eden (1998) reports that she has "heard of versions of this technique being passed down in various cultures for thousands of years" (p. 330). Some studies have compared a repeated exposure method with the same procedure but with the addition of eye movements and found that this component produced significant decreases in levels of distress and psychophysiological arousal (Lohr, Tolin, & Kleinknecht, 1995, 1996; Montgomery & Ayllon, 1994). Siegel (2002) reports that when he used non-bilateral, or non-alternating sensory stimulation with patients who had previously shown positive responses to EMDR, they no longer experienced relief and relaxation. Studies of eye movements alone, without the other components of EMDR, indicate that these do have effects, such as decreasing physiological arousal and reducing the vividness of memory images (Andrade, Kavanagh, & Baddeley, 1997; Barrowcliff, MacCulloch, & Gray, 2001; Kavanaugh, Freese, Andrade, & May, 2001; Muris, Salemink, & Kindt, 2001; Sharpley, Montgomery, & Scalzo, 1996; van den Hout; Wilson, Silver, Covi, & Foster, 1996) However, other studies, involving a variety of designs and outcome measures, have produced equivocal results. Smyth and Poole (2002) argue that EMDR's focus on the trauma image, body sensations, affect, and beliefs is essentially that of emotion processing and cognitive elements of cognitive behaviour therapy, so that EMDR minus the eye movements "can be considered a parsimonious integration of all the core elements of old and new behavioural treatments" (Smyth & Poole, 2002, p. 159). As yet, substantial research on other forms of bilateral stimulation has yet to be carried out. Maxfield (2002) has summarized the current position regarding research findings concerning EMDR, including the role of eye movements, as well as indicating areas requiring further research. Those who are familiar with EMDR in practice are unlikely to be doubtful about the contribution of bilateral stimulation; sometimes they will have encountered the "whoosh" effect, as emotion floods out when eye movements commence.

Integrating left and right brain functions

Clinicians were not slow to recognize the possible connection between the eye movements of EMDR and rapid eye movement (REM) stages of sleep (Shapiro, 2001). Both dreams and EMDR are to do with processing emotional information, and the REM stages of sleep may be concerned with moving information from storage as episodic memory in the hippocampus to more generalized knowledge, or semantic memory, in the neocortex (Stickgold, 2002). One patient described this very clearly: she reported having noticed that after some sessions of EMDR she was no longer troubled by intrusive memories of specific incidents of childhood sexual abuse, but instead was left with just a knowledge that this was what had happened in her childhood; and in this way she felt free of her past. A further hypothesis concerns the facilitation of communication between right and left hemispheres, brought about by bilateral sensation that stimulates each hemisphere alternately. The hypothesis that eye movements are associated with activation of the opposite side of the brain was supported in work presented by Kinsbourne thirty years ago (Kinsbourne, 1972, 1974). Siegel (2002) points to the finding that people tend to look to the left when retrieving an autobiographical memory (indicating activation of the right hemisphere) and that flashback traumatic memories seem to involve intense activation of the right hemisphere (and the visual cortex), while the linguistic left hemisphere is deactivated. Factual and semantic elements of memory seem to involve the left hemisphere. Thus, the hypothesis emerges that the rhythmic bilateral stimulation brings about an activation of both hemispheres and thereby facilitates integration of different elements of memory, perhaps also allowing the formation of new synaptic pathways in place of the previous perseverative patterns of traumatic arousal. The facilitation of intercourse between the emotion-processing right brain (Schore, 2003a, 2003b) and the linguistic left brain, combined with the requirement that the client provide a brief verbal report at the end of each set of bilateral stimulation, seems likely to foster an integration of emotion and language—resulting in a story that can be told, rather than an experience to be endlessly relived like a waking dream.

A further perspective is provided by the argument that traumatic stress brings about brain disorganization, particularly involving a shutting down of the integrative pathways of the corpus collosum and anterior commissure, linking the left and right hemispheres (Krebs, 1998). The result is that logic and rational thinking cannot be brought to bear on the emotional experience, and the visual image and verbal representation of an experience (processed in the left and right hippocampus respectively) may not integrate adequately. Various cognitive dysfunctions may flow from this, and, in the case of children, learning difficulties may develop. Eye movements, rather similar to those used in EMDR, have been used to correct this kind of neurological disorganization (Dennison & Dennison, 1994; Krebs, 1998).

Implications for the understanding of psychopathology

Shapiro states:

> The central thesis of EMDR therapy is that the physiological storage of earlier life experiences is the key to understanding behaviour, personality, and attendant psychological phenomena. According to this view, the perceptual information of past experiences, both negative and positive, is conceptualised as stored in memory networks. Natural learning takes place as unimpeded adaptive

associations are made. However, if a trauma occurs the system can become imbalanced and the experience is stored dysfunction- ally. If an experience is dysfunctionally stored, it has within it the original perceptions, including disturbing emotions, and physical sensations that were experienced at the time. [Shapiro, 2002, p. 42]

This summary statement by Shapiro emphasizes the point that experience is embodied, rooted in physiology—perhaps calling to mind Freud's statement that the ego is "first and foremost a body ego" (1923b, p. 27). Freud's early investigations were of the body: his first patients were those with hysterical disturbances of body function, and his theorizing concerned neurobiological processes, zones of bodily excitation, and the bodily pathways of the libido. Freud hypothesized (in "Project for a scientific psychology", 1895) that biologically driven desire would, in the course of encounters with reality, give rise to pain or pleasure, and the organism would learn to avoid pain by initiating various defences inhibiting or diverting instinctual excitation. Through this process of adapta- tion, personality would develop. For Freud, as for Shapiro, psy- chopathology (and dreams) are constructed out of networks of memories; the original troubling memories of painful childhood experience being subject to strategies of avoidance, yet ever-ready to be triggered, with accompanying physiology, when an associa- tive cue is encountered. This is the psychodynamic mind. Therapy consists of accessing and reassessing, with adult awareness, the desires and the memories or phantasies of pain associated with them. Both EMDR and Freudian-based psychoanalysis do this.

What is energy psychology?

Energy psychology is the generic name for an emerging family of experimental rapid-effectiveness tools that utilize the body's energy pathways (meridian acupoints system), energy centers (chakras) and biofield (aura) to assist in addressing psychological, spiritual, mind–body, and peak performance goals. [Grudermeyer, 2003, p. vi]

This is the dawning of the new age in psychological therapy. Enjoy the sunrise. [Gallo, 2002, p. xii]

Origins

The term "Energy psychology" refers to a genre of therapies that link psychological and physiological distress with disturbances or blockages in the subtle energy fields of the body (Grudermeyer, 2002). Most of these therapies are inspired by the seminal contributions of psychiatrist John Diamond, who discovered the links between the energy meridians and emotions (e.g., Diamond, 1985) Usually the approach is for the client to stimulate acupressure points while holding in mind a particular aspect of distress or emotional difficulty. There are many variations, but the two most well known now are "thought field therapy" (TFT), and a modified and simplified version of this called the "emotional freedom techniques" (EFT). The former was discovered when a clinical psychologist, Roger Callahan, after months of fruitlessly trying to treat Mary, a patient with a long-standing, severe water phobia— "using every psychotherapeutic method I knew" (Callahan, 2001a, p. 7)—had a sudden inspiration "on a whim, and out of my own desperation" (*ibid.*, p. 8). Drawing upon his knowledge of Chinese medicine and the theory of the meridians of energy flows, he asked her to tap on an acupressure point under the eye while thinking of her phobia. Mary's anxiety had tended to be located particularly in sensations in her stomach, and Callahan knew that the point under the eye was the location of an end of the stomach meridian. After two minutes of tapping, Mary declared, in amazement, that the phobia had gone, and Callahan reports that two decades later Mary is still free of her phobia. Following this astonishing experience, Callahan began to explore the phenomenon and develop it as a therapeutic approach. Although the technique sometimes worked with remarkable effect, Callahan's initial success rate was "only about 3 percent" (*ibid.*, p. 10). Gradually he found that sequences of tapping points were required for most patients, and that different psychological problems required different tapping formulas or "algorithms". He also noted that the method, that he began to term thought field therapy, brought about physiological changes, and one of his outcome measures has been heart rate variability (Callahan, 2001b,c; Pignotti & Steinberg, 2001). As Callahan refined his method, its success rate improved greatly. One of Callahan's students, Gary Craig, designed a simplified universal tapping sequence that could be applied to more or less any psychological problem, and this was termed the emotional freedom techniques (Carrington & Craig, 2000).[2] Details of EFT and training materials can be found on Gary Craig's website: www.emofree.com

Disruptions in the energy field

One of the important implications of Callahan's and Craig's clinical findings is that emotional distress and disturbance may not lie essentially in the person's neurobiology, their traumatic memories, cognitions, internal models of relationships, persisting phantasies, and so on, but most fundamentally in their energy fields. The patterns of information in the energy fields then determine the recurrent reverberations throughout the psychosomatic system.[3] It is hard to escape this conclusion if the reports of extremely rapid and lasting changes, brought about by stimulating the energy meridians, are to be taken seriously. Thus, Callahan argued that the root cause of emotional distress is a *perturbation* in a thought field. This perturbation "contains active information (a quantum physics concept) of a highly specific sort—a subtle but clearly isolable aspect of the Thought Field—that is responsible for triggering the negative emotions." (Callahan, 2001a, p. 25). Similarly, Craig, in his teaching materials, presents the formula: "The cause of ALL negative emotions is a disruption in the body's energy system". This idea of information residing in the body's subtle energy field is somewhat similar to the concept of morphogenic fields, which provide a kind of blueprint for the organism, as proposed by some biologists. Sheldrake describes these as "self-organising fields of influence, analogous to magnetic fields and other recognized fields of nature" (Sheldrake, 1999, p. 258) and he sees these as having memory. Such ideas have been embraced by quantum physicist David Bohm (Bohm & Sheldrake, 1985), and Callahan, too, makes links with Bohm's theories of the "implicate order". The hypothesis of an organizing field of energy around the body, containing information, and capable of memory and evolution, provides a potential link between many diverse and otherwise puzzling phenomena, including telepathy and group learning (Hawkins, 1995; Sheldrake, 1985, 1988, 1999; Sheldrake, McKenna, & Abraham, 1998). It may also go some way to explaining the well-known but perplexing process whereby significant traumatic experience early in a person's life tends to be repeated later in thematically similar ways, often to an extent that appears quite uncanny. There are many radical implications of considering human relationships in terms of energy transactions (see Hartmann, 2003b, 2004). Another interesting and original idea is that the energy body/mind contains a template of the person as he or she would be if born into an adequately facilitating environment (Hartmann, 2004).

If the immediate cause of emotional disturbance is a disruption in the body's energy system, then it follows that this disruption is the primary level requiring intervention. A full reliving of the *contents* of a traumatic memory is not necessary, provided the energy disruption is released. Thus, although a memory, or a thought, or a phantasy, may trigger emotional distress, this is not a direct effect; the crucial intermediary is the disturbance in the energy body. The focus on this intermediary distinguishes EFT and TFT from other psychological therapies, including psychoanalysis, cognitive therapy, and EMDR. However, the energy approach may be helpfully combined with aspects of EMDR and other approaches (Benor, 2002; Hartung & Galvin, 2003; Lane, 2002; Weil, 2002).

The subtle energy field and the acupressure points

Although the methods of energy psychotherapy are very new, the ideas and knowledge are also ancient and are found in many parts of the world (Gallo, 1999). Subtle energy, known as *chi* in the Chinese system, and *prana* in the Indian yoga system, can be detected and measured by appropriate devices, such as Kirlian photography and the Coggins aura camera (Tiller, 1997). The subtle energy is thought to pass along fourteen main meridians, connecting with seven major *chakras*, or energy centres. Pert (1999, 2000) describes neurophysiological correlates of the *chakras*, which she hypothesizes are "minibrains", centres where electrochemical information is received and processed. Many forms of complementary medicine/therapy draw upon ideas of the energy fields. Acupuncture and acupressure have received significant levels of research support for their efficacy in relation to a variety of conditions, including mental health (Apostolopoulos & Karavi, 1996; Stux, &

Pomeranx, 1995). Moreover, the validity of acupressure points is supported by findings of a marked difference between these and other points of the skin in terms of electrical resistance (Cho, 1998; Cho & Chung, 1994; Liboff, 1997).

Precursors of energy psychology

There were two notable modern precursors of Callahan's TFT and Craig's EFT. In the 1960s, a chiropractor, George Goodheart, developed the method of "applied kinesiology" in which the strength of muscles is used as a test in response to various kinds of enquiries about health and illness. This approach came to be linked with the theory of the energy meridians and was developed in a variety of directions (see Krebs, 1998 for an informative account, also Durlacher, 1995). A little later, psychiatrist John Diamond (1979, 1985, 1988), whose background included Kleinian psychoanalysis, applied muscle testing to psychiatry and found that different emotional states appeared to be associated with different meridians. He treated emotional problems by using muscle testing to locate the relevant meridian and then asking the client to place a hand over the associated organ of the body and repeat an affirmation in order to correct the imbalance in the energy meridian. By systematically correcting disturbances in relevant meridians, he found he could rapidly unravel *layers* of unconscious psychodynamic conflict.

Psychological reversal and other obstacles

Diamond also discovered a phenomenon that was to prove vitally important in later energy psychotherapies: that people would very often react against their own positive intentions—a process he called "reversal of the body morality" (1988, p. 15), later termed by Callahan and Craig "psychological reversal", and thought of as some kind of polarity reversal in the meridian system. When reversal is operating, muscle testing gives paradoxical, or perverse, results—such that love tests as bad, and hate tests as good—and a wish to be ill or to die will be revealed. This clearly has some

similarity to the psychoanalytic ideas of resistance, negative therapeutic reaction, and the death instinct. I have found rather striking
instances of psychological reversal when using EFT with patients
who have been extensively abused in childhood. For these people,
relaxation is felt to be dangerous, like letting one's guard down in
a hostile environment; the relaxing effect of EFT then induces a
paradoxical increase in anxiety and general agitation. However,
there may be many and varied reasons and motivations that lead to
psychological reversal (Gallo, 2000).

Experimenting with muscle testing, and drawing upon the ideas
of Goodheart and Diamond, Callahan developed methods of coun-
tering psychological reversal, as well as identifying and finding a
treatment for a similarly obstructive phenomenon called the
"collarbone breathing problem"—also termed by other energy therapists and applied kinesiologists "neurological disorganisation"
(Walther, 1988). Another, later, observation was that in a minority of
cases a complete failure of the expected clearing of the thought field
appears to be due to the presence of some kind of toxin; when this
is removed, the normal rapid processing is able to take place. This
initially surprising idea perhaps makes more sense when it is
considered that the energy fields of the body may well be suscepti-
ble to interferences from toxins and, in addition, the process may
work in the opposite direction as well, so that some recent energy
methods are reported to bring about a reduction in allergy reactions
(e.g. Radomski, 2000, 2002; Scott & Goss, 1988; Tenpenny, 2002).
Callahan makes the point that Thought Field Therapy works so
rapidly and clearly that the therapist can more or less instantly
know whether the correct acupressure points have been chosen or
whether some other factor, such as psychological reversal, is interfering; this contrasts with traditional psychotherapy that works so
slowly and inefficiently that it is rarely possible to know with any
certainty whether the method or its focus is correct or not. He
comments:

> The reason conventional psychotherapy has such a poor track
> record is that it has been playing the "wrong game". The problem
> is not fundamentally in the cognitive system, in past experience, or
> in the brain or nervous system. It is in the Thought Field. [Callahan,
> 2001, p. 39]

Tuning the thought field

While Callahan emphasized the specificity of sequences of tapping, Craig developed EFT as a more universal sequence intended to cover all the points that might be necessary. Craig, drawing on his engineering background, uses an analogy of a car displaying a fault; one approach might be careful diagnosis; another might be to give the car a thorough service so that any fault will be thereby found and eliminated. However, what Craig does emphasize is the importance of tuning the mind to the correct and specific aspect of the emotional problem. EFT does not work if it is applied too broadly. Instead, relevant experiences and, sometimes, each emotional aspect of an experience, state of mind, or bodily sensation, must be identified and tapped. The aim is to try to identify the most important core emotional issues, and at times considerable clinical skill may be required in locating and exploring these. My own practice often is to spend considerable time in conventional verbal exploration, gradually identifying significant nuances of traumas, anxieties, and conflicts, and then to invite the client to tap on these, using the client's own words and phrases. If the correct focus is not found, the tapping may have no effect. So while each tapping sequence takes only seconds, complex problems may require many rounds of tapping as different aspects of an emotional situation are identified. Layering of emotions is also commonly observed, so that as one is cleared another emerges.

If not recognized, this layering of emotions can obscure the processing of trauma; after a round of tapping the person may report that the target experience remains at the same level of distress—but what has happened is that one emotion has been processed and now another similarly distressing emotional aspect has emerged. For example, EFT was being used to help a woman process a traumatic experience with her mentally ill son. After various emotional aspects, such as shock, confusion, anxiety, and anger, had been addressed with tapping, she reported that the experience still felt just as troubling to recall. However, on enquiring what now seemed the worst part, she said it was seeing her son immensely distressed and being unable to reach him. After tapping while tuned to this aspect, she again reported a high level of distress. Now she said it was to do with the thought that she was afraid of her son. This too was addressed with tapping. Still she reported a high level of distress. On being asked what particularly troubled her now, she said it was the thought that she was angry with her son and she felt she should not be angry with her own son. After tapping for this aspect she finally reported the event no longer felt distressing. This necessity of focusing or tuning the tapping to specific emotions or features of an experience distinguishes EFT from EMDR. The latter is able to bring about processing in a much more "broad sweep" kind of way; eye movements or other bilateral stimulation will move the processing along, from one emotional aspect to another. EFT may require more vigilance from the therapist in spotting the subtly changing aspects.

Sometimes EMDR may be helpful in generating the more specific aspects that can then be processed with EFT. For example, a woman reported feeling "tearful" when she thought about a serious road traffic accident that had left her with both physical and psychological difficulties. Tapping to the thought of "tearful" brought no change whatsoever, and she was unable to identify any other emotion. However, a set of eye movements quickly brought up the following thoughts and feelings: she was angry at the impact on her family; she was angry and sad at the fact that because of the need for further surgery she and her husband would have to delay starting a family; she was fearful of the pain of further surgery; she was angry that she was suffering all these consequences of an accident that was not her fault; she was angry that the other driver was probably unaware of what she was suffering. It was then possible to process each of these aspects with EFT.

Despite the importance of tuning to the specific emotion when using the energy methods, it is not necessary for the client to experience the full intensity of the distressing experience; it is enough for consciousness just to dip into the surface of the emotion while the tapping is applied. In this respect, also, it is unlike EMDR, which tends to take the client fully into the intensity of the target traumatic experience.

EFT and related methods often seem to work very well when applied to physical symptoms. While these obviously cannot directly cure tissue damage or serious physical illness, significant relief often occurs, especially if pain is partly due to tension and stress. Many instances of this are described on Gary Craig's website (www.emofree.com). On experiencing good progress in resolving emotional issues using EFT, a patient recently asked if it might help with her blocked sinuses that had been troubling her all week. As we tapped on the thought of "blocked sinuses" she began to laugh and reported a sudden sensation of mucus clearing. A second round of tapping left her feeling her sinuses had cleared completely. Such experiences are not uncommon.

Research reports

In addition to the many case reports in books on thought field therapy and the emotional freedom technique (e.g. Callahan, 2001a; Figley & Carbonell, 1995; Hartmann, 2002; 2003a; Lynch & Lynch 2001), there are a number of studies published in journals—particularly a special issue of the *Journal of Clinical Psychology* (2001, Vol. 57, No. 10). Thus, the application to a wide variety of clinical problems in a general psychiatric setting was reported by Sakai *et al.* (2001). Its use in relation to war trauma was described by Johnson, Shala, Sejdijai, Odell, & Dabishevci (2001). Heart rate variability as an interesting outcome measure for TFT was discussed by Callahan (2001b; 2001c) and Pignotti & Steinberg (2001). Swingle, Pulos, and Swingle (2001) reported on the use of EFT with road traffic victims suffering PTSD and described significant changes in the patient's brain waves, as well as experienced symptoms of stress. Reductions in seizure frequency in children diagnosed with epilepsy, following two weeks of daily EFT at home, were reported by Swingle (2001). Carbonell (1997) reported on the use of thought field therapy in relation to acrophobia. Criticism of some of these studies and scepticism regarding the theory of meridian therapies have also been expressed—e.g. Lohr (2001) and Herbert & Gaudiano (2001). One well-designed and detailed controlled study of the effectiveness of the emotional freedom technique has been published (Wells, Polglase, Andrews, Carrington, & Baker, 2003), demonstrating that a single thirty-minute session of EFT can significantly and lastingly reduce simple phobias.

More complex problems and reactions

EFT certainly works. The challenge is to apply it to complex psychological problems. This requires clinical experience and a knowledge of psychodynamics, psychopathology, and developmental processes, as well as an understanding of the layering and linking of emotional memories. As with EMDR, there are many subtly different ways of using EFT. The psychoanalytically minded clinician is more likely to use the method free-associatively, as a very rapid journey of healing through myriads of memories, fantasies, emotions, and strategies of defence. The emotional relief provided by tapping the acupressure points enables the client to make contact with potentially disturbing areas of experience without being affectively overwhelmed. The absence of emotional intensity means that psychic material can be covered very quickly.

Although EFT is usually remarkably relieving and non-distressing, and is welcomed by most clients, I have noticed more reactions of hostility and rejection of the method in the case of EFT than with EMDR. Partly the problem may be the startling effectiveness of a method that seems both simple and bizarre, and which is thereby so incongruent with people's expectations. While many clients will express astonishment and delight as their emotional distress is rapidly lifted, often wanting to smile and laugh, some react with anger and hostile bewilderment, occasionally even suggesting that the therapist is playing a trick on them. The person registers that something has happened but cannot make sense of it. He or she may also be unused to experiencing the body without the energy disruption, and be alarmed at the changes brought about so rapidly. These hostile reactions, which may contain elements of paranoid transference, as well as aspects of psychological reversal, can be addressed with further tapping and explanation of the process.

Other forms of energy psychology

There are many variants in the recently emerging field of energy psychology (see Hover-Kramer 2002, and www.energypsych.org). One of the most well known has been developed by acupressure practitioner Tapas Fleming—Tapas Acupressure Technique (TAT)

(Fleming, 1999; www.unstressforsuccess.com). This involves the use of a particular pose of the hands, applying one hand to pressure points at the end of the eyebrow by the nose and to the "third eye" *chakra*, while the other hand holds the back of the skull, in the region of the occipital part of the brain. The person then proceeds through a series of profound inner affirmations regarding healing of the target experience and forgiveness of self and others. Some people find this meditative approach very beautiful and indeed healing. A similar acupressure pose, known as the emotional stress defusion technique (ESD)—involving holding one hand against the two bumps in the forehead and the other hand against the base of the skull (frontal occipital holding)—was developed out of *Touch for Health* (Thie, 1979) and Stokes and Whiteside's *Structural Neurology* (1985) as a means of integrating unresolved emotional problems; it drew upon observations of the "neurovascular reflex", originally described by Terence Bennett (Martin, 1977; Walther, 1988). Another widely cited method is that of clinical psychologist Larry Nims, who calls his approach "Be Set Free Fast". Like Gary Craig, he developed a comprehensive tapping algorithm, but gradually simplified this further to the point of deriving an overall processing instruction to the unconscious mind (Nims, 2001; www.BeSetFreeFast.com) Other energy approaches focus on the *chakras* rather than acupressure points (e.g. Clinton, 2002; Millet, 2001). Asha Clinton's "Seemorg Matrix" work is a very comprehensive *chakra*-based approach addressing deep belief systems—matrices of core beliefs—deriving from childhood traumatic experience (Clinton, 2002). An approach that depends upon Sheldrake's ideas of morphogenetic fields is Attractor Field Technique (Hawkins, 1995; www.the-tree-of-life.com) In the UK, the most innovative and radical developments have come from Silvia Hartmann (Hartmann, 2002, 2003a,b, 2004). As well as outlining advanced patterns of EFT, she has also explored the perspective resulting from discarding assumptions about meridian pathways and instead focusing on softening and releasing existing energy patterns, in whatever form these might be within the energy body—a method she calls "Emo-Trance". This involves having the client notice and pay attention to the sensations within the body—rather like aspects of the EMDR approach and the "mindfulness" stance advocated in some other recent psychological therapies (e.g. Segal, Williams, & Teasdale,

2002). EmoTrance may be combined with the use of tachyon energy cells (Quinn & Hartmann, 2002; Wagner & Cousens, 1999). All these energy approaches point to possibilities of bringing about deep and profound psychobiological changes far faster than previously imagined.

And what is psychoanalysis?

It should be the task of a libido theory of neurotic and psychotic disorders to express all the observed phenomena and inferred processes in terms of the economics of the libido. [Freud, 1905d, p. 218]

... the final outcome of the struggle we have engaged in depends on quantitative relations—on the quota of energy we are able to mobilize in the patient to our advantage as compared with the sum of energy of the powers working against us. ... The future may teach us to exercise a direct influence ... on the amounts of energy and their distribution in the mental apparatus. [Freud, 1940a, p. 182]

Psychoanalysis is an energy psychology

Contemporary psychoanalysis has developed in many different directions, not all of which seem rational or therapeutically helpful (see Chapter 4). Personally I find the original theories of Freud to be more helpful and clear than those of most later analysts—with the exception of Kohut, whose writings were firmly rooted in Freud (Rubovitz-Seitz, 1999). Since my account of psychoanalysis below is somewhat different from many contemporary versions, I have liberally included quotations from Freud in order to indicate the authenticity of this perspective. I hope it will thereby become apparent that Freudian psychoanalysis was both a free-associative trauma therapy, like EMDR, and an energy psychology, concerned with disturbances in the flow and distribution of a subtle, yet elusive, excitation—the libido. This remained the case, I believe, alongside all of Freud's other discoveries and theoretical developments, such as the meaning of dreams, the mode of action of the unconscious, the concept of the life and death instincts, his distinction between traumatic anxiety and signal anxiety, and his structural model of the mind.

With the development of "object relations" theories, such as Fairbairn (1952), attachment theories, and the Kleinian theories of instinctually-driven relationship phantasies, it is easy to lose sight of what the editor of the standard edition of Freud's writings describes as the "most fundamental of all his hypotheses" (Strachey, 1962, p. 63):

> that in mental functions something is to be distinguished—a quota of affect or sum of excitation—which possesses all the characteristics of a quantity . . ., which is capable of increase, diminution, displacement and discharge, and which is spread over the memory-traces of ideas somewhat as an electric charge is spread over the surface of a body. . . . This hypothesis can be applied in the same sense as physicists apply the hypothesis of a flow of electric fluid. [Freud, 1894a, pp. 60–61]

Freud never ceased to be preoccupied with the distribution and flow of quantities of excitation, and the anxiety that may occur when these quantities increase beyond a tolerable level.

Disruption of association

This early paper, on "The neuropsychoses of defence", outlines Freud's observations and hypotheses that formed the basis of his later theorizing. He describes the impression that he and Breuer had formed of a breakdown, in states of hysteria, of the normal synthesis or integration of consciousness. Breuer had proposed that some individuals develop "peculiar dream-like states of consciousness with restricted capacity for association" (Freud, 1894a, p. 46), which were termed "hypnoid states". Ideas that emerged during hypnoid states were "cut off from associative communication with the rest of the content of consciousness" (ibid., p. 46). Psychopathology developed in these states was termed "hypnoid hysteria". Another form of hysteria was thought to occur when there had been insufficient abreaction of a traumatic experience, and was thus termed "retention hysteria". However, Freud considered that in other cases a splitting of consciousness occurs as a result of an "act of will" intended to banish a distressing idea from consciousness:

> their ego was faced with an experience, an idea or a feeling which aroused such a distressing affect that the subject decided to forget about it because he had no confidence in his power to resolve the contradiction between that incompatible idea and his ego by means of thought-activity. [Freud, 1894a, p. 47]

Freud argued that the ego's task of treating the incompatible idea as "non arrivée" cannot be fulfilled, but as an approximation of this goal the objectionable idea is robbed of its affect, so that it becomes a weak rather than a powerful idea and will thus "have virtually no demands to make on the work of association" (*ibid.*, p. 49). However, the "sum of excitation" has then to be channelled in some direction. In the case of hysteria it "proceeds along the line of motor or sensory innervation which is related—whether intimately or more loosely to the traumatic experience" (*ibid.*, p. 49). Further "hysterical attacks" will occur when fresh impressions break through the barrier or repression and provide the weakened idea with renewed affect. In the case of obsessional states, the troubling idea remains in consciousness, but the affect is separated from it. Separated from its affect, the idea will not press towards association, but "its affect, which has become free, attaches itself to other ideas which are not in themselves incompatible; and thanks to this "false connection", those ideas turn into obsessional ideas" (*ibid.*, p. 52).

Thus, here Freud formulated the problem of hysteria and obsessional states partly in term of a blocking of the normal associative activities of the mind. The impedance of association is brought about by a severance of the idea from the affect. Freud's treatment of the associative disorder was his novel technique of free association. The patient is asked to speak freely of whatever comes to mind, and then when disruptions in the flow of associations become apparent, the analyst endeavours to discern the nature of the inhibitions, or "resistances". This focus on an underlying *associative disorder* is startlingly similar to Shapiro's emphasis, within the EMDR framework, upon the need to facilitate the blocked associative processing and her hypothesis that the bilateral stimulation

provokes intercourse between the linguistic left hemisphere (corresponding to Freud's verbal "idea)" and the emotion-processing right
hemisphere (corresponding to Freud's severed affect). In many
ways Freud's concept of repression could be viewed in terms of an
inhibition of right brain/left brain communication.

The basis in trauma

A little later, in his "Five lectures" (1910a), Freud formulated his
psychoanalytic principle as follows: "our patients suffer from
reminiscences. Their symptoms are residues and mnemic symbols
of particular (traumatic) experiences" (p. 16).

Explaining his concept of "mnemic symbols" he refers to the
monuments and memorials found in large cities—such as the
monument designed as a memorial of the Great Fire of London. He
asks what one might make of a Londoner who stopped and shed
tears before the monument, then adds:

> Yet every single hysteric and neurotic behaves like . . . [such an]
> unpractical Londoner. Not only do they remember painful experi-
> ences of the remote past, but they still cling to them emotionally;
> they cannot get free of the past and for its sake they neglect what
> is real and immediate. This fixation of mental life to pathogenic
> traumas is one of the most significant and practically important
> characteristics of neurosis. [Freud, 1910a, p. 17]

Thus, Freud emphasized that neurosis has a basis in trauma—
and, by implication, that the problem lies in the failure to process
the trauma, locate it as an event in the past, and be able to live in
the present. This perspective may be closely compared with the task
of EMDR, which is to enable the intrusive traumatic memories to be
processed in such a way that they can be relinquished to normal
autobiographical memory, leaving the person free to attend to the
present.

In Freud's account it is apparent that the hysterical and neurotic
symptoms are not caused directly by the unacceptable idea itself,
nor by the ego's attempt to banish it, but by the disruption in the
normal flow of affect:

One was driven to assume that the illness occurred because the affects generated in the pathogenic situations had their normal outlet blocked, and that the essence of the illness lay in the fact that these "strangulated" affects were then put to an abnormal use. [Freud, 1910a, p. 18]

Freud points out that normally affect is expressed both psychically and somatically, but in hysteria the conscious experience of emotion is blocked so that the excitation is channelled much more along somatic paths.

Hysterical conversion exaggerates this portion of the discharge of an emotionally cathected mental process; it represents a far more intense expression of the emotions, which has entered upon a new path. When the bed of a stream is divided into two channels, then, if the current in one of them is brought up against an obstacle, the other will at once be overfilled. [Freud, 1910a, p. 18]

Thus Freud portrayed neurosis as arising from energetic blockages.

The energy of sexuality

Freud believed that the conflicts that give rise to neurosis always had roots in the energies of infantile sexuality, in what he described as the "widespread and copious but dissociated sexual life of children in which each separate instinct pursues its own acquisition of pleasure" (Freud, 1910a, p. 44).

Much of the sexuality of childhood is subject to repression.

extremely energetic repressions of certain instincts have been effected under the influence of education, and mental forces such as shame, disgust and morality have been set up, which, like watchmen, maintain these repressions. So that when at puberty the high tide of sexual demands is reached, it is met by these mental reactive or resistant structures like dams, which direct its flow into what are called normal channels and make it impossible for it to reactivate the instincts that have undergone repression. [Freud, 1910a, p. 45]

Remembering through transference

The adult does not consciously recall the sexual conflicts of child-hood that are causing him or her distress, but in the course of psycho-analytic treatment these are now relived in relation to the analyst:

> The patient . . . directs towards the physician a degree of affection-ate feeling (mingled often enough, with hostility) which is based on no real relation between them and which—as is shown by every detail of its emergence—can only be traced back to old wishful phantasies of the patient which have become unconscious. Thus the part of the patient's life which he can no longer recall to memory is re-experienced by him in his relation to the physician; and it is only this re-experiencing in the "transference" that convinces him of the existence and of the power of these unconscious sexual impulses. [Freud, 1910a, p. 51]

The trauma of helpless overstimulation

In his early writings Freud considered that some anxiety states could be a direct result of the inadequate discharge of sexual exci-tation—the *actual* (meaning "current") neuroses. Essentially the same result—the damming up of libido—would occur in the "defence neuroses", but as a result of repression. He theorized that anxiety was a transformation of libido. However, in 1926 he revised this view of anxiety, now proposing that infantile sexuality and aggression were unconsciously perceived as threatening danger, and that this perceived threat of danger was the cause of anxiety. The ultimate danger, Freud reasoned, was a state of helplessness in the face of mounting excitation, the prototype of this being the experience of birth. Freud described (1926d, p. 146) a series of anxi-ety situations corresponding to different stages of childhood: birth, loss of the mother, loss of the mother's love, fear of castration in retaliation for aggressive rivalry with the father, fear of the father (the internalized father). He theorized that each of these danger situations is perceived as threatening a return to the original trau-matic situation of helplessness in the face of mounting tension, and this threat created "signal anxiety" that motivates the individual to avoid the danger, whether its source is internal or external. Nevertheless, Freud still thought that anxiety could arise directly from unrelieved mounting excitation.

> It is still an undeniable fact that in sexual abstinence, in improper interference with the course of sexual excitation or if the latter is diverted from being worked over psychically, anxiety arises directly out of libido; in other words, that the ego is reduced to a state of helplessness in the face of an excessive tension due to need, as it was in the situation of birth, and that anxiety is then generated . . . Analysis of the traumatic war neuroses . . . would probably have shown that a number of them possess some characteristics of the "actual" neuroses. [Freud, 1926d, p. 141]

Although, later, Freud stated "We shall no longer maintain that it is the libido itself that is turned into anxiety . . ." (1933a, p. 94), he still considered that anxiety could arise "directly from traumatic moments, when the ego meets with an excessively great libidinal demand . . . on the model of birth" (ibid., p. 94). Thus, he reasoned that there was traumatic anxiety and signal anxiety when the danger of trauma was perceived: "I can see no objection to there being a twofold origin of anxiety—one as a direct consequence of the traumatic moment and the other as a signal threatening a repetition of such a moment" (ibid., pp. 94–95).

Negative therapeutic reaction

Just as the energy psychologists later discovered that sometimes the expected positive response to therapy does not occur, so Freud identified puzzling paradoxical reactions with some patients.

> There are certain people who behave in a quite peculiar fashion during the work of analysis. . . . Every partial solution that ought to result, and in other people does result, in an improvement or a temporary suspension of symptoms produces in them for the time being an exacerbation of their illness; they get worse during the treatment instead of getting better. They exhibit what is known as a "negative therapeutic reaction". [Freud, 1923b, p. 49]

Freud concluded that these negative therapeutic reactions that occur in some, but not all patients, were a result of an unconscious sense of guilt. By this he meant that the superego, or ego-ideal, is unconsciously directing aggression towards the ego. He viewed the superego as partially derived from an identification with the law-giving father, but also as containing the person's own aggression:

> ... the more a man controls his aggressiveness, the more intense becomes his ideal's inclination to aggressiveness against his ego. It is like a displacement, a turning round upon his ego. [Freud, 1923b, p. 54]

Thus, Freud considered that the negative therapeutic reaction occurs as a result of a reversal of the natural flow of aggression outwards. Instead of responding assertively towards an external other, the flow of aggressive energy is reversed.

Freeing the energy

Throughout Freud's evolving theorizing regarding the psycho-dynamic mind, the psychoanalytic method consisted of using free association to explore the patient's conflicts and blocked affects: i.e. to explore disruptions of association. Current inhibitions and anxieties were related to earlier infantile wishes, phantasies, and experiences perceived to be associated with danger. Anxiety was seen always as ultimately related to the threat of trauma—a state of helpless overstimulation. It was this threat that gave rise to repression. The repressed content could not then be integrated or processed through the conscious or preconscious mind, but would be cut off from the associative network. Through the analyst's interpretation of disguised derivatives of unconscious desires, the repressions and resulting disruptions in the flow of instinctual energy could be undone. The ego, which "struggles to master its economic task of bringing about harmony among the forces and influences working in and upon it" (Freud, 1933a, p. 78) is thereby helped to find reality-adapted ways of expressing the energy of the id.

Thus, Freud's psychoanalysis was the original therapeutic method of exploring and resolving the emotional conflicts of the mind, the layering and networking of memories of trauma, and the disruptions in the flow of instinctual energy. The method of investigating the disruptions of association was that of free association. Freud's approach was always concerned with the economic dimension—the distribution of quantities of excitation within the psychosomatic system. In these respects, psychoanalysis displayed elements found in both EMDR and energy psychology.

Comparison of EMDR, energy psychology, and Freudian psychoanalysis

All three approaches target traumatic experiences and bring about processing of these. The bilateral stimulation of EMDR seems to bring about a general facilitation of emotional processing. Free-associative access to the traumatic experience, or networks, and layers of experience, is an inherent component. When applying bilateral stimulation it is rather as if an accelerator pedal for the free-associative function had been pressed. The full psychodynamic complexity of the mind is revealed as EMDR proceeds. EFT, or other energy approaches, release the affect bound up in traumatic memories, just as does EMDR. However, unlike EMDR, EFT has to be focused rather precisely, in terms of the target thought, feeling, or bodily experience. Sometimes considerable exploration, or clinical intuition, is required in order to find the crucial aspect to hold in mind while tapping. One way in which EMDR and EFT can usefully be combined is to employ sets of eye movements in order to generate and reveal more of the various aspects of the emotional problem and then to target each of these with EFT, using the precise words, phrases and metaphors that the client has produced. Freudian psychoanalysis (but not necessarily all the contemporary derivatives) also seeks to locate and process trauma, particularly those from early childhood. Freud's psychoanalysis always focused on the traumas and developmental conflicts of early childhood—much more so than EMDR or energy psychology.[4] These conflicts and traumas are expressed and revealed in the transference relationship to the analyst; this is the principal arena in which they are to be brought to the client's consciousness and, as far as possible, resolved or modified. This is a slower process than that involved in EMDR or energy

psychology. However, it may allow a richer conscious understand-   ⋎
ing of developmental conflicts. Freud's perspective was concerned
with the distribution of energy and impedances in its flow—and a
psychoanalytic interpretation, which frees the analysand from the
grip of a hitherto unconscious conflict, does release energy. Where
psychoanalysis excels is in its capacity to track the surface symptom
or problem to its, perhaps quite unconscious, sources, following the
disguises and transformations it has undergone before being manifest at the surface of the mind. However, one limitation of psychoanalysis is that it cannot always bring about processing and   ✓
resolution of the traumas and psychodynamic issues painstakingly
identified through the method of free association.

Both psychoanalysis and energy psychology recognise paradoxical reactions that on occasion occur in place of the expected
recovery—in psychoanalysis called the "negative therapeutic reaction", and in energy psychology called "psychological reversal".
Such phenomena undoubtedly occur also during EMDR, but would
be processed along with every other psychodynamic manifestation.
The inherent bilateral stimulation and alternating movements of
EMDR may also function somewhat like the "cross crawl" (hand to
opposite knee) correction for polarity reversal, as used in applied
kinesiology (Walther, 1988), and thus EMDR may act as a continual
counterbalance to whatever factors within the psyche may oppose
healing.

Notes

1. The attention to bodily experience is increasingly perceived as an
    important component of effective psychotherapy. For example, Roz
    Carroll comments:

    All the major theoreticians in neuroscience are moving—in their
    different ways—towards recognising psychological process as
    fundamentally embodied . . . This is part of the cultural and scien-
    tific paradigm shift and is reflected in the growing interest in the
    role of the body in psychotherapy. Body psychotherapy, for exam-
    ple, includes the explicit use of the feedback from the body to the
    brain to enhance and clarify object relations. [Carroll, 2003, p. 201]

2. A similar, but somewhat less well-known approach was developed by Jim Durlacher (1995), termed the "Acu-Power" treatment.

3. It seems reasonable to suppose that recurrent early interactions with care-givers become patterned into the energy system. Psychoanalytic theories that emphasize object relations, or attachment, could be viewed as describing the establishment of information regarding patterns of expected relationships with significant others. Ponomareva (2003) explores the patterns of energy transactions, initially between mother and infant, and later between lovers. Of all post-Freudian analysts, Kohut most clearly described the way in which the child uses the care-giver to help regulate energy, this function being denoted by Kohut's term the "selfobject". Thus, Kohut described states of energy overstimulation (e.g. Mr Z receiving too many desperately wanted psychological gifts from his father all at once, represented by the dream of trying to prevent his father entering through the door [Kohut 1979]), understimulation (depleted self), and various states of undischarged narcissistic tension (Mollon, 2001).

4. Many contemporary psychoanalysts would argue that their approach is actually to focus essentially on the conflictual relationship patterns, the persisting phantasies, or internal models of relationships, as revealed in the present interaction with the analyst. Such a method emphasises the need to modify the relationship conflicts in the present, with relatively little concern for the significant early experiences that gave rise to these patterns of conflict. However, I do not believe this was Freud's view.

CHAPTER TWO

The waking dream: from Freud to EMDR

"Affective states have become incorporated in the mind as precipitates of primaeval traumatic experiences, and when a similar situation occurs they are revived like mnemic symbols"

complexes

(Freud, 1926d, p. 93)

"It would be not quite so bad if these memories were like memories of the past—but when I get them it is like they are happening now." Thus remarked a patient whose recurrent flashback memories of childhood sexual abuse had been triggered by the experience of giving birth. Her traumatic memories had more the vivid "here-and-now" quality of dreams than of memories located in a past perspective. Such flashback reliving of a past event, typical of traumatic memory, is like a waking dream. The events are experienced in the present, with a full sensory involvement, while the realistic awareness of the present is temporarily compromised. The reality-displacing experience of the flashback is a state of temporary psychosis wherein the present is invaded by the past. Conversely, the actual dreams of traumatized people may often be close to the reality of the past.

The "here-and-now" quality of flashback memories is also displayed sometimes in the form of bodily enactment. One patient's recollections of childhood abuse partly took the form of states of panic, followed by fainting, and then writhing around as if attempting to fight off a sexual assault.[1] She also experienced consciously many other elements of remembering the trauma, but the fainting appeared to be associated with the more severe episodes of abuse. It seemed likely that the fainting repeated states of dissociation or unconsciousness that she had developed during the original trauma as a defensive/adaptive response. Such remembering in the form of a sensory–motor enactment is a form of implicit memory (Mollon, 2002a). It is not experienced as a verbally accessible narrative within autobiographical memory, but instead is a sensory–motor repetition, often evoked not by intentional introspection, but by triggering cues inadvertently encountered (e.g. hearing or reading of sexual abuse reports in the media, having one's own child, re-encountering the scene of abuse, or a sight or smell reminiscent of the abuser). These are termed situationally accessible memories (SAM), as opposed to the verbally accessible memories (VAM) that form our autobiographical memory (Brewin, 2001, 2003).

Freud's views on repeating, remembering, dreaming, and the origin of the ego

Throughout most of his writings and theoretical explorations (from 1895 onwards), Freud envisaged a mind (or a psychosomatic system) that aimed primarily to unburden itself of internal tensions arising from instinctual wishes.[2] This "primary process" came up against the external reality that real satisfaction requires delay, attention, and selection of appropriate behaviour. These "secondary process" functions require the development of an "ego". Instinctual desires that would lead to pain would be blocked by the ego. These desires, travelling along their neuro-paths would be forced into side paths ("side cathexes)". These side paths would be particularly apparent during dreams and in the formation of neurotic symptoms. Freud regarded this process of blocking of the primary process by the ego as essential to health—its absence would "provoke a disturbance analogous to a traumatic neurosis" (Freud,

1920g, p. 35). In this interesting comment, Freud implicitly links his own predominant model of the psyche (in a state of inherent conflict between instinctual wishes and the external reality) with the model of a traumatized psyche. Current views on traumatized states of mind also suggest that failure of the movement of excitation along side channels—a failure of associative assimilation—is a crucial part of the disorder.

Another point of contact between Freud's model of the mind and that of a traumatized mind is that he emphasized the tendency for repressed wishes and experiences associated with pain to be repeated rather than remembered—just as the traumatic experience tends to be relived rather than experienced as memory. In Freud's psychoanalysis, as in contemporary treatments for post traumatic stress disorder, the aim was to help the patient shift from repeating, or reliving, to remembering, and, thus, to be able to function optimally in the present without excessive distortion by experiences of the past.

Transference as resistance to remembering

The distinction between remembering and repeating, commonly noted in discussions of post traumatic stress disorder, is close to Freud's original thoughts on transference as a resistance to remembering. It is clear that Freud viewed transference as what we would today call a form of implicit (non-verbal and non-explicit) memory. For example, he wrote

> . . . we may say that the patient does not remember anything of what he has forgotten and repressed, but acts it out. He reproduces it *not as a memory but as an action*; he repeats it, without, of course, knowing that he is repeating it. . . . As long as the patient is in the treatment he cannot escape from this compulsion to repeat; and in the end we understand that *this is his way of remembering*. . . . We soon perceive that the transference is itself only a piece of repetition, and that the repetition is a transference of the forgotten past not only on to the doctor but also on to all the other aspects of the current situation. We must be prepared to find, therefore, that the patient yields to the compulsion to repeat, which now replaces the impulsion to remember, not only in his personal attitude to his doctor but also in every other activity and relationship which may occupy his life at the time . . . [Freud, 1914g, pp. 150–151, my italics]

The action of repression

It is absolutely clear from above passage that Freud viewed transference as a form of unconscious (or implicit) memory. However,
the reason for the memory appearing implicitly, rather than explicitly and consciously, was the action of repression and resistance
functioning to avoid "unpleasure" and anxiety. Thus it was the
disguised expression of repressed material that was repeated in
the transference.

> We have learned that the patient repeats instead of remembering,
> and repeats under the conditions of resistance. We may now ask
> what it is that he in fact repeats or acts out. The answer is that he
> repeats everything that has already made its way from the sources
> of the repressed into his manifest personality—his inhibitions and
> unserviceable attitudes and his pathological character-traits. He
> also repeats all his symptoms in the course of the treatment. [Freud,
> 1914g, p. 151]

From repeating to remembering in psychoanalysis

In a later paper, Freud indicates that psychoanalysis aims to shift
the balance from repeating to remembering.

> He is obliged to *repeat* the repressed material as a contemporary
> experience instead of, as the physician would prefer to see, *remem-
> bering* it as something belonging to the past. These reproductions,
> which emerge with such unwished-for exactitude, always have as
> their subject some portion of infantile sexual life . . . and they are
> invariably acted out in the sphere of the transference, of the
> patient's relation to the physician. When things have reached this
> stage, it may be said that the earlier neurosis has now been replaced
> by a fresh, "transference neurosis". It has been the physician's
> endeavour to keep this transference neurosis within the narrowest
> limits: to force as much as possible into the channel of memory and
> to allow as little as possible to emerge as repetition. [Freud, 1920g,
> pp. 18–19]

In certain respects, transference could also be described as a
form of *procedural memory*. This term "procedural" refers to those
kinds of implicit memory that are to do with learning how to do

something, and thus covers a vast and varied range of human learning. Transference could be described in part as the patterns developed through childhood of learning how to respond and relate to others—how to "proceed" in relation to others.

However, Freud viewed transference as the patient's alternative to remembering directly his or her early desires, feelings, anxieties and other experiences, *necessitated by repression*. Thus, for Freud, transference was an implicit memory as a result of defence. Repression rendered the infantile feelings unconscious, so that they could emerge only in implicit form. Similarly, symptoms could be viewed as implicit expressions of repressed feelings—feelings that are not verbally accessible. However, in his "Project" (1895), Freud made clear that an additional factor beyond repression alone may intervene to produce symptoms (originally hysterical symptoms)—the action of displacement, whereby the original source of affect and anxiety is repressed and the affect displaced on to another element, thereby concealing the original source.

Freud's puzzlement over traumatic dreams.

In his paper on the death instinct ("Beyond the pleasure principle", 1920g), Freud considered puzzling features of traumatic dreams, whose nature posed a problem for his assumptions about the psyche being governed by the pleasure principle (albeit modified by the reality principle). He wrote

> Now dreams occurring in traumatic neuroses have the characteristic of repeatedly bringing the patient back into the situation of his accident, a situation from which he wakes up in another fright. This astonishes people far too little. They think the fact that the traumatic experience is constantly forcing itself upon the patient even in his sleep is a proof of the strength of that experience: the patient is, as one might say, fixated to his trauma. . . .

> Anyone who accepts it as something self-evident that their dreams should put them back at night into the situation that caused them to fall ill has misunderstood the nature of dreams. It would be more in harmony with their nature if they showed the patient pictures from his healthy past or of the cure for which he hopes. If we are not to be shaken in our belief in the wish-fulfilling tenor of dreams by the dreams of traumatic neurotics, we still have one resource

open to us: we may argue that the function of dreaming, like so much else, is upset in this condition and diverted from its purposes, or we may be driven to reflect on the mysterious masochistic trends of the ego. [Freud, 1920g, pp. 13–14]

Trauma acts as if it were a wish

Thus, Freud implicitly suggests that in some strange way trauma acts within the psyche *as if it were a wish*. It appears that trauma functions as a kind of foreign body within the mind. By definition, trauma implies some kind of breach of normal protective and regulatory boundaries. Perhaps we can draw a partial analogy with the activity of a virus—an intruder that hijacks some of the body's own functions. Or, to use another analogy, we might say that just as the body responds to a physical wound by surrounding the site of the breach with protective cells of the immune system so as to isolate and contain potential infection, so the psyche acts to isolate and contain trauma. This containment means that the trauma is not absorbed—is not digested—but remains active, albeit sequestered. Given any relaxation of the containing defences, it will again press towards consciousness and hallucinatory representation. Thus, the trauma will not be experienced as an aspect of autobiographical memory but will act as if it were an event taking place in the present—a waking dream.

Trauma hijacks the body

Traumatic experience does indeed hijack the body. In contrast to ordinary memories, which do not involve a re-experiencing of all the physical sensations and sensory modalities of the original event, the evoking of traumatic memory does involve a physical sensory reliving. Van der Kolk (2002), writing of the "subcortical imprints" of trauma, notes that

> Numerous studies have shown that people with PTSD, when confronted with reminders of the original trauma, have psychophysiological reactions and neuroendocrine responses indicating that they have been conditioned to respond as if they are being reexposed to the actual trauma itself [van der Kolk, 2002, p. 65]

It seems that once there has been trauma, the part of the limbic system called the amygdala is continually inclined to interpret any reminders of the trauma as a signal of its return, these conditioned emotional reactions being relatively indelible (LeDoux, 1996). Moreover, the normal "top-down processing" (LeDoux, 1996; van der Kolk, 2002), whereby subcortical brain responses and associated physiological processes are regulated, inhibited, or "screened" from conscious awareness (Damasio, 1999) by higher cortical areas (Freud's "ego"), cannot cope with the persisting responses to trauma. The higher cortical functions of words and verbal insight are of little use when the traumatized person cannot link their experience with language, perhaps due to the decreased activation of Broca's area and increased activation of the limbic system in the (non-linguistic) right hemisphere (Rauch *et al.*, 1996).

The primary process opposed by the ego

In Freud's original model of the psyche—"The project for a scientific psychology" (1895)—it is only endogenously arising wishes and biological needs that can press towards (disguised) representation in dreams. This is a psyche governed by the "unpleasure principle", modified by the reality principle. Endogenously arising impulses/wishes will press free-associatively towards discharge— the primary process—cathecting a pleasurable memory image, giving rise to hallucinatory fulfilment. This primary process is inhibited by the cathected ego (or "coherent ego"[3]), a system of continuously cathected neurones that acts to block the direct passage of excitation in order that more reality-based work can take place that can lead to actual (as opposed to hallucinatory) gratification. The "freely mobile" cathexes of the primary process are inhibited and channelled by the "bound cathexes" (or "tonic" cathexes) of the ego. Without this inhibiting function of the ego, the psyche would be overwhelmed with excitation pressing towards discharge, and functioning in the external world would be severely compromised. Moreover, the psyche would be, in effect, traumatized. Freud emphasizes this in "Beyond the pleasure principle" (1920g), as follows:

> ... the impulses arising from the instincts do not belong to the type of *bound* nervous processes but of *freely mobile* processes which

press towards discharge. . . . it would be the task of the higher strata of the mental apparatus to bind the instinctual excitation reaching the primary process. **A failure to affect this binding would provoke a disturbance analogous to a traumatic neurosis**; and only after this binding has been accomplished would it be possible for the dominance of the pleasure principle (and of its modification, the reality principle) to proceed unhindered. Till then the other task of the mental apparatus, the task of mastering or binding excitations, would have precedence—not, indeed, in *opposition* to the pleasure principle, but independently of it and to some extent in disregard of it. [Freud, 1920g, pp. 34–35, my bold emphasis]

Thus, Freud appears to be saying here that "mastering or binding excitations"—the maintenance of order within the psyche—is more fundamental than seeking pleasure and avoiding pain. He acknowledges that mastery through repetition can itself be pleasurable: "None of this contradicts the pleasure principle; repetition, the re-experiencing of something identical, is clearly in itself a source of pleasure" (*ibid.*, p. 36).

Further problems with the model of a wish-fulfilling psyche

However, Freud then points to further difficulties for his model of a wish-fulfilling psyche. He noted that often a patient's behaviour during psychoanalysis did not yield pleasure.

In the case of a person in analysis, on the contrary, the compulsion to repeat the events of his childhood in the transference evidently disregards the pleasure principle in every way. The patient behaves in a purely infantile fashion and thus shows us that the repressed memory traces of his primaeval experiences are not present in him in a bound state and are indeed in a sense incapable of obeying the secondary process. It is to this fact of not being bound, moreover, that they owe their capacity for forming, in conjunction with the residues of the previous day, a wishful phantasy that emerges in a dream. [Freud, 1920g, p. 36]

Thus, Freud indicates that the emotional pains and unresolved developmental issues of the childhood past press forward for expression in the present, disregarding to a large extent both the pleasure principle and the reality principle. Why should this be the case? Freud's own explanation was in terms of the compulsion to repeat, which he linked to his emerging impressions of "the conservative nature of living substance" (*ibid.*, p. 36), which he speculatively designated the "death instinct".[4]

> *It seems, then, that an instinct is an urge inherent in organic life to restore an earlier state of things* which the living entity has been obliged to abandon under the pressure of external disturbing forces; that is, it is a kind of organic elasticity, or, to put it another way, the expression of the inertia inherent in organic life. [*ibid.*]

Regardless of the merits of Freud's theory of the death instinct, it is clear that this work, "Beyond the pleasure principle", is essentially concerned with the problems of trauma, repetition, and the apparent seeking of pain, and reflects Freud's recognition that trauma challenges the assumptions of a pleasure-seeking psyche.

The psyche unburdening itself of tension: the importance of "side cathexes"

Freud's model of the psyche, beginning with the "Project", was of an organization tending to unburden itself of tension (Pribram & Gill, 1976). The immediate process of discharge, through the freely mobile cathexes of the primary process, would be inhibited by the bound or tonic cathexes of the "coherent ego", in order that real rather than hallucinatory satisfaction can be achieved, and also so that "hostile mnemic images" are not cathected—i.e. to avoid following a path that had previously led to "unpleasure". This defensive inhibition of the primary process of discharge is brought about by means of "side cathexes". By activating (cathecting) neurones at the side of the main pathway, the mobile cathexes are drawn away, in a manner analogous to the leaking of an electrical circuit—Freud's model of neuronal connection being in line with Hebb's (1949) later formulation that neurones that "fire together wire together". If the sources of tension were successfully discharged, either through eventual successful motor action in the world or through absorption and distribution amongst side cathexes, there would presumably be no need for experience to be repeated or re-enacted, since there would be no motivating force.

The origin of the ego

In the following passage, Freud describes the origin of the ego—the organizing and regulating executive of the psyche—through the process of learning the difference between hallucinatory satisfaction and real satisfaction of a wish. This development of the ego is based on the principle of avoiding pain or "unpleasure".

> . . . we find ourselves . . . before the most obscure problem: the origin of the "ego"—that is, of a complex of neurones which hold fast to their cathexis . . . The ego consists originally of the nuclear neurones, which receive endogenous (excitation) through paths of conduction and discharge it along the pathway to internal change. The experience of satisfaction has brought about an association between this nucleus and a perceptual image (the wishful image) and information of a movement . . . The education and develop-ment of this original ego takes place in a repetitive state of craving, in *expectation*. It (the ego) learns first that it must not cathect the motor images, so that discharge results, until certain conditions have been fulfilled from the direction of the perception. It learns further that it must not cathect the wishful idea beyond a certain amount since otherwise it would deceive itself in a hallucinatory manner. If, however, it respects these two barriers and directs its attention to the new perceptions, it has a prospect of attaining the satisfaction it is seeking. . . . It only remains to enquire about the origin of the two barriers which guarantee the constant level of the ego and, in particular, of that against motor images, which prevents discharge. . . . All we can say is that when this barrier was not yet in existence and when motor discharge took place along with the wish, the expected pleasure regularly failed to appear and the continuance of the release of the endogenous stimuli finally evoked unpleasure. Only this threat of *unpleasure*, which became attached to premature discharge, can represent the barrier in question. . . .
>
> Everything that I call a *biological acquisition* of the nervous system is in my opinion represented by a *threat of unpleasure* of this kind, the effect of which consists in the fact that those neurones which lead to a release of unpleasure are *not* cathected. This is *primary defence*, an understandable consequence of the original trend of the nervous system. Unpleasure remains the only means of education." [Freud, 1895, pp. 369–370]

The mind in intrapsychic conflict versus the traumatized mind

Thus Freud saw "unpleasure", or pain, as arising from endogenous excitation leading to motor discharge that fails to achieve gratification—thus pain arises from internal pressures. It is a model of the mind in (intrapsychic) conflict, employing defences against endogenous instinctual excitation. This is somewhat different from a model of a traumatized and violated mind (Mollon, 1996); the excitation of violation arises exogenously and is not the result of activation arising internally. In the psyche as envisaged by Freud in his "Project" and in "The interpretation of dreams"—the model that he held to essentially throughout his later theorizing—there would be conflict and disturbance only under the pressure of endogenously arising instinctual excitation, which cathects repressed wishes that could lead to "unpleasure". When the instincts were quiescent the psyche would be at peace. By contrast, what we find in the case of the traumatized psyche is that often it is when the person is relatively satisfied and lacking distraction that he or she begins to remember or re-experience the episodes of trauma. In reality, of course, a person's mind may be traumatized *and* in conflict.

A contemporary perspective on trauma, dreams,
and the primary process

Freud (1900a) described how the underlying wishes expressed in dreams may be displaced along chains of signifiers—the freely mobile cathexes of the primary process—so that the eventual manifest experienced dream may bear no resemblance to the original wishful idea. During sleep the repressive power of the ego is weakened, with the result that forbidden wishes are able to embark on their neuro-journey, but the ego is still able to block their direct expression and instead to direct the path of excitation along "side cathexes". Dreams would be the compromise result of the interplay between the primary process (with its mobile cathexes and pressure towards direct discharge) and the secondary (inhibitory) processes of the ego and its bound cathexes. Freud saw this as a process of "defence", functioning to preserve sleep, but this shift to less direct associative pathways is also the means of mentally digesting trauma proposed by Shapiro (2001):

The resolution of traumatic memories begins when activation of the memories of dysfunctional material leads to a chain of events different from that normally initiated by recall of the material . . . allowing the brain to identify and strengthen new associations to the traumatic memories and eventually to weaken the hold of the familiar, stereotypical associations and emotions that had blocked the adaptive resolution of the traumatic memories. [Shapiro, 2001, p. 327]

It is precisely the stereotyped and repetitive quality that characterizes traumatic flashbacks and dreams. Traumatic dreams tend to have a literal and direct link to the original experience. They have not been channelled along the less direct associative pathways. In Freudian terms one might say that traumatic dreams and flashbacks display a failure of the ego to force the primary process along the displaced associative pathways—the "side cathexes".

The function of dreams

While Freud saw the function of dreams only in terms of preventing the disturbance of sleep by the emergence of repressed wishes, a modern perspective would consider the possibility that dreams may have a variety of functions and determinants. One important function might be that of processing or "digesting" the emotional experiences of the day—sorting through the meanings and implications of various episodes. This might involve making comparisons with previous experiences, sorting into categories, and drawing out the less immediate and conscious meanings and perceptions of interpersonal encounters. For example, a woman dreamt of a friend who had the appearance of a tramp and was living in a derelict caravan; she realized that this reflected her subliminal perceptions and worries about her friend's mental state that she had not registered consciously. Such processing of emotional–interpersonal information requires free-associative access to related images that have connotative links with the original perception or experience. Thus the normal (non-defensive) processing of emotional information may depend on the same means of primary process displacement and "side cathexes" as the defensive manoeuvres of the ego described by Freud.

Facilitation of weak associative pathways

If this hypothesis regarding the processing of emotional information is correct, then the task in relation to traumatic experience
would be to facilitate weaker associative neuro-pathways (analogous to Freud's "side cathexes") and to lessen the tendency to flow
along the original direct neuro-pathways. There is evidence that
this happens during dreaming: REM sleep facilitates activation of
weak associations whereas non-REM sleep activates exclusively
strong associations (Stickgold, 2002; Stickgold, Scott, Rittenhouse, &
Hobson, 1999). In contrast, there is evidence that traumatic dreams,
often containing a near-literal repetition of the original situation,
take place during non-REM sleep (Hartmann, 1996)[5]. Moreover, the
high levels of norepinephrine released during traumatic stress may
tend to increase signal to noise ratios in cortical neurons and to
inhibit weak association (Foote, Bloom, & Ashton-Jones, 1983), a
process perhaps selected by evolution because it favours clarity
regarding life-threatening situations; this may act to prevent traumatic experience being assimilated in the way that other experiences are, thus providing a partial explanation of the persisting and
intrusive quality of traumatic memories. A further relevant factor is
the contrasting tendencies of the two hemispheres in relation to
weak and strong associations; the left hemisphere gives more
emphasis to strong associations, whereas the right hemisphere facilitates weaker associations (Chiarello & Richards, 1992; Nakagawa,
1991). This is consistent with popular ideas about the "creative" and
holistic functioning of the right hemisphere compared with the
linear and linguistic mode of the left hemisphere.

   Just as the rapid eye movements of normal dreaming seem to
involve the facilitation of weak, as opposed to strong, associations
of thoughts and images, so the action of EMDR appears to foster the
release of trauma-related sensory experience into the wider neuro-
network. An analogy might be with the way that, although a
concentrated quantity of a toxin may be poisonous, if it is released
into the vastness of the ocean it becomes relatively innocuous.
Without EMDR, or effective REM activity, the traumatic sensations
simply perseverate along a narrow associative neuro-path, trapped
as episodic sensory memories within the hippocampus[6] (Stickgold,
2002). They are not digested. The memories remain implicit and

procedural—they are not experienced as autobiographical verbally accessible memories (i.e. are not explicit memories), but are patterns of neurophysiological response concerned with action (procedure) in response to severe danger (Mollon, 2002a). After successful EMDR therapy, these traumatic implicit procedural memories become experienced as recollections of past events, no longer associated with overwhelming physiological concomitants of emotion. They have become explicit memories.

Shapiro describes the action of EMDR as one of facilitating the physiological (brain and body) system in adaptive information processing. Under normal circumstances the adaptive information processing system establishes appropriate associations between the recent experience and other experiential information, so that constructive learning can take place. In this way the experience is integrated into positive emotional and cognitive schemas. Traumatic information, by contrast, is trapped in the nervous system, maintained in its raw sensory–motor and state-specific form, readily triggered by a variety of internal and external stimuli. EMDR helps the disturbing emotional information to be moved at an accelerated rate further along the appropriate neurophysiological pathways.

This view of the action of EMDR, in moving experience from a state in which it is continually repeated to one in which it is recognized as a memory of an event in the past, is remarkably close to Freud's position regarding the need to replace repeating with remembering—for example, when he wrote of the analyst's endeavour "to force as much as possible into the channel of memory and to allow as little as possible to emerge as repetition" (Freud, 1920a, p. 19).

Summary

Traumatic memories tend to be experienced not as features of autobiographical memory but as flashback re-experiencing. Similarly, Freud described transference as a form of repeating rather than an experience of remembering. In relation to both transference (as Freud viewed it) and traumatic experience, the therapeutic aim is to facilitate a shift from repeating to remembering. Traumatic experience continually presses into consciousness, although this movement is opposed by mental efforts to avoid re-experiencing pain. Freud noted that this is true of traumatic dreams, and he noted that such phenomena seem inconsistent with his model of a wish-fulfilling and pain-avoiding psyche. Trauma appears to hijack the body and mind, and act *as if it were a wish.*

In Freud's model, the psyche evolves towards adaptation to reality by creating an "ego" which blocks the primary process and the direct expression or discharge of desire, forcing the movement of neuro-cathexis along side-paths. This diverting of the movement of cathexis is apparent in the structure of dreams, which display the operation of displacement. Traumatic dreams seem to overwhelm the ego and force a direct expression of the traumatic experience in consciousness. From the perspective of both EMDR and Freud's model of the psyche, the assimilation of neuronal charge along side-paths, in place of a direct path to consciousness, is required for healthy adaptation. This is analogous to physical digestion. EMDR facilitates precisely this kind of assimilation, as may do the free-associative processes of Freudian psychoanalysis.

Notes

1. The patient's recollections of childhood sexual abuse trauma were her reason for seeking psychological help; they were not *evoked* by any form of psychological therapy.
2. There are obvious exceptions to this general point—particularly the two early papers on hysteria (1896b & 1896c)
3. This term was used in Freud's 1920g paper "Beyond the pleasure principle":

   We shall avoid a lack of clarity if we make our contrast between the coherent ego and the repressed. It is certain that much of the ego is itself unconscious, and notably what we may describe as its nucleus . . . [*ibid.*, p. 19]

   This idea was developed further in his "The ego and the id" (1923b).
4. Freud's speculations are remarkably similar to contemporary observations of the process of apoptosis, or programmed cell death, whereby the individual cell's potential suicide is inhibited by the messages of the surrounding cells.

One cell helps to preserve the life of another . . . We might suppose that the life instincts or sexual instincts which are active in each cell take the other cells as their object, that they partly neutralise that death instincts (that is, the processes set up by them) in those cells and thus preserve their life; while the other cells do the same for them, and still others sacrifice themselves in the performance of this libidinal function. [Freud, 1920g, p. 50]

5. Hartmann (1996) comments:

I believe that the repetitive post-traumatic nightmares . . . are not nightmares at all and should be considered a different class of phenomena and perhaps given a different name such as "memory intrusions". I will argue that they differ completely from nightmares in their contents, their repetitive quality, their time of occurrence, and their underlying biology insofar as we know it. They do not participate in the "connecting" furthermore, and they tend to occur in different sorts of people. [*ibid.*, p. 105]

6. Stickgold (2002) makes an important point regarding the idea of memory "storage":

In reality, the concept of memory storage is at best metaphorical. What occurs in reality when we "store a memory" is that we alter a system so that a certain pattern of brain activity and hence perception or thought is more likely to be reinstated in the future. [*ibid.*, p. 64]

CHAPTER THREE

What happens during an EMDR or EFT session?

Clinicians who are familiar only with conventional (psycho-analytically derived) verbal psychotherapy may experience difficulty in grasping what takes place during eye movement desensitization and reprocessing (or the procedurally similar methods of "energy psychology"). Those from a behavioural or cognitive background may be misled by the word "desensitization" in the name; this may give the impression that EMDR is a variant of behavioural desensitization therapy, which indeed initially it was. Although Francine Shapiro, a cognitive-behavioural clinical psychologist and originator of EMDR, first developed the method as a treatment for post traumatic stress disorder, she soon found that much more than desensitization was occurring and that the method revealed much about aspects of the structure of the mind and its processing of emotional information. Ironically, what began as a quasi-behavioural treatment for anxiety took Shapiro back to phenomena that Freud had been exploring a hundred years previously—particularly free association, the unconscious, networks of memory, the layering of traumatic experience, the representation of trauma in the body, and the importance of intrapsychic processing. She also discovered something new and astonishing—that given a little help, the mind has its own natural healing process. This feature of the mind is quite at odds with assumptions that have been prevalent in many areas of psychoanalysis; e.g. that the minds of many patients are in the grip of destructive and anti-developmental forces. What EMDR reveals is that the apparently destructive dynamics and organizations of the mind are functioning as defences against unbearable pain and anxiety.[1]

Using bilateral stimulation

Shapiro originally explored the therapeutic potential of actual eye-movements—side-to-side, saccadic movements. However, it was soon found that other forms of "bilateral stimulation" were also effective in inducing a more rapid processing of disturbing emotional information. These include auditory stimulation (stereo headphones that provide alternating sounds or beats to either ear), tactile (tapping alternate sides of the body, e.g. hands, knees, or shoulders, by either client or therapist), and kinaesthetic (moving either side of the body alternately, walking being one normal instance of this). Equipment is now available in place of the original reliance on a moving finger or tapping by hand; e.g. light bars with moving points of light, auditory equipment, and tactile stimulators of various kinds. Different forms, intensities and speeds of bilateral stimulation suit different clients, and some experimentation may be necessary. For example, one client found the light bar extremely disturbing because the lights reminded him of the headlights of the car that had hit him; he responded much better to auditory stimulation. Although the various technological devices save the therapist from developing "EMDR shoulder" resulting from repeated arm waving, the original "by hand" method does have some advantages in allowing a more direct and sensitive engagement with the client's emotional and somatic processing, as well as enabling movements, such as figure of eight, which a light bar cannot replicate. By becoming, in effect, entrained with the client's autonomic nervous system, it is possible to respond immediately to the subtle changes in his or her psychosomatic state, increasing or reducing the speed, sweep and direction of the eye movements as required. For example, as a client recalls the most harrowing moments of a trauma, his or her eyes may freeze, indicating that processing has become blocked at that point; the therapist can then facilitate the stalled processing by slowing and reducing the finger movement and then gradually stepping up the movements again as the client's eyes are "caught"—a sort of mirroring and leading process. Similarly, it is often apparent when the client has success-fully completed processing an area of experience because his or her eyes begin to move much more freely, and the therapist can mirror this with wider finger movements. On the other hand, some clients (particularly those who have experienced sexual abuse) may experience the therapist's hand movements as too intimate and intrusive, and may be more comfortable with the neutrality and distance of watching a light bar or listening to bilateral auditory stimulation.

While bilateral stimulation alone tends to be relaxing, the therapeutic effect requires that the "thought field"[2] be tuned to the target problem—essentially by asking the client to think about the distressing experience or anxiety and to notice the emotions and physical sensations. If the clinician were following the standard protocol established by Shapiro (2001), then the client would be asked to rate the severity of distress on a ten-point scale—the subjective units of disturbance (SUDs), originally devised by Wolpe (1990)—and also there would be an endeavour to establish the "negative cognition", in terms of the injury to self-esteem and self-image associated with the trauma (e.g. "I am weak and pathetic"). Having established the SUDs and the negative cognition, the client's success in processing the trauma and associated self-referencing thoughts can be measured by comparison with these original ratings. However, these steps are obviously not essential to the process and some clinicians may find them constraining at times.

A form of bilateral stimulation is then applied and the client is asked simply to notice the thoughts, feelings, images, and so on that come to mind. Before proceeding to address the trauma or other distressing experience, there may be an initial step of establishing a "safe place", involving the client's selection of a place in memory or imagination where he or she would feel safe and relaxed. By focusing on this, using the bilateral stimulation, and noticing the sights, sounds, smells, and other physical sensations of the "safe place", the feelings of safety and relaxation are enhanced. The purpose of this is to enable the client to experience relaxation, partly as a resource that he or she can access if required and to which he or she can return at the end of the session. Again, it is not inherently an essential part of EMDR work, and if the focus of the therapy does not concern a severe trauma some clinicians may choose to discard this step.

The work can then begin to focus upon the target problem—either a known trauma or the symptom. The client is asked to think about this while engaging with the eye movements or other bilateral stimulation. Sometimes the processing of emotion may be very rapid and startling, as if floodgates were suddenly opened in response to just three or four eye movements. In other cases the client may report that nothing much has come to mind. Usually, however, there is some new emotional information emerging during the first set: a strong emotion or bodily sensation, or a particular detail of the experience, or a thought about what happened. As processing proceeds, the client's level of distress will start to rise, subsiding later. At the end of each set of bilateral stimulation, the therapist may ask the client what came to mind, or may ask "what comes to mind now?", thus placing the emphasis upon continued free association. The client may then give a brief indication of what feelings, body sensations, images, or thoughts have passed through his or her mind, or may sometimes wish to give a lengthier discourse. Usually the therapist will then say something like "OK, just go on with that", and continue with the next set of bilateral stimulation.

If the target problem is a known trauma, the client will almost certainly, sooner or later, begin to access distressing emotions and images. His or her level of distress (the SUDs) will begin to rise through the sets of bilateral stimulation, before gradually subsiding. Quite often, a simple trauma suffered by a previously psychologically healthy person, can be resolved in a single session (perhaps an hour) of EMDR. Many problems are more complicated, as the more recent traumatic experience links into other unprocessed distress, including childhood trauma. Each area of difficulty must be dealt with systematically, processing the emotions and the self-related thoughts and fantasies. Often the client will spontaneously move to thinking of an earlier, thematically-related, trauma once the more recent experience has been processed. Another pattern is for the client to become stuck, failing fully to process the initial target trauma as expected. It may be that the reason for the impasse is the link to another, earlier trauma. If this does not spontaneously emerge, the clinician may ask "when have you felt like this before?", using the current affect as a bridge to the past. One of the lessons of EMDR is that processing the traumas of the past is indeed necessary, contrary to some contemporary psychoanalytic perspectives that advocate an exclusive focus on the client's current mental models and unconscious conflicts (e.g. Fonagy, 1999).

Stimulating the acupressure points in EFT

The procedure used in the energy psychology method of EFT is very similar to that of EMDR, except in place of bilateral stimulation, the client engages in tapping or pressing a sequence of acupressure points, mainly around the face and hands[3] (for more details see www.emofree.com; or Hartmann, 2003a; or Lynch & Lynch, 2001; or Llewellyn-Edwards & Butterell, 2003) Where the emphasis can be a little different is that with EFT it is more important to focus on a specific aspect of an experience or emotional constellation, processing one small bit at a time. EMDR seems to process with a broader focus. Another difference is that EFT begins with an initial procedure designed to counter the frequent tendency for "psychological reversal"—the resistance, self-sabotage, or negative therapeutic reaction that commonly impedes psychological healing. This step involves bypassing internal fighting by making a statement of higher order self-acceptance while tapping a particular acupressure point. In EMDR, the internal arguments and forces of self-sabotage are processed along with every other emotion and cognition as they arise during the bilateral stimulation.

Free associating through traumatic experience:
the thematic linking thread

An eighteen-year-old woman, Jean, sought help because of depression and self-harm (cutting her arms). Initial assessment suggested that an abusive sexual relationship at age fourteen had left a residue of anger and shame, with some symptoms of persisting post traumatic stress (intrusive angry thoughts and anxiety relating to this relationship). Currently she was in a supportive and committed relationship and lived with her boyfriend; she was upset at the intrusions into this from her first abusive relationship.

Experiences within the abusive relationship were targeted for EMDR and these were satisfactorily processed in one session. Subsequently she reported feeling much less troubled by memories of this relationship. However, her anxiety was still very apparent in the second session. As this anxiety was tracked with EMDR, she then reported a previously undisclosed disturbing experience. A couple of years previously she had been participating in an internet chat room when a message appeared declaring that the writer knew that she was Jean and where she lived and what she looked like. Since she was naturally not using her actual name, nor disclosing any identifying details while "chatting", she was extremely puzzled and alarmed as to how someone would know who she was. This was followed by a threatening phone call. Other incidents gave Jean the impression that she was being stalked—whether by her first boyfriend or some other person she had no idea. As these experiences were processed Jean appeared utterly terrified. Her anxiety at being alone in a room with the male therapist was acknowledged and processed.

Following this, Jean reported some diminishment in her anxiety and depression. A further EMDR session focused upon current issues in her life, mainly to do with instances in which she felt pressured by others and experienced a lack of agency. Jean then spoke more about her episodes of self-harm. She experienced cutting herself as a pleasurable relief of tension and self-punishment. Initially she was unclear about her motivations for the self-harm, but her introspection revealed that it was also associated with intense feelings of anger. Although she had stopped actually cutting herself, she reported a recent instance of experiencing an urge to do so. This had been when she had spoken to her boss about the possibility of returning to work; her boss had been somewhat unpleasant. While making the eye movements, I asked Jean to hold the feeling of anger in mind and to search for earlier instances of feeling the same way. She reported recalling experiences with the childminder who cared for her when she was aged four. Apparently this woman was quite sadistic, imposing her will on the children through various physical punishments, while presenting a front to the parents of being very kind and caring. Jean's initial attempts to communicate her fear and anger to her mother were repudiated by the childminder, but eventually she had become so overwhelmed with rage that in front of her mother she had insisted on her accusations and declared that the childminder was lying—at which point her mother did believe her. As she continued the processing, Jean thought again about her boss, a woman who seemed similarly punitive and controlling. It became clear that Jean's difficulties at work, her increasing depression culminating in a prolonged period of sickness leave, were a result of experiences with her female boss that resonated with abusive experiences with the sadistic childminder, as well as with the abusive and controlling first boyfriend. Thus the linking thematic thread concerned experiences of coercion by sadistic others.

Rapid locating of traumatic experience

Sometimes the client's associations during bilateral stimulation are quite startling, cutting through to core determining experiences. For example, a middle-aged man presented with hypochondriacal anxiety and panic, triggered by the development of some relatively minor cardiac condition. Several sessions of conventional psychotherapeutic exploration threw little light on the origins of this, although some meaningful lines of enquiry emerged; for example, that his narcissistic personality structure was threatened by ageing and awareness of mortality. However, after just a few sets of eye movements, he suddenly recalled, in vivid detail and accompanying affect, an experience when he was aged eighteen. He had inadvertently taken an overdose of an illicit recreation drug and developed an acute cardiac condition, necessitating emergency treatment in hospital. Prior to the EMDR he had not consciously thought about this episode and its links with his current anxiety. After a few sets of eye movements this traumatic experience was processed and he no longer suffered hypochondriacal anxiety.

Often the underlying pathogenic experience is not initially known, but targeting EMDR upon the origin of the symptom or behavioural difficulty will reveal the source of the problem. For example, Mrs R, a young, married, professional woman presented with a hysterical symptom of being unable to speak in certain situations. This had become a problem at work, where she was regarded generally as a highly competent professional. The difficulty in speaking had first occurred at a funeral of a family friend. She had become extremely upset, to a degree that she could not understand in terms of her relationship with the deceased. When she tried to talk to the daughter of the deceased man she found herself unable to speak. In talking about this, Mrs R recalled her own father's funeral ten years previously when she was aged thirteen. She expressed puzzlement that she had not felt much emotion at this funeral in contrast with her overwhelming feelings at the more recent funeral. It was agreed to begin EMDR with Mrs R's thought field tuned to the situation when the symptom appeared. Mrs R's tears poured out in a flood after just a few eye movements. She associated immediately to her father's funeral. She recalled that she had, in fact, been extremely upset before the funeral. However, her mother and others in her family had shamed her, telling her she must stop crying otherwise she would not be allowed to attend the funeral. As a result, Mrs R had struggled to suppress her feelings and her tears, and subsequently had felt numb during the actual funeral. Then in the days following the funeral there had been visits from many relatives, and the family culture was such that she was expected to assist in polite hospitality for the visitors, leaving her with little opportunity to express her own grief. These memories and emotions were processed in a single session, following which Mrs R's symptom was fully resolved.

Even when the target experience is known, new and surprising details may emerge once processing starts. Mr Z had been witness to a very serious assault in a pub, in which his friend had suffered a life-threatening injury. An initial attempt at EMDR failed because he repeatedly became overwhelmed with distress that showed no sign of diminishing, and therefore it was not possible to proceed beyond the very first stages of the incident. At this time, Mr Z was drinking heavily in an attempt to cope with his severe post traumatic stress. Often it seems that heavy alcohol consumption significantly interferes with processing emotional trauma—a point perhaps related to the finding, from Callahan and others in the field of energy psychology, that sometimes toxins can prevent emotional healing. After Mr Z had undergone alcohol counselling and had managed to stop drinking, we tried EMDR again. This time he reacted quite differently, rapidly proceeding through the sequence of the assault with appropriate but tolerable affect. Then he was astonished to recall details of his own actions that he had hitherto forgotten. Apparently he had acted rather heroically, managing to land a hefty punch on the assailant's chest, resulting in the latter running out of the pub. Then, since the ambulance had not arrived, he put his badly injured friend in his car and drove at high speed to the hospital, and when stopped by the police after he jumped a traffic light, he shouted that it was an emergency and was given a police escort with sirens and blue lights, with the result that his friend's life was saved. Prior to the EMDR, Mr Z had no recollection of this sequence of events and he had been left with self-images of being weak and helpless. After the incident was processed, in a single EMDR session, he was left with a restored self-esteem.

Processing trauma

As the person's thought field is tuned to the trauma, he or she will usually begin to recall the sequence of events, accompanied by appropriate affect and trauma-related thoughts. These will be processed by the bilateral stimulation and the general psychological movement will be towards lessened distress. However, the level of distress (the SUDs) will initially rise before subsiding. Usually the best strategy is to keep repeating the sets of bilateral stimulation until the SUDs reduce. The aim is to process the experience until the SUDs are at zero—i.e. that the experience can be recalled as a memory, an unfortunate event in the past that is no longer relived when it is thought of. At such point the experience has passed into autobiographical memory. Usually there will be one part of the event that evokes most distress, and this will be the area on which to focus particular attention. As the entire episode is processed, a final check can be undertaken by asking the client to scan through the experience and to notice any remaining aspects that cause distress, and also to scan the body for areas of remaining tension. If areas of residual distress or tension are noticed, then further bilateral stimulation is applied while the client's thought field is tuned to these. This careful testing of the client's response on recalling the trauma is important, since the work is not complete until the SUDs are at zero and there is no disturbance experienced in the body.

Self-image, self-esteem, and beliefs about the self

Another crucial part of the work is to explore the trauma-related cognitions—the beliefs about the self that have derived from the traumatic experience. These might include beliefs such as: "I am weak"; "I am unable to cope"; "I am damaged goods"; "I am disgusting"; "I am worthless", etc. Having identified these, the client may be asked to hold the thought in mind while engaging with the bilateral stimulation. Usually the thought will begin to alter spontaneously—in a positive direction. However, the method advocated by Shapiro was to derive from the existing "negative cognition" a counter "positive cognition" and then to apply bilateral stimulation while the client holds this in mind. It is important to derive a positive cognition that represents a plausible alternative to the negative cognition. Thus it must not run counter to reality; for example, "I can beat off any attacker" (for a rape victim) or "I can be completely safe when I drive" (following a road traffic accident). Instead, cognitions such as "I managed to survive", or "I can aim to drive as safely as possible", or "I can learn from past experiences", or "I can become a loving person", are more likely to be experienced as plausible and acceptable. An interesting variant of this procedure is used in the emotional freedom techniques, where the formula is "Despite this anxiety/feeling of weakness/self-hatred (etc.), I deeply and completely accept myself", used to induce a state of acceptance that relinquishes resistance to the healing process. In using Shapiro's technique, the client is asked to rate the "validity of cognition" (VOC 7 point scale) of the positive cognition—and then, using bilateral stimulation, the aim is to raise the subjective validity of the positive thought. Whether or not the therapist bothers with the procedure and concept of deriving the negative and positive cognitions, attention to the client's thoughts about the trauma, especially thoughts about the self, is important— sometimes more important than processing (desensitizing to) the actual trauma. The damaged self-image and self-esteem often seems a crucial component of the impairment resulting from the trauma.

Disintegration anxiety

At times a particularly strong resistance to altering the self-image and beliefs about the self may be encountered. This occurs when the person's mental structure seems organized around a particular view of the self. As a result of this organization, the prospect of altering a fundamental pillar of the self-organization gives rise to fragmentation (or disintegration) anxiety (Chapter 5). The nature of such anxiety is rarely conscious, but, if identified and explained, is usually readily grasped by the client. This fragmentation anxiety can then be processed through EMDR like any other anxiety. Similar anxieties may arise when the rapid therapeutic process is incongruent with a person's strongly held beliefs about the mind or the world in general (e.g. beliefs that psychological change is necessarily always slow and involves much pain and suffering). This may occur particularly in relation to the often astonishingly rapid methods of energy psychology[4] (Hartung & Galvin, 2003), which in certain respects do not conform to conventional Western scientific assumptions.

Emotional layering

There may be different levels or aspects of a presenting problem, like layers of an onion. As one is cleared, the next emerges. The following is an example, using the EFT energy technique (www.emofree.com), taking place in the context of ongoing psychotherapy.

A very disturbed woman who had suffered extensive abuse from her mother would often enter states of extreme anxiety, panic, paranoia, and confusion. Despite her chaotic mental world, she had established a lasting and very loving committed relationship (albeit volatile, from her side) and planned to be married. As her wedding day approached she became increasingly disturbed and requested an emergency session. Since it was clear that the context for her current disturbance was the proximity of her wedding, it was agreed to use EFT to reduce her anxiety. Initially she was so agitated she could hardly speak coherently. However, after the first sequence of tapping, she was noticeably calmer. She was then able to identify a more specific anxiety: that she would not be able to say her vows correctly in front of all the people present. After the next sequence of taps she decided her anxiety was that she might not be able to speak at all—an experience she was prone to when feeling very stressed. Following the next sequence she reported no longer feeling anxiety when she thought about the actual wedding, but spoke of her worry about not being able to get *to* the wedding—of being in such a state of anxiety that she could not function. With the further set of taps she spoke of her sudden realization that she was "scared of being scared", and this too was processed. By this point she began to report various intense physical sensations: of feeling hot and tingling, of feeling sick, of tightness in her chest, of constriction in her throat, and of pains in her muscles. She was asked to notice the various physical sensations as she proceeded with the tapping sequence. As the sensations began to subside, she suddenly reported a further feeling, that of confusion. After the next sequence of taps she realized that the feeling of confusion was related to her states of paranoia, and that she was very frightened of becoming overwhelmed by her paranoid confusion, as had often happened. The next set of taps allowed her to feel more tolerant of her confusion and paranoia. By this point she was feeling much calmer, although exhausted and looking forward to going to sleep. Thus the emotional processing began with general anxiety, then focused on social performance anxiety, next moved to the "fear of fear" that often underlies states of panic, and then mobilized a great deal of physical tension, before descending to the more fundamental paranoid confusion.

The rapid and sequential unravelling of layers of anxiety can sometimes allow the clinician to arrive at a much clearer impression of the structure of a particular form of psychopathology. For example, the use of EMDR with one particular patient enabled the author to identify the dynamics and structure of "psychic murder syndrome" (Mollon, 2002b), which could then be recognized in a number of other patients whose therapy did not involve EMDR.

Transference and other routine phenomena of psychotherapy

Despite the common initial impression that EMDR and EFT are very odd procedures, all the ordinary and normal features of psychotherapy and psychoanalysis do have a place in the work—although the emphasis may be different since the processing is essentially internal (or intrapsychic) rather than arising from the patient–therapist interaction. Thus, the therapist's capacity to create a receptive and empathic atmosphere in which to allow the client's unconscious to speak is crucial. If the client's psychological problems are complex and pervade his or her personality, then periods of more conventional psychoanalytically-informed psychotherapy may be interspersed with EMDR and/or EFT. In my experience, such a combination is vastly more effective and efficient than psychotherapy alone. Insight is important, but seems to emerge as a *result* of the processing, rather than being in itself the cause of psychological change. Similarly interpretation, of hitherto unconscious contents and processes, takes place, but is often achieved by the client rather than the therapist. The process of transference (of past to present) can be seen as an aspect of the general way in which insufficiently metabolized trauma (whether in childhood or later in life) tends to hijack perception of the present, creating areas of phobic avoidance of both internal and external triggers of traumatic affect. Thus, the present is misperceived through an automatic assimilation to the past. As the past experience is processed through EMDR or EFT, the patient is released to see self and other in a fresh way.

Transference is often quite central in EMDR and EFT, although it tends to be more transitory in its manifestations than it is in regular psychoanalytic work. The temporary preoccupation with the psychotherapist as a transference figure gives way quite rapidly and spontaneously to a focus on processing the original childhood experiences and emotional conflicts that have formed the basis of the transference perception. This is demonstrated in the following example.

A woman with social anxieties

A middle-aged woman presented initially with social anxieties. Ordinary free-associative discussion of these was relatively unproductive. However, during EMDR, using the light bar, she rapidly began to disclose more of the concerns that lay behind her anxieties. She indicated that she was continually preoccupied with the question of what role she was meant to play for other people, and whether she was carrying out this role satisfactorily. After several sets of eye movements during which these issues emerged, she remarked that she was now worried about whether she was carrying out the eye movement procedure correctly and whether I was happy with her performance. I did not make any comment or interpretation about this, but simply indicated that we should proceed with the processing. She then began to speak of her childhood concerns about pleasing her mother and her worries that she was responsible for her mother's state of happiness (recollections and remarks that both point to the origin of some of her anxieties, and also illuminate her wish to please the therapist now).

A further session developed as follows. Each numbered line is the patient's response at the end of a set of eye movements. The author's comments are in italics. Again the patient begins with an anxiety in the transference and then proceeds spontaneously to explore its childhood precursors.

1. I'm worrying that I wouldn't have enough to say—not think of enough to say to someone whom I consider more intelligent than me. *Her typical social anxieties are apparent in relation to the therapist.*

2. I'm wondering why I need to be correct in everything I think and do. *She is asking herself a question. EMDR seems spontaneously to evoke apt questions and then to prompt new insights and answers.*

3. I think I admire intelligence. My Dad has something to do with it. He worked on a building site but he used to read a lot. He used to say he was surrounded by incompetents. He grew up in a boys' home—he had to fight for himself—he would always pick people he could lecture to.
She identifies that her anxieties have something to do with childhood fears of evoking her father's scorn.

4. I have such high expectations of myself. I always think people are judging me.
She recognizes her generalized expectations of self-in-relation-to-other.

5. I am thinking of fears of blushing.
Her fears of her embarrassment being embarrassingly apparent

6. Can I learn a different behaviour—or am I stuck with it?

7. Where does my anxiety come from?
She continues to search for origins.

8. I remember anxiety starting school—I was terrified.
This is presumably a mixture of social and separation anxieties.

9. My mother was anxious. If someone knocked on the door we would all run into the bathroom to hide.
The family appears to have been in the grip of a shared anxiety about the world outside the home.

10. I couldn't integrate with the other children. I would stand in the corner.

[The therapist comments, "You describe a fear of being judged by others—as if the world is full of versions of your father who would think you stupid, incompetent, etc."]

Yes. My dad would get verbally aggressive—he would shout the person down. It's hard for me to put across my point calmly.

11. My mother is terrified of doctors—she's not been for 41 years—she used to threaten to take me to the doctors.
She now seems to be shifting tack to a consideration of her mother's anxieties.

12. I think my mother is terrified of finding a solution to this—that she'd have to justify not getting better herself if I overcome it.
She begins to hint at a symbiotic relationship with her mother, such that the latter requires her to remain joined with her in their shared view of a dangerous world.

13. New people worry me—I'm not sure if I can get them on my side.
Again she expresses a paranoid view of the world.

14. If I get better I would be likely to be letting my mother down. A fleeting thought—I feel as if we are joined together.
A very clear expression of the malignant symbiosis with her mother.

[The therapist asks, "A difficulty in developing a separate identity from your mother?"]

Yes, she reinforces my anxiety—I should have stayed like a child— she's tried to keep me there—I've always felt like her protector.

[The therapist asks, "You've sacrificed your own life for your mother?"]

I've never thought of that—it's given me something to think about.

This single session covers a great deal of rather condensed psychodynamic ground, moving from an initial transitory focus on anxiety in relation to the therapist to a spontaneous review of relevant experiences with her scornful father, before arriving at the more crucial recognition of her anxiety at the prospect of disrupting the symbiotic relationship with her mother. The content and process is clearly of a *psychodynamic* nature, concerning conflict and anxiety that has evolved from relationships with parents, but the method is quite different from that of verbally based psychoanalytic psychotherapy in that, although the therapist does offer some facilitating reflections, the essential process clearly does not rest upon interpretations by the therapist. After four EMDR sessions along these lines the patient reported noticeable lessening of her social anxiety.

A not uncommon phenomenon is for a person who has undergone years of conventional psychoanalytic psychotherapy to find that a session or two of EMDR may release and process distress that had remained locked into their psychosomatic system, as in the following example. Such patients who have undergone lengthy psychoanalytic therapy are often able to make particularly rapid and effective use of EMDR. This appears to be because rigid defences have been loosened and considerable insight has already been achieved, allowing relatively easy access to unconscious anxieties and phantasies.

A woman with anxieties about giving birth

A thirty-year-old woman who had previously benefited from psychoanalytic psychotherapy, once per week for four years, sought further help during a pregnancy because of anxieties about giving birth. It is not necessary to provide extensive details of the patient's history, except to say that she appeared to have experienced her childhood family environment as somewhat emotionally brutal and depriving of affection.

The following EMDR transcript indicates how she rapidly accesses and processes primitive and vivid mental material coalescing around the prospect of birth: fears of giving birth to a monster; wishes to regress to being a baby who stays in the womb for ever; childhood medical trauma involving pain and humiliation; secondary gain from childhood illness—wishes to gain father's attention and love (since her father was a doctor); shame and guilt about childhood masturbation and oedipal phantasies; an attitude of triumphant withholding.

1. It's stuck. I don't want it to come out.

2. I am scared of two things. Scared it will be a monster, and scared it will rip me.
At this point the baby is experienced as threatening and persecutory.

3. I don't know if it is about me as the baby or about the actual baby. It doesn't want to come out. It's so nice inside.
Here she shows a rapid insight into how her feelings and phantasies about the baby are linked with an identification with the baby—the baby part of herself.

4. I am thinking of hospital at age four. Catheters . . . my legs spread . . . people watching . . . being hurt. Then I think of B watching at the last birth, taking photographs.
She has shifted quickly to recalling an associated childhood trauma, before then turning to a previous experience of giving birth. This moving between childhood and adult experiences is both typical and necessary for the working through of the associative networks of trauma and conflict.

5. I hate my body there [pointing to her "bump"]—it's so ugly and disgusting.
Now she has moved to a focus on her dysphoric feelings about her body, and she goes on to associate to childhood experiences and phantasies regarding her body.

6. [Why?] It's all so ugly . . . I'm ill . . . something is wrong with my wee . . . they keep looking at it . . . the shame . . . pleasure and pain . . . they said I was attention seeking when my kidneys went wrong . . . its all mixed up with masturbation . . . pain and pleasure jumbled up together.
She is describing childhood confusions of different feelings and phantasies— pain, but also pleasure through the secondary gain of illness, combined as well with phantasies linking urinary problems with masturbation.

7. What comes out of me is bad and diseased. They want to get it out of me—by force . . . I tried to give it to them voluntarily . . . so I pissed . . . I gave it to them . . . they screamed . . . it has to come by force.
Here are clear indications of the roots of her fear of giving birth. In her phantasy, birth involves forceful extraction from her body—a process in which her autonomy is overridden.

8. Nasty thought that I had as a child that I was going to hold on to everything . . . never let go of anything again . . . really evil.
Anal-sadistic feelings and phantasies are provoked by the shame and humiliation of her body being examined and intrusively controlled by others.

9. Ugly thoughts . . . triumphant withholding . . . a wish to be raped . . . I can't surrender . . . especially if they watch.
The link between childhood hostility towards doctors and nurses and her more contemporary resentment towards midwives becomes very clear.

10. The midwives want to poke fingers in . . . they really hurt me . . . I wanted to put my own fingers in . . . to feel the baby's head . . . it felt shameful. B watched them poking their fingers in when I didn't want them to . . . he didn't help me. Masturbation in hospital . . . I abused another child . . . pain and pleasure.
Here she begins to allude to anxiety and guilt about sexual phantasies and activities. These are linked to efforts to re-establish her own autonomy.

11. Pregnancy is pure and angelic . . . but there is corruption . . . I hate the look of that part . . . the shame and ugliness.

12. Shame at being female. I'm thinking of very early sexuality . . . mixed up with my brothers and father.

13. That feeling of corruption . . . having been dirtied . . . not being a child.

14. [Where does the sense of corruption come from?] I feel you are angry . . . that my thoughts aren't right . . . that I'm not doing it right . . . that my thoughts are all wrong . . . my love for the baby and sexuality all mixed up.
Her expectation of disapproval comes into the transference. She then goes on to associate to childhood wishes in relation to her father. This is typical of the way in which here-and-now transference feelings and anxieties rapidly give way to associations with the relevant historical experience.

15. If I try to get love from my father I will be punished.

16. I feel I'm doing it all wrong . . . I'm supposed to be talking about the birth . . . like I thought I was being very clever with my father . . . being ill to get his attention . . . but then I get punished.

17. An awful thought . . . enjoyment of attention from other doctors . . . resentment of my father's patients who get his attention. An evil sense of triumph . . . I get several doctors' attention . . . I feel so impure.
She articulates her resentment of her father's attention to his patients, and her triumphant secondary gain from illness.

18. [Why impure?] Because the love has become corrupt. I feel I'd played a game . . . I'd become very haughty . . . not looking at him . . . I thought my father would come begging . . . but he didn't . . . he died.

19. My thoughts turn back to B at the birth. He turned into my father . . . watching me while other people manipulated my body. It's like my father looking on in a detached way.

20. I couldn't touch my father's heart any more and couldn't touch B's heart. Giving birth is like giving so much love . . . all the things I've built up . . . my haughtiness, abrasiveness . . . all just go . . . I can't stand that. I want to be able to be soft and vulnerable . . . and to be held . . . I want to be a baby again.

She describes how she developed a haughty narcissistic aloofness as a protection against longing for love from her father. This aloof state of mind is undermined by the vulnerability of giving birth, and the vulnerability of the baby.

21. Giving birth . . . the whole idea of opening up . . . being open . . . something terrible will happen . . . like death.

22. I feel I'm losing my sexuality . . . can't bring together surrender and innocence with sex . . . mother with lover . . . I'm a mother with a baby . . . therefore I'm gone.

She confronts the difficulty of reconciling sexuality and motherhood, the paradox for the child of the sexual mother (Bollas, 2000).

23. If the baby comes out of me, am I going to be corrupt? Being pregnant is being sexual . . . but if I become a mother that doesn't have good associations for me either.

24. Fears of rejection . . . I am the baby . . . fears of my father's rejection . . . terrible fears.

25. Will I still be loved when the baby is born?

26. [Ask yourself that question.] I didn't feel loved when both of D's children were born. I think I will be loved this time.

27. [Can you review what you've been saying?]

I feel all my life I've tried to manipulate and control . . . I've tried to control my body and my emotions . . . but the only way I can receive and hang onto love is by letting go and surrendering.

This concluding remark is interesting because she recognizes what might have appeared to be a persisting malignant and destructive character attitude. The overall impression left by EMDR is that destructive motivations, while prevalent, are not primary.

Subsequently the patient reported that the birth had been very good and unproblematic, and that her baby seemed particularly alert, happy and healthy.

Facilitation and installation of positive resources

In addition to processing traumatic experience and psychodynamic conflict, EMDR is often used to enhance or install positive resources. The common establishment of a "safe place" before proceeding with processing trauma is an example of this, but there are many others. One of the lessons of EMDR is that mental processing naturally moves in a positive direction if given facilitation. Thus "negative cognitions" will tend to metamorphose into "positive cognitions" if bilateral stimulation is applied. Once a more positive view has become potentially acceptable to the mind, then its felt validity can be enhanced by EMDR. Sometimes this installation of the positive becomes more crucial. It may happen that a person cannot feel he or she has the mental of behavioural resources to accomplish a particular task, or a paucity of positive interpersonal experiences in childhood may have left a legacy of psychological deficit manifesting as low ego strength. In such instances bilateral stimulation may be applied while the client's thought field is tuned to such positive experiences and achievements as there have been. For example, a man sought help with disabling post traumatic stress, including severe anxiety and depression, following a road traffic accident in which he nearly died. His childhood had been difficult, with much trauma and neglect, and he was extremely fearful that any attempt to process the experience of the accident would trigger unmanageable feelings from these early adverse circumstances. Instead of targeting the accident, EMDR was used to access previous experiences of success and of overcoming adversity. He began to recall various areas of real achievement, including his skill as a driver. As a result there was a marked improvement in his mood and feelings of confidence, which then allowed subsequent processing of the accident to be undertaken satisfactorily.

A natural psychoanalytic concern about this emphasis upon the instalment of positive resources is the possible danger of bypassing the full encounter with the negative—a collusion between client and therapist to avoid despair or other deep emotional pain. While this could occur, it should not if the principles of EMDR are followed carefully. Resort to the "positive" as an *avoidance* of processing the negative would be bad practice in EMDR, just as it would in psychoanalysis.

Summary

EMDR draws upon phenomena congruent with the original principles of psychoanalysis, including free association, networks of memory, trauma, and psychodynamic conflict. However, the emphasis is upon resolution through intrapsychic processing rather than predominantly by means of the therapist's interpreting the transference. This intrapsychic processing is facilitated by bilateral stimulation, which can take the form of visual, auditory, or tactile stimulation that directs attention alternately to either side of the body and, by inference, to each cerebral hemisphere. The mind–brain shows a natural tendency to process trauma and move towards an emotionally positive resolution when assisted by bilateral stimulation. An important part of this processing is the shift in self-related thoughts and beliefs. Psychopathology may be revealed to be structured in layers and networks, and each aspect can be processed systematically. As well as processing trauma, EMDR can be used to install or enhance positive mental resources—but, as in conventional psychoanalytic therapy, a focus on the positive should not be used as a defensive avoidance of the negative. Transference manifestations may be apparent during EMDR, but these are not regarded as the crucial vehicle of healing. The therapist's task is to facilitate the internal processing, but, in general, to be extremely sparing in his or her comments and introduction of content. Similar principles apply in the case of energy work, except that the processing appears to take place at a higher level in the psychosomatic system.

Notes

1. Although this might seem an obvious and well-recognized feature of mental life, based on simple principles of psychodynamic conflict and defence, it is actually absent in many influential contemporary psychoanalytic positions, e.g. Joseph, 1985.
2. This rather apt term is actually derived from an energy psychology method called "thought field therapy" (Callahan, 2001a)
3. The acupressure tapping points used in EFT:
   Thirteen points are used: an additional one, linked to the liver meridian, is normally omitted because of its difficulty in accessing, particularly for women. There is also a place on the chest, below the collar bone (on

either side), known as the "sore spot", the name deriving from the fact that it is often somewhat tender. This is not actually a meridian acupressure point, but is the site of a lymphatic node; its exact relationship with the meridian system seems a little obscure. It is used in connection with correcting reversed polarity/psychological reversal.

The thirteen main tapping points are as follows: (1) (bladder meridian) start of the eyebrow, where the bone above the eye turns into the bridge of the nose; (2) (triple warmer meridian; gall bladder meridian) corner of the eye, on the bone at the side; (3) (stomach meridian) under the eye, on the bone, in the centre underneath the pupil; (4) (large intestine meridian) under the nose; (5) (central vessel) between chin and lower lip; (6) (kidney meridian) collarbone, in the angle formed by collarbone and breastbone; (7) (spleen meridian) under arm, in line with male nipple or female bra strap; (8) (lung meridian) thumb, on the outer edge, on the side, next to base of the nail; (9) the same place on the index finger; (10) (pericardium meridian) the same place on the middle finger; (11) (small intestine meridian) the little finger; (12) the side of the hand (karate chop); (13) (heart meridian) "gamut point", between knuckles of ring finger and little finger, a centimetre or so back—its name deriving from the way that a "gamut" of procedures, including various eye movements, counting, and humming, may be applied while tapping this point.

The rationale behind stimulating all these points is that all the major meridians of the energy body are thereby covered—so that wherever the disturbance in the body's energy system is located it will be released by tapping one or more of the meridians. In his latest teaching, Craig tends to abbreviate the tapping sequence and often omits the "gamut" procedures. He emphasizes learning to sense intuitively where to tap.

The steps of the full EFT treatment protocol:

(a)   The first steps include the obvious ones of establishing rapport, enquiring about the problem, taking a history, etc. Information is sought concerning the origin of the problem. If the circumstances of the origin are not clear, the presenting problem itself can be addressed with EFT; the origins may come to mind as the processing takes place. The nature of the energy method is explained, including a description of the tapping points if EFT is to be used.

(b)   The client's own words are used as a description of the problem—preferably words or a phrase that is a vivid personal metaphor rather than a more neutral or polite description.

(c) The various aspects of a problem are identified. These may be the various emotions, or other components of a situation or experience. Each of these is addressed with EFT in turn.

(d) For each aspect, a subjective units of disturbance (SUDs) rating is taken. This is the client's subjective rating on a scale of 0–10 of the intensity of the distress, as experienced at that moment (or in recalling the troubling situation at that moment).

(e) The "set-up" statement and tapping is used before tapping for each aspect. This is designed to counter the tendency towards psychological reversal. The phrase that is used is "Even though ... [the problem or aspect] ... I deeply and completely accept myself". There are two options for tapping while repeating this statement (normally three times): the karate chop point, or the "sore spot"; client preference may determine which is used, but Gary Craig suggests the sore spot may be marginally more effective. In his later work, Craig often introduces various reframing or interpretive comments into this stage.

(f) The tapping sequence is followed, using a short "reminder phrase" at each point. This full sequence includes the "nine gamut" procedure (of eye movements (down to the left and right, round in a circle both ways), counting (1, 2, 3, 4, 5), and humming a bar of any tune—all of this while tapping the gamut point) within the EFT "sandwich". The eye movements, counting, and humming, are designed to engage various modalities of brain function and to facilitate the interaction between the hemispheres, as in EMDR.

(g) Following a round of tapping, an SUD rating may be taken. If the rating is not yet zero, further rounds of tapping should be undertaken. The aim is to reach a rating of zero, since a level of distress that is merely lowered can leave roots or hooks that can grow again.

(h) As well as taking the SUDs, other methods of testing may be used, such as asking the client to imagine being in the target situation, or, if appropriate, for the client actually to confront the previously feared situation. If the test reveals remaining anxiety or other distress, then further tapping can be done.

(i) Often testing may reveal further aspects to the problem. These can then be addressed in the same way.

(j) If the target fails to respond to the tapping procedure, various "fail-safes" can be tried. These include collarbone breathing (recommended by Gary Craig), Cook's Hook-ups or Cross Crawl (both physical movements derived from applied kinesiology to correct polarity reversal [Walther, 1988; Dennison & Dennison, 1994; Krebs, 1998]), drinking water, breaking state (moving around etc.), or muscle testing to explore the source of the problem (Diamond, 1979; Krebs, 1998).

Frequently asked questions about EFT.

How do you tap?

There are many subtle variations on style, force and speed of tapping. Normally two fingers may be used, at a speed perhaps of 2–4 per second, lightly but with a certain percussive rhythm and resonance. "Touch and Breathe" is a gentler version that some clients may prefer (Diepold, 2002). The client may tap their own body, as guided by the therapist.

How long do you tap for?

There is no hard and fast rule for how many times to tap at each point, but often it would be about seven times. The number of rounds of tapping required may vary considerably.

Which side of the body do you tap?

It does not matter which side of the body is tapped, since the meridians are bilateral (or central). Gary Craig has suggested that occasionally tapping both sides may possibly be of benefit, but this is not normally done.

How many times must a round of tapping be repeated?

The aim is to reduce the SUDs to zero, so ideally the EFT treatments are repeated until this is achieved. Sometimes a single round of tapping is sufficient. With very severe problems many rounds of tapping may be required.

4. Callahan (2002) calls this the "apex problem", but I find his rationale for this particular term somewhat obscure, although the phenomenon is clear enough. The brain cannot track the process of change in the way that it can in conventional psychotherapy, working with experienced thoughts and emotions. The resulting state of perplexity may give rise to anxiety, hostility, and confabulation in certain clients.

CHAPTER FOUR

The abandonment of memory, trauma, and sexuality: the excessive preoccupation with "transference", and other problems with contemporary psychoanalysis

> "We thus reach the idea of a quantity of libido ... whose production, increase or diminution, distribution and displacement should afford us possibilities for explaining the psychosexual phenomena observed"
>
> Freud 1905d, section added 1915, p. 217

I n its origins, Freud's psychoanalysis gave us a psychobiological theory, involving concepts of psychodynamic conflict, energy (libido), the bodily roots of the mind (the libido theory), and trauma. Freud postulated that the flow of libido, with its roots in bodily pathways, could be blocked by anxiety, conflict, and trauma. This block resulted in symptoms. Moreover, blocks in the forward flow of libido resulted in regression, a flowing backwards along the paths of libidinal development, the ensuing threatened emergence of abandoned and unacceptable infantile forms of sexuality giving rise to further repression of the libido. All these fundamental concepts appear to have been discarded by contemporary post-Freudian psychoanalysis. No longer is there any talk of libido, or any other form of bodily-based energy. The psychoanalyst who took Freud's concept of the psychobiological libido most seriously and focused on the bodily basis of "character defences"—Wilhelm Reich—was expelled and derided, even though his theories (and the bioenergetic therapies flowing from them), which seemed so eccentric at the time, can now be viewed as highly congruent with contemporary energy psychology and research on biological energy (Becker & Selden, 1985; Bischof, 1995; Reich, 1942).[1] Symptoms are no longer understood as compromise formations, resulting from repression but allowing some leakage of libido along distorted channels. Regression is similarly rarely mentioned. The idea of the "transference neurosis", in which all the repressed libido would gather around the figure of the analyst, whereby the psychological blocks to the healthy free flow of libido along realistic paths could be resolved, is more or less completely ignored.

Another fundamental psychoanalytic concept called into question within some forms of modern technique is that of free association, seen by Freud as the crucial means of revealing the blocks in the flow of libido. Thus, Fonagy has stated, "I come to bury free-association, not to praise it" (quoted in McDermott, 2003), arguing that the patient's verbalizations are not free, but fundamentally rule-bound and always to be understood in the context of communication within the relationship with the analyst, shifting the emphasis from Freud's essentially intrapsychic focus to the interpersonal and relational. Instead of Freud's model, what is now found in British psychoanalysis typically is a preoccupation with the patient's attachment or dependence relationship with the analyst, this being seen as an example of the patient's characteristic problems in relationships. In place of the libido, the concern is with the patient's alleged destructive attacks on dependence. Sexuality is generally ignored, unless it is construed as "perversion" and therefore an expression of the "death instinct" (as opposed to the libido). Psychodynamic conflict is often not considered (see discussion of Joseph, 1985 below), certainly not in the form of compromise formations between the forces of libido and the forces of repression. Astonishingly, this transformation of Freudian (psychodynamic and psychoeconomic) psychoanalysis into a relationship-based form of psychotherapy, loosely structured on a theory without roots in the body and the libido, has taken place seemingly without much awareness of how radically current practice has torn away from its origins. While the study of attachment and "object relations", and the internal models derived from early relationship experiences, are undoubtedly important, something is surely lost in the abandonment of Freud's libido theory and his concepts of psychic energy. *Jung*

The importance for Freud of the energy–libido model is indicated in the following quote. He is discussing the infant's separation anxiety.

> The reason why the infant in arms wants to perceive the presence of its mother is only because it already knows by experience that she satisfies all its needs without delay. The situation, then, which it regards as a "danger" and against which it wants to be safeguarded is that of non-satisfaction, of a growing tension due to need, against which it is helpless. . . . The situation of non-satisfaction in which the amounts of stimulation rise to an unpleasurable height without it being possible for them to be mastered psychically or discharged must for the infant be analogous to the experience of being born . . . What both situations have in common is the economic disturbance caused by an accumulation of amounts of stimulation which require to be disposed of. [Freud, 1926d, p. 137]

Thus, Freud is describing here the functions of the mother in regulating the infant's states of tension and arousal—what Kohut (1971) would later call the "selfobject" functions. Later he continues:

> Finally, being grown-up affords no absolute protection against a return of the original traumatic anxiety-situation. Each individual has in all probability a limit beyond which his mental apparatus fails in its function of mastering the quantities of excitation which require to be disposed of. [Freud, 1926d, p. 148]

Throughout Freud's writings, from the "Project" onwards, he was concerned with the vicissitudes of quantities of energy, as they flowed through the body and mind, or as they suffered blocks in their normal paths with consequent build-up of tension. How can a theory and therapy that discards this central psychodynamic and psychoeconomic theme claim still to be grounded in Freudian psychoanalysis?

In certain respects, a closer approximation to Freud's theory is found in EMDR and energy psychology. EMDR sees impaired

psychological functioning (when it is non-organic) as rooted in
trauma and blocked emotion processing; the trauma becoming, in
effect, trapped in the nervous system and in the body. Desires and
thoughts (internal), or reminders (external), that could potentially
lead to stimulation of the stored experience of trauma, give rise to
anxiety and inhibition of thought and feeling. These blocks prevent
the free flow of energy and information within the mind and body.
Processing through EMDR allows the normal digestion of experience and flow of energy to be resumed. Similarly, methods of
energy psychology (Hartung & Galvin, 2003) postulate that psychological impairment arises in blocks in the flow of energy and information in the body's meridian system. These blocks result from
psychological trauma, but the problem is not the actual memory of
the trauma, but the disturbances in the energy flows that have
resulted from the trauma. Both these approaches recognize resistance to treatment and to the releasing of the flow of energy, as in
Freud's theory. In energy psychology, the resistance is conceptualized in terms of "psychological reversal"—a kind of reversal of
polarity in the energy system, with results similar to those described by Freud in terms of "death instinct", "repetition compulsion", "resistance", and "negative therapeutic reaction". What is
not found in EMDR and energy psychology is a particular preoccupation with transference (of infantile conflicts on to the figure of
the analyst), but it may be questioned whether Freud saw the
phenomenon of transference as crucial to psychoanalysis or simply
could not see any other way of eliciting and releasing the libido.
There is no necessary theoretical reason why interpretation of transference should be the only means of resolving problems within the
psychodynamic mind and body. In terms of Freud's overall model
of the psyche-soma, transference seems rather peripheral, regarded
as just part of the psychodynamic processes of the mind whereby a
"false connection" (Breuer & Freud, 1895d, pp. 301–304) is made
between a repressed idea and a preconscious idea (Freud, 1900a,
p. 562) or an external figure. Indeed, he wrote relatively little about
technique in relation to transference (Freud, 1912b, 1915a), and he
certainly did not discourse at length about "counter-transference"
in the manner so often encountered today.

    As an analyst I have for many years listened to detailed accounts
of contemporary psychoanalytic treatment with some growing

unease and puzzlement concerning what appears to me to be an excessive preoccupation with a particular view of transference (and particularly negative transference). Often it seems that the analyst's interventions are not based on an attempt to convey empathically an understanding of psychodynamic conflict and states of tension within the patient's mind, in order to bring about a release of blocked energy, but instead are focused on hypotheses regarding the patient's unconscious *activity* (usually seen as expressing some kind of hostility) in relation to the analyst. Related to this point, there may, in some versions of contemporary British technique, be a position of seeming antagonism between patient and analyst rather than the working alliance that is consistently found in research to be the factor most crucial to successful therapeutic outcome (Bordin, 1979; Garfield, 1995; Gaston, 1990; Orlinsky, Grawe, & Parks, 1994). The widespread trend for relentless interpretation of the so-called "transference" concerning the here-and-now activity of the patient in relation to the analyst, while particularly linked with some of the Klein group, now cuts across the three groups of the British Society.[2] This fashion in technique is associated with certain assumptions: that only "transference" interpretations relating to immediate anxieties experienced in relation to the analyst are "mutative"; that interpretative comments outside the immediate transference are overly intellectual and likely to involve a collusive retreat from anxiety; that reconstruction of early relationship experiences is unreliable since the patient's perception of parents would have been distorted by projective phantasy; that the idea of the "working alliance" and related concepts are misleading since the entire relationship of the patient to the analyst is pervaded by transference; that all of the patient's communications and activities in the consulting room are unconsciously an expression of the transference. For all these reasons, it is often considered that the only useful kind of analytic activity is that of commenting upon the patient's unconscious transference activity in relation to the analyst.

However, it is possible that these widespread assumptions and associated technique, while motivated by the highest concerns for rigour, may be misguided. While we still lack good research to tell us which forms of psychoanalytic technique are most helpful and which might be harmful, there are studies suggesting that excessive transference interpretations are associated with poor outcome in psychoanalytic psychotherapy. For example, Høglend (1993) reported that his research team found that psychotherapy associated with few transference interpretations led to a better outcome than therapy with a high frequency of transference interpretations, when the patients were followed up at two and four years. He also comments:

> One might speculate that a persistent analysis of the patient-- therapist interaction leads to a temporary deterioration but in the long run (years) leads to more insight and translation of that insight into creative action and sustained adaptive behavioural change. This study does not provide any support for this popular incubation theory. [Høglend, 1993, p. 504]

Piper, Hassan, Azim, Joyce, and McCallum (1990) reported a "significant inverse relationship between the proportion of transference interpretations provided by the therapist and both measures of therapeutic alliance and therapy outcome" (p. 951). They also add:

> Advocates of the use of transference interpretations, such as Strachey, have at times been identified with the extreme position that only transference interpretations should be made or that the more transference interpretations the better; this was not Strachey's position. He maintained that the normal course of events during therapy is an oscillation between transference and extratransference interpretations and that transference interpretations may occupy only a small portion of treatment. [ibid., p. 952]

Connolly et al. (1999) similarly found that "relatively high levels of transference interpretation can lead to poor treatment outcome for some patients" (p. 491). Of course, we must be cautious in drawing conclusions for psychoanalytic practice from these studies— they were not examinations of five times per week analysis, and the content of transference interpretations may vary considerably according to one's psychoanalytic theory and geographical location. Nevertheless, they do raise questions about the therapeutic value of transference interpretation—and the quality of clothing worn by the Emperor of the here-and-now.

What are the sources of this British technique? Partly it seems to stem from a misreading and distortion of Freud's (1912b) position and that of Strachey (1934), both of whom emphasized the importance of transference interpretation but did not envisage it as the exclusive focus of the analysis. A second source seems to have been the direct application of child analytic technique to work with adults, especially when combined with the Kleinian view of the internal world of phantasy and the projective model of transference. Another influence seems to have been the Sandlers' (1983, 1984, 1994) concept of the distinction between the past unconscious and the present unconscious, their emphasis being that it is impossible to have access to the original past unconscious and that the analyst must only address the present unconscious as played out in the transference. The Sandlers' basic idea, in so far as I understand it, is as follows. The past unconscious is not conceptualized as a reservoir of repressed instinctual wishes, but as a complex and organized world of a young child. This organized child forms the template for psychodynamic processes in the adult, within the present unconscious; but, crucially, the psychically organized child of the past unconscious is structurally unavailable to the adult and the analyst. Thus, the Sandlers state:

> An unconscious wish arising in the depths of the PRESENT UNCONSCIOUS can be regarded as modelled on the inner child's wishes, but the objects involved are objects of the present. So, to give a very simple example, if in an analysis an unconscious hostile wish towards the analyst arises in a patient's PRESENT UNCONSCIOUS, then it would not be, in the light of argument put forward here, a hostile wish towards the father displaced onto the analyst. Rather it might be seen as a hostile impulse arising in the person's current life towards the analyst, one possibly modelled on the inner child's relation to the father. In other words, the conscious or unconscious transference wish . . . is not a transferring from parent to analyst, but rather an attempted interaction with the analyst . . . which functions in the present according to rules set down in the patient's early years. [Sandler & Sandler, 1997, p. 176]

It appears, then, that in this model all that is left available of the early years is the "template" that forms the basis of the present unconscious: a set of procedural rules rather than actual experiences or childhood desires.[3] There is no direct transference of the infantile past to the present. Indeed, the infantile past is structurally inaccessible. In a similar way, this model also implies that regression to an infantile position is structurally impossible. It is also difficult to see how specific traumatic events of childhood, as opposed to generalized procedural rules deriving from repeated experiences with care-givers, can breach the structural barrier of the present unconscious. Thus, this kind of theorizing cannot easily accommodate psychoanalytic reports where a specific early trauma appears to be re-experienced in the transference—such as Casement's (1985) account of a patient who had suffered burning with boiling water as a preverbal child. Casement describes a point in the analysis when the patient became extremely distressed when he continued talking to her after she had held up her hand for him to stop; subsequently she explained that at that moment he had become the surgeon who had carried on with a skin operation under local anaesthetic regardless of her distress. A specific experience of this kind cannot be represented within a generalized template, as the Sandlers envision the present unconscious.

A recent variant of the Sandler position has been expressed by Fonagy (1999), who declared that memory is "therapeutically inert" and argued that therapeutic change results from the experience of "self with other" in the here-and-now transference, a position (strongly criticized by Blum, 2003) that is obviously incongruent with the observation, from EMDR and other therapies, that states of post traumatic stress disorder require processing of the memory of the trauma. Thus, the Klein group and elements of the Contemporary Freudians have, in effect, constituted a pincer movement to foreclose the legitimacy of any analytic work other than here-and-now transference interpretation. The Independent Group has failed to sustain a coherent alternative. Perhaps all this is a long-term outcome of unresolved issues in the "controversial discussions" (King & Steiner, 1991; Scarfone, 2002).

This contemporary fashion in technique within the British Psychoanalytic Society is very different from the original approach to analysis. Arthur Couch (2002) describes his analysis with Anna Freud as follows:

> In many sessions when I talked about childhood memories or accounts of my present life, interspersed with associations and self-reflections, Anna Freud would frequently remain silent until she

made a penetrating point. By these long silences I sensed that she placed a high value on my own efforts to gain insight without her help. This stance reflected a faith in the psychoanalytic process itself as a curative factor. . . . Anna Freud was a listening companion of my current life and a knower of my past life. She never commented on the here-and-now interaction between us. Such interpretations about the ongoing communications would have seemed very foreign to the analysis that was focused on our task of working together. It would have seemed a violation of the integrity and authenticity of our analytic relationship if the meaningfulness of my communications about inner and outer life were re-interpreted in terms of here-and-now transference references. [*Ibid.*, p. 65]

In a recent article in the *Journal of the American Psychoanalytic Association*, Jacob Arlow remarks,

Repeatedly I have observed how exclusive concentration on possible transference derivatives skews the way analysts listen to their patients. As a result an artificial insensitivity seems to impose itself on the discourse in the psychoanalytic situation . . . They are not listening *to* the material; they are listening *for* material, transference material. At a workshop on technique I heard a case presentation in which consideration of some of the patient's most painful experiences was bypassed and attention focused instead on some minor transference issue. [Arlow, 2002, p. 1141]

He goes on to give several examples where a focus on transference is actually defensive against the more disturbing feelings regarding the actual parents. In these instances, if the analyst pursues the here-and-now interaction excessively, the material is severed from its genetic context. The crucial point here is that just as turning to developmental history can be a defensive flight from difficulties in the here-and-now, so the preoccupation with the here-and-now interaction can be a defensive avoidance of the pain of the past.

A somewhat startling example of the defensive flight to the here-and-now was presented by a patient undertaking EMDR. This man had suffered severe burns early in his life, resulting in a lengthy period in hospital involving much painful changing of dressings. As he was beginning to process some of these early memories, he suddenly exclaimed that he wanted to rip the female therapist's skin apart. This formed part of a pattern in which whenever these early medical trauma were approached he would suddenly shift to a preoccupation with aggressive fantasies concerning the therapist in the here-and-now.

In listening to presentations of analytic work, it is sometimes interesting to ask oneself what appears to be the analyst's *implicit* theory of the analytic process. My impression is that the implicit theory behind the modern here-and-now technique is that the patient improves by becoming able to establish a healthy relationship with the analyst (see the discussion of Joseph's 1985 paper below). Ironically, this becomes, as Pearl King has pointed out (personal communication), a kind of relational psychotherapy rather than psychoanalysis as traditionally understood. Crucially, there is a loss of the "as if" perspective regarding transference. Those using the "modern" technique speak and write as if it is the real relationship with the analyst, albeit with unconscious conflicts and anxieties, that is the vehicle of the analytic process. There is, it seems to me, a loss of a distinction between the real relationship and the transference; it is all called transference. By contrast, in the classical mode of analytic work it is the coexistence of the real and the transference relationship that brings the latter into focus.

To believe that everything the patient says is unconsciously concerned with the analyst is clearly an unsound assumption. To give obvious examples, the patient's thoughts and discourse may be concerned with a crisis in his or her life, a bereavement, a significant moment in a relationship, or a childhood memory of an important event. Patients who are not training as analysts may find the excessive transference focus of some analysts very strange, and may perceive the analyst, unconsciously if not consciously, as paranoid and narcissistic.

The object relationship is not always in the centre of the analysand's conscious and unconscious preoccupations. Instead it may be the functions of the analyst and the setting of the analysis that are of importance, particularly their tension-regulating functions. These are denoted by Kohut's (1971) concept of the selfobject, Balint's (1968) emphasis on the unobtrusive analyst, and Winnicott's (1958) concept of "being alone in the presence of the other". If the analyst is continually dragging the patient into object-relating, these silent selfobject transferences are not allowed to develop. There is no space for the patient to explore meanings and aspects of experience that have nothing to do with the relationship with the analyst directly, meanings that relate more to the experience of self, its internal tensions, and its past traumas.

In some variants of modern British technique there is also a lack of attention to developmental history. This is a missing third, leaving the patient trapped in the dyad with the analyst. The disregard of history can lead to serious distortions in the understanding of the patient. For example, the significance of severe abuse or other trauma in a patient's childhood may be missed if the focus is exclusively on the here-and-now interaction.

My own working hypothesis regarding transference (based on both classical psychoanalysis [e.g. Greenson, 1974] and self psychology [Kohut, 1971]) tends to be as follows. The transference contains two components: it is a vehicle for exploring and resolving the developmental past and its traumas; and it is an opportunity for new relational and selfobject experience in the present. Thus, as the patient attempts again an anxiety-laden (and often shame-laden) developmental initiative, there is the *fear* of a repetition of the original traumatizing response and the *hope* of encountering a new and more benign response. These two strands of transference are intertwined. It seems to me that addressing one without the other will not work; I hypothesize that it is the continual moving between the past and present that is curative. Another way of putting this is to say that the mind generally displays two opposite tendencies—the developmental move forwards, and the backwards pull of unresolved trauma. Given a facilitating environment (whether through psychoanalysis or EMDR), the patient is continually (unconsciously) trying to bring the past into the present in order that trauma and developmental disturbance can be resolved. Until trauma is resolved, the present will tend to be assimilated to the past, but when the processing of trauma is achieved then the patient is free to live in the present. However, one of the lessons of EMDR and energy psychology is that much important processing of emotional information may not necessarily occur within the domain of transference at all, and to try to drag it into a presumed arena of transference may impede rather than facilitate its resolution.

A consideration of a contemporary psychoanalytic approach to technique: Betty Joseph's paper "Transference. The total situation", 1985.

While Freud's theorizing can easily mesh with the phenomena of EMDR, some forms of contemporary psychoanalysis are fundamentally incongruent with a therapeutic approach that addresses past trauma. A striking example of a version of psychoanalysis that seems to me to have the potential to repudiate childhood trauma is a famous paper on transference by Betty Joseph. This is important to consider for two reasons: first, Miss Joseph is arguably the most well-known practitioner of the technical approach that privileges a focus upon the immediate interaction between patient and analyst in contrast with the wider focus of traditional psychoanalysis; second, this particular paper seems to have been quite influential and is seen as epitomizing Joseph's approach. I have heard this paper cited approvingly even by analysts who would not locate themselves within the Klein group. Certainly it appears congruent with the "here-and-now" Contemporary Freudian position advocated by Fonagy (1999). More generally, it illustrates how far some current versions of psychoanalysis have evolved from the psycho-economic and psychodynamic theory of Freud and how it is possible to develop a kind of psychoanalysis that appears completely to avoid addressing and processing the stresses, strains, and traumas of childhood.

Joseph's framework of transference and projection

Joseph begins:

> My intention in this chapter is to discuss how we are using the concept of transference in our clinical work today. My stress will be upon the idea of transference as a framework, in which something is always going on, where there is always movement and activity. [Joseph, 1985, p. 156]

She then refers to Strachey's (1934) contribution, which she says described

> the way in which projection and introjection colour and build up the individual's inner objects, [and] showed that what is being

transferred is not primarily the external objects of the child's past, but the internal objects, and that the way that these objects are constructed helps us to understand how the analytic process can produce change. [Joseph, 1985, p. 156]

Thus, Joseph states her assumption that transference is essentially to do with the projective transfer of the patient's internal objects. Within a framework derived from Abraham and Klein, it is possible to assume that innate phantasy, determined by the child's own instinctual life, is the primary determinant of the internal objects, latching in a secondary way on to aspects of external reality. Once this assumption is made, then the real character of the care-givers of childhood becomes relatively irrelevant. This may partly explain the impression sometimes given of a dismissive and distrustful attitude towards reconstruction among some analysts within the Klein group. However, while Strachey is often credited with being the first to emphasize the "mutative" nature of transference interpretations, compared to those that are extratransferential, Joseph's method of analytic work differs markedly from his. Strachey quite definitely did not believe the analyst should *only* make transference interpretations:[4] as he said, "A cake cannot be made of nothing but currants . . ." Moreover, Joseph's view of transference marks a profound departure from that of Strachey and Freud, as I indicate below.

To explore the technical style that Joseph advocates, I will examine her account of work with the patient she calls N, whom she says was in analysis with her for many years. Her description illustrates her concept of transference, her use of counter-transference, her approach to dreams, her assumptions about the nature of psychopathology, and her particular way of focusing on the interaction between patient and analyst.

Joseph's view of transference

First, Joseph describes a counter-transference experience with N, of feeling "vaguely comfortable . . . as if I quite liked this patient's sessions". She explains that she decided this must correspond to

an inner conviction on the patient's part that whatever I interpreted he was somehow all right . . . that he had some very special place

... that, I, the analyst, had a particular attachment to or love for him, and that for my own sake I would not wish to let him go ... [Joseph, 1985, p. 159]

Joseph does not say a lot about N's history, except that he was "the youngest child, the favourite of his mother, who had a very unhappy relationship with his father, a rather cruel man, though the parents remained together throughout their lives" (*ibid.*, p. 159).

Joseph states that it would have been easy to link N's feeling of having a special place with the history of having been the favourite of his mother. However, she argues, "But had I done this, it would have played into my patient's conviction again that interpretations were 'only interpretations' and that I did not really believe what I was saying" (*ibid.*, p. 160). Such a comment is not uncommon among contemporary analysts in Britain, where there is (as I perceive it) a general distrust of any conversation with the patient that could be viewed as "intellectual" rather than embracing the raw impact of anxiety in the "transference"—indeed, it is so common that its extraordinary implications may be missed. Joseph appears to be saying that if she were to link the patient's experience in the consulting room with childhood experiences then the patient would think the transference was *not real*; the patient would perceive her interpretations as "only interpretations". The argument seems to be that the "transference" must be experienced as real and not "as if". This is precisely the opposite to an assumption, which I believe to be rooted in both classical analysis and Strachey's position, that one of the tasks of analytic enquiry is to identify the desires, anxieties, and phantasies in relation to the analyst, but then to release the patient from the grip of these illusions by revealing them to be *merely transference* based in childhood experience. From a classical position, and from the point of view of Strachey, transference *is not real*; it is *illusion*; the task of analysis is to free the patient from transference illusion. As Strachey put it:

If all goes well, the patient's ego will become aware of the contrast between the aggressive character of his feelings and the real nature of the analyst, who does not behave like the patient's "good" or "bad" archaic objects. The patient, that is to say, will become aware of a distinction between his archaic phantasy object and the real external object.[5] [Strachey, 1934]

This point about the transference illusion seems to me often to be lost in contemporary analytic approaches within British psychoanalytic circles. The stance advocated by Joseph seems to consist of maintaining the patient in the childhood phantasies and assisting him or her in achieving a better relationship with the analyst *within this framework of childhood phantasy*. A related point is the absence in much modern technique of concern for what was classically considered the "real" relationship alongside the transference. It is as if the entire interaction between patient and analyst is now viewed in terms of "transference", but then, if there is no contrasting concept of the real relationship (and the therapeutic alliance), the concept of transference loses its meaning (of illusion) and becomes concrete; the transference is experienced as real.

Joseph's use of a dream

Joseph relates a dream that is quite central to her account. She does not give the patient's associations and thus her approach is very different indeed from Freud's way of working with dreams (Loden, 2003). The dream is:

> ... there was a kind of war going on. My patient was attending a meeting in a room at the seaside. People were sitting round a table when they heard a helicopter outside and knew from the sound that there was something wrong with it. My patient and a major left the table where the meeting was going on and went to the window to look out. The helicopter was in trouble and the pilot had baled out in a parachute. There were two planes, as if watching over the helicopter, but so high up that they looked extremely small and unable to do anything to help. The pilot fell into the water, my patient was wondering whether he would have time to inflate his suit, was he already dead, and so on. [Joseph, 1985, p. 160]

Joseph then states,

> I showed him how we could see the war that is constantly raging between the patient and myself, which is shown by the way in

which he tends to turn his back, in the dream, on the meeting going
on at the table, on the work going on from session to session here.

She interprets the two planes as the analyst with two arms and
breasts watching over him, but unable to help because he is
absorbed in his fascination with his masochism, preferring this to
an enjoyment of the help offered by the analyst: "Here I mean that
he shows his preference for getting absorbed into situations of
painful collapse rather than turning to and enjoying help and
progress" (*ibid.*, p. 161).

The following day, the patient says he felt disturbed after the
previous session's work on the dream. After talking about various
aspects of the session, he remarks that "whatever goes on in the
analysis he seemed somehow to get caught up in this rejection and
fight" (*ibid.*, p. 161). He talks some more about events of the day, but
Joseph tells him that all that he is saying is "being used against
progress in the session, as if a particular silent kind of war against
me was going on, which I showed him". The patient replies in a
gloomy voice that there seemed to be no part of him that wanted to
work and cooperate. Joseph then states that the situation between
them reflects the way that the dream is now lived out in the transference.

At this point I will comment on what Joseph has recounted. First
of all, she interprets the dream entirely in terms of the interaction
in the consulting room, taking the manifest content as an allegorical representation of the transference. While this may have some
validity, it can easily appear to the reader who is not already
persuaded of the correctness of Joseph's technical stance as rather
arbitrary. As Loden (2003) points out, the original psychoanalytic
view was that the unconscious meaning of a dream is likely to be
extremely hidden and not discernible immediately from the manifest content. However, even if we follow the modern assumption
that the dream may have allegorical meanings, other obvious possibilities arise. It might, for example, refer partly to childhood experiences, such as the war between the parents, the vulnerable child
self being in a very precarious position, unable to be rescued by the
two parents far above, preoccupied with their own war. Might the
child be seeking contact with a father, the major? This alarming
childhood situation might be re-experienced in the transference,

giving rise to a phantasy of an analyst–mother who is preoccupied with her need for the patient to need her and not go off with the major–father, while the child's real predicament is neglected by the parents' involvement in their war. Some might wonder whether the patient's communication of feeling disturbed by the session might be an indication that the analyst could be on the wrong track, but from Joseph's perspective it can be taken as further confirmation of her construction. She interprets his remarks about other events as a "silent war" against her. Perhaps not surprisingly, the patient sounds "gloomy". He states that there seems to be no part of him that really wants to work, and we might wonder whether this reflects his feelings of hopelessness about the therapeutic impasse. His remark could be taken as compliant, as if he has learned Joseph's theory. Thus, it may be that the dream does indeed refer in part to the interaction between analyst and patient, but it may be the patient's unconscious commentary on how he experiences the here-and-now style as a distressing repetition of his childhood predicament with his possessive mother and the war between his parents.

Joseph's response to a childhood memory

Joseph continues her account of the session after her dream interpretations. She tells us that the patient suddenly remembered childhood occasions at boarding school, where he was very miserable, when he would hide a tobacco tin and go off on his own into the countryside and smoke; this was the beginning of his smoking, although there seemed no real pleasure in the cigarettes. Joseph tells the patient that this relates to how he traps her with remarks about how no part of him wants to cooperate and how he has been addicted to the excitement of this fight with her; however, she tells him he has difficulty in acknowledging his improvement (the reduction in his addiction) because this would mean giving up his pleasure in defeating her; she tells him he is not yet ready to enjoy using the helping hands of the two planes in the dream. The patient "tended to agree with this" (Joseph, 1985, p.162), but then suggested that perhaps he felt resentment and sadness that the analyst had moved too quickly away from the memory of the cigarette box, which he had felt was vivid and important. Joseph says she "went back to the cigarette box memory, and had a look at his feelings that I had missed something of its importance" (*ibid.*). However, she also tells him again that the emergence of the memory is to do with his excitement and pleasure about defeating her, and his resentment that his feelings had shifted as a result of her work. N agrees with this, but tells her he still thinks she moved too fast away from the memory. He explains that it was as if the analyst had become a kind of Pied Piper and he had allowed himself to be seduced along by her. Joseph then states: "I pointed out that it sounded as if he felt that I had not really analysed his problem about being stuck, but had pulled and seduced him out of his position" (*ibid.*, p. 163).

Note here that Joseph assumes that the patient felt she had seduced him out of a particular problem, that of being stuck. However, this was not what the patient had said. He had said she had moved him away from his important memory of his childhood misery and loneliness and how he consoled himself with smoking. It was the analyst who was preoccupied with an idea that the patient was "stuck", and one hypothesis might be that the state of being stuck was an iatrogenic result of the analyst's perseverative interpretative focus on an aspect of their interaction. At this point the patient adds that he is also worried about getting caught up with excited warm feelings. Joseph tells him that both these are old anxieties that he is using at that moment "so that he could project them into me in order not to have to contain and experience and express the actual good feelings and particularly the warmth and gratitude . . ." [*ibid.*, p. 163), which she links with what she saw as a helpful quality in the planes overhead in the dream.

Projective processes distorting the patient's history

Somewhat surprisingly (to this reader), Joseph then describes all this as "rather straightforward material" (Joseph, 1985, p.163). She states again that the dream was lived out in the session "where we can see the patient's specific and willing involvement with misery and problems rather than meeting up with his helpful and lively objects, the planes, which are minimized, small" (*ibid.*, p. 163). Furthermore, she states that "his own capacity to move warmly towards an object is quickly distorted and projected into me: it is I who pull and seduce" (*ibid.*, p. 163). Thus, the patient's communication of her Pied Piper activity in leading him away from his own history is interpreted as his projection of his own warm feelings. A few lines later, Joseph states "we can see here how the transference is full of meaning and history" (ibid., p. 164), but then the example she gives is as follows: "We can get an indication of one way in which, by projecting his loving into his mother and twisting it, he has helped to consolidate the picture of her as so seductive . . ." (ibid.). She then both acknowledges and dismisses the patient's actual early experience by adding "Of course we can add that she may well have been a seductive woman towards her youngest son, but we can see how this has been used by him" (ibid.).

The absence of a concept of psychodynamic conflict

While an analyst rooted in the classical tradition might consider that psychopathology (symptom formation) is an unconscious attempt to avoid *anxiety* associated with infantile needs, desires, and emotions, and might view the therapeutic process as one in which the patient discovers, by means of the transference, that the desires and anxieties of childhood are no longer appropriate to the present, it is striking that Joseph does not seem to focus on anxiety. For example, she links the dream with what she considers N's "preference for getting absorbed into situations of painful collapse rather than turning to and enjoying help and progress" (Joseph, 1985, p. 161). What kind of psychodynamic hypothesis is this? Where is the conflict, involving a desire or need, an anxiety and a neurotic compromise? In place of psychodynamic conflict, Joseph refers to the patient's "preference". Summarizing the work she presents with N, she states, "The patient gets insight, I believe, into what is almost a choice between moving towards a helpful object or indulging in despair—his defences are mobilised and he goes the latter way . . ." (ibid., p. 163). Despite often using the language of psychodynamic conflict by speaking of "defences", Joseph does not at any point state what anxiety these "defences" are acting against. When the patient himself refers to his (now conscious) anxieties (to do with the Pied Piper aspects of the analyst and his worries about his excited warm feelings), Joseph seems to dismiss these: "I thought they were being used at that moment so that he could project them into me in order not to have to contain and experience and express the actual good feelings and particularly the warmth and gratitude . . ." (*ibid.*, p. 163). Thus, Joseph appears to see her task as one of showing the patient his *preference* for destructive modes of emotional relating towards the analyst, in order that he can give these up and develop a healthier mode of relating towards the analyst.

Differing views of reconstruction of developmental history

Most of Joseph's examples focus entirely on the "here-and-now" interaction, and she explicitly avoids looking to the patient's history and memories as clues to what is repeated in the present. Where she does refer to the patient's childhood memories, she is dismissive of the possibility that these relate to real externally-derived experience. For example, she states that N's perception of his mother as seductive is based on his "projecting his own loving into his mother and twisting it" (Joseph, 1985, p. 164). Thus, although Joseph does say that "the transference is full of meaning and history" (*ibid.*) and that it is "essentially based on the patient's past and the relationship with his internal objects or his beliefs about them and what they were like" (*ibid.*), the understanding of the neurotic present, in terms of images, beliefs, desires, and anxieties of the childhood past, is not reflected in her clinical accounts. Since the patient is seen as having created the original experience through projective phantasies (and, in the case of N, through his turning away from the feeding breast in his preference for his masochistic excitements), then presumably there is no reason to seek illumination in memories and reconstructions of history and experiences with actual caregivers; there is nothing to be found. The patient's inner world drama is all happening in the present, in the interaction with the analyst—and that is where it is to be addressed. By implication, if the patient can get his or her relationship right with the analyst (by appropriate feeding and gratitude), then the psychopathology is resolved, but this is not psychoanalysis as classically conceived. How is the patient to change his relationship pattern? Since there are no true psychodynamics in Joseph's view of her patient's difficulties, there can be no releasing of libido or other energy through interpretation of unconscious conflict, so presumably change must come about essentially through the patient's coming round to the analyst's point of view and realizing the pathology of his ways. The interpretation seems intended not to free blocked energy or repressed feelings and impulses, but instead to encourage the patient to think differently about his or her mode of relating in the present interaction.[6]

Comparison with classical analysis

The relentless pursuit of the interaction, characteristic of the modern British approach, seems a far cry from the more relaxed style of the classical analyst (Couch, 2002), who would allow the transference to unfold alongside the real relationship, and would interpret the distortions in the patient's perceptions of the present resulting from the transference intrusions of childhood images, desires and anxieties. Since the transference was considered an "as if" phenomenon, an illusion rather than reality, the classical analyst would view his or her own importance in the process as more limited, consisting in the repeated juxtaposition of reality with the play of the transference theatre. For Freud, the transference was a vehicle for exploring and resolving the sexual traumas and conflicts of the infantile past, an endeavour seemingly abandoned by Joseph and many other contemporary analysts.

The EMDR and energy psychology perspective on transference

What significance does EMDR have in relation to these shifts in understanding and technique concerning transference, from the original Freudian view to the modern here-and-now emphasis? First, EMDR shows that processing the original trauma, painful experience, or anxiety, is crucial to the resolving of the psychological dysfunction. A focus on present experience and behaviour will inevitably tend to keep attention away from the original trauma.[7] Working only through the secondary, indirect, derivatives of the trauma or anxiety is bound to be an inefficient means of resolution of the underlying problem. First, not all aspects of an original traumatic experience (or other kind of distorting experience) can easily be expressed or represented in the relationship with the therapist; it depends on what features of the analyst and the setting are available to form potential hooks for the transfer of past traumatic experience. Second, even when aspects are transferred to the present, addressing them solely in the here-and-now, without linking to the original experience, is like treating metastases without dealing with the main tumour. Another analogy might be as follows: a severely abused child is placed in a foster home; he or she displays a mixture of anxiety and provocative behaviour; no interest is shown in hearing about the child's past experiences of trauma; instead, the focus is upon modifying the child's behaviour in the new setting. In such a situation, the child may learn that he or she will not suffer the same abuse in the present setting, but the original traumatic experience will remain unresolved and reminders of the trauma will evoke anxiety and avoidant responses. By contrast, the EMDR paradigm is to track backwards from the current manifestation of dysfunction to the earlier contributing experiences, processing and resolving these, with the result that behaviour and emotional reactions in the present are then altered. From this perspective, the transference in the present is just a clue to the experiences of the past that need to be addressed.

The vantage point of energy psychology suggests a further analogy illustrating how an excessive focus on transference may be relatively unhelpful. In certain ways transference is a kind of unconscious drama, enacted within the theatre of the consulting room and the analytic relationship. Identifying this and making it conscious can certainly help to free the patient from transference illusions that distort his or her perception of the present, and can also enable aborted strands of early development to be rewoven into the fabric of the personality. However, such a process might be viewed as rather like imprisoning two actors in a basic dramatic template that contains no resolution, giving them some permission to discuss and improvise, and hoping that they will eventually evolve a satisfactory outcome and may even be able to end the play. A more direct and quicker resolution would be to change the script itself—the information patterned into the energy system, which cascades through the various lower neurobiological, experiential, physiological, and behavioural levels—so that the extensive working through of the drama might not be necessary.

Conclusion

Modern British psychoanalytic technique has moved very far from the classical approach. In some variants of the here-and-now emphasis, the abandonment of core features such as interpretation of psychodynamic conflict, reconstruction of developmental history, and exploration of the latent content of dreams, as well as the shift towards a view of transference as real rather than illusion, would render the method barely recognizable as psychoanalysis from a classical perspective. This approach, of working entirely with the present relationship, seems unlikely to be an effective or efficient form of therapy since it does not contain any means of processing trauma and other damaging experiences. While the assumptions and observations of Freud's psychoanalysis are congruent with the phenomena found in the practice of EMDR and energy psychology, those of much contemporary psychoanalysis are not.[8]

Notes

1. The experience of streamings of biological energy within the body, decribed by Reich, will be readily recognized by energy therapists today. Myron Sharaf, a student and patient of Reich, reports the following in his biography of Reich:

   What really staggered me in therapy was experiencing what Reich called at various times the "vegetative currents", "bioelectric currents", and—by 1949—"orgonomic streamings". These currents were often particularly strong after intense sobbing. I would lie there, breathing more easily, and would feel this beautiful, sweet, warm sensation of pleasure in my genitals and legs. It was glorious, I had never felt anything like it. I had never read anything about it . . . [Sharaf, 1983, p. 25]

   Reich considered that neuroses and functional psychoses resulted from undischarged sexual energy, or anger, or anxiety—rather similar to Freud's concept of the "actual neuroses". This "biopsychic energy" becomes locked into the body's musculature, forming the physical component of character defences. He describes the case of a man he treated whose resistance to uncovering passive homosexual phantasies took the form of an extreme stiffness of the neck. Suddenly the man's resistance gave way, in an alarming manner. The colour of his face continually changed from white to yellow to blue, he suffered severe pains in the neck, his heartbeat was rapid, and he experienced diarrhoea, these symptoms persisting for three days. This vivid experience clarified a principle for Reich: "Affects had broken through somatically after the patient had yielded in a psychic defense attitude" (Reich, 1949).

2. Loden (2003) comments: "The idealization of exclusive and aggressive focus on transference now permeates all three groups in the British Society—Kleinian, Independent, and Contemporary Freudian—and has many advocates elsewhere" (p. 49).

3. This view is rather similar to the reformulation of transference and the "prereflective unconscious" developed by Stolorow and colleagues: "Thus transference, at the most general level of abstraction, is an instance of organising activity—the patient assimilates . . . the analytic relationship into the thematic structures of his personal subjective world" (Stolorow, Brandchaft, & Atwood, 1987, p. 36).

4. It must not be supposed that because I am attributing these special qualities to transference interpretations, I am therefore maintaining that no others should be made. On the contrary, it is probable that a large majority of our interpretations are outside the transference—though it should be added that it often happens that when one is ostensibly giving an extra-transference interpretation one is implicitly giving a transference one. A cake cannot be made of nothing but currants; and, though it is true that extratransference interpretations are not for the most part mutative, and do not themselves bring about the crucial results that involve a permanent change in the patient's mind, they are none the less essential. If I may take an analogy from trench warfare, the acceptance of a transference interpretation corresponds to the capture of a key position, while the extratransference interpretations correspond to the general advance and to the consolidation of a fresh line which are made possible by the capture of the key position. But when this general advance goes beyond a certain point, there will be another check, and the capture of a further key position will be necessary before progress can be resumed. An oscillation of this kind between transference and extratransference interpretations will represent the normal course of events in an analysis. [Strachey, 1934]

5. Strachey considered that the analyst functioned as an "auxiliary super-ego", on to which the patient would transfer his/her harsh superego derived partly from his/her own aggression. As the patient discovers, through the analyst's interpretations that the auxiliary superego is not hostile to his/her id impulses, a more benign superego is re-introjected:

> The most important characteristic of the auxiliary superego is that its advice to the ego is consistently based upon *real* and *contemporary* considerations and this in itself serves to differentiate it from the greater part of the original superego. [*ibid.*]

Strachey further notes:

> The analytic situation is all the time threatening to degenerate into a "real" situation. But this actually means the opposite of what it appears to. It means that the patient is all the time on the brink of turning the real external object (the analyst) into the archaic one; that is to say, he is on the brink of projecting his primitive intro-jected imagos on to him. In so far as the patient actually does this, the analyst becomes like anyone else that he meets in real life—a phantasy object. [*ibid.*]

6. Fonagy (1999) has expressed this point of view as follows:

> . . . it is important for the analyst to be aware that the changes sought are not changes in the patient's awareness of past events but rather changes in procedural and implicit memory. Thus recovery of past experience may be helpful but the understanding of current ways of being with the other is the key to change. [Fonagy, 1999, p. 19]

7. Of course, this avoidance of the original experience may be what many patients (unconsciously) wish to do, and an excessively here-and-now technique may function to collude with this.
8. The views and arguments articulated here are a truthful expression of the author's perception of current trends in psychoanalysis in Britain. However, it must be acknowledged that many colleagues would disagree. Some of my comments may appear provocative, or even offensive. This is not my intention. However, it is necessary to state the arguments somewhat starkly in order to demonstrate how classical, as opposed to contemporary, psychoanalysis is compatible with the findings of both EMDR and energy psychology.

CHAPTER FIVE

Disintegration anxiety: the bedrock resistance to psychological change

D isintegration anxiety is hidden, obscure and not easily understood. It may form a formidable resistance to successful processing with EMDR, or indeed to any form of psychological therapy. It is most likely to be found in those individuals whose early environments were particularly unsupportive. ✳ The signs of disintegration anxiety may include various forms of rigidity of thought and attitude, muscular tension, fears of "letting go", dream and free-associative allusions to chaos, breakdown of structure and decay, and, in the case of EMDR or EFT, a failure to show the normally expected processing leading to relaxation. It ✳ may form a significant component of what in energy psychology is called "psychological reversal". Since EMDR and related methods potentially bring about rapid change, disintegration anxiety can be stronger and more clearly an obstacle during these forms of work.

To understand disintegration anxiety, it is necessary to consider insights derived from conventional psychoanalytic theory and technique, particularly drawing on the work of Kohut and Lacan. For some years I have been puzzled by two related common phenomena. The first is the way that people seem very often to have established within their psyche alien and oppressive mental structures,

Kohut also Kalsched

97

based partly upon the characteristics of hostile care-givers; alien structures that they then defend vigorously as their own self. The second is the way in which there is often a rigid clinging to funda- mental beliefs and assumptions, even when these are maladaptive and cause pain. For example, a patient often complained that I surely did not really care about him since I saw him only because he paid me. Recently, he referred to this again, using an odd form of words. He said, "I continually look to assure myself that you do not care about me." While his conscious meaning had been the familiar one, he agreed that his phrasing was ambiguous and could appear to be saying that he looked to *reassure* himself that I did not care about him. It then struck him that if he found evidence that I cared about him, this could be very alarming, because it would threaten one of his core beliefs that people do not really care about one another. Core beliefs can always be recognized because they are clung to with particular vehemence and are relatively immune to modification in the light of evidence. Similarly, core transference perceptions may be main- tained despite evidence incompatible with the transference image. As my patient talked about his alarm at the idea of a fundamental belief being challenged, I was reminded of a schizophrenic patient who once remarked that she could not contemplate giving up her persecutory internal voices because they constituted the "skeleton" that held her psyche together. The preservation of psychic structures appears to be a compelling human need.

The following basic paradigm describes the origins and function of this bedrock resistance. From a substrate of the fragmented self, the urge to form an organization is powerfully compelling. In the absence of "selfobject"[1] organization (Kohut, 1971) around the care- giving functions of the mother, based on empathy and respect for the child's developmental needs, the child will form oppressive organizations and internal structures using whatever psychological material is available. The task of psychoanalytic therapy, perhaps enhanced with EMDR, is to help free the patient from these oppres- sive structures so that the authentic unknown self can be released.

The invisible threat of fragmentation

One of the unusual features of Kohut's writings was his emphasis upon disturbances of structure and arousal alongside the more common psychoanalytic concern with content (of fantasies, desires, etc.). He regarded the overt content—even that which is unconscious to the patient but can be discerned by the analyst—as driven by the hidden or invisible breakdown of structure, the structure of the self held by the selfobject functions provided by the care-giver (or later by the spouse, friends, culture, etc.). The unconscious impulses and fantasies that typically and historically have been the focus of psychoanalytic work were seen by Kohut as merely the shrapnel of disintegration and defences against this. Thus, he came to view unconscious impulses and conflicts as themselves defences against a deeper and more unspeakable dread—that of disintegration—and, as he commented (1984), ". . . the attempt to describe disintegration anxiety is the attempt to describe the indescribable . . ." (p. 16).

In his paper on narcissistic rage (1972), Kohut describes certain kinds of patients as follows:

> These patients initially create the impression of a classical neurosis. When their apparent psychopathology is approached by interpretation, however, the immediate result is nearly catastrophic; they act out wildly, overwhelm the analyst with oedipal love demands, threaten suicide—in short, although the content (of symptoms, fantasies, and manifest transference) is all triangular oedipal, the very openness of their infantile wishes, the lack of resistances to their being uncovered, are not in tune with the initial impression . . . [Kohut, 1972, pp. 625–626]

Thus, Kohut describes how, in some cases, the apparent analytic material covers, and is driven by, something much less visible. The "drive" is an absence, a hole where the core self should be. It is perhaps analogous to an astronomical black hole, invisible and discernible only through its secondary effects. He goes on:

> The nuclear psychopathology of these individuals concerns the self. Being threatened in the maintenance of a cohesive self because in early life they were lacking in adequate confirming responses ("mirroring)" from the environment, they turned to self-stimulation in order to retain the precarious cohesion of their experiencing and acting self. The oedipal phase, including its conflicts and anxieties, became, paradoxically, a remedial stimulant, its

very intensity being used by the psyche to counteract the tendency toward the breakup of the self—just as a small child may attempt to use self-inflicted pain (head banging, for example) in order to retain a sense of aliveness and cohesion. [*ibid.*, pp. 626–627]

Kohut suggests that psychodynamic conflict is used itself as a defence against the deeper danger—the breakup of the self. He refers to the cohesion of the experiencing and acting self as "precarious". Thus, the fundamental danger is of fragmentation. Kohut did not have much to say about states of fragmentation *per se*, appearing to view them as characterizing psychosis and inherently beyond the reach of analysis. He was more concerned with the *threat* of fragmentation and defences against this. To continue the astrophysical analogy, it is as if Kohut began to look beyond the visible and manifest (albeit unconscious) realms of the psyche and found the areas of dark matter and black holes that account for what is observed. The selfobject transferences, of mirroring, idealizing and twinship, tend to be invisible until they are disrupted. It is through the breakdown products of their destruction that their existence is discerned.

Disintegration anxiety is difficult to articulate and communicate, compared with other more specific anxieties (such as the series Freud described: loss of the object, loss of love, fear of the superego, castration). Kohut (1977) wrote:

> . . . the expression of the ill-defined yet intense and pervasive anxiety that accompanies a patient's dawning awareness that his self is disintegrating (severe fragmentation, serious loss of initiative, profound drop in self-esteem, sense of utter meaninglessness) . . . may initially be veiled; the analysand may attempt to express his awareness of the frightening alterations in the state of his self through the medium of verbalizations about circumscribed fears— and it is only gradually and against resistances that his associations will begin to communicate the central content of his anxiety, which, indeed, he can only describe with the aid of analogies and metaphors. [Kohut, 1997, p. 103]

A woman whom I have been seeing in psychotherapy for about twelve years, and who is having to face ending because of her geographical move, remarked "the only thing between me and disintegration is you". She had a dream in which the house that she and her husband are moving to was riddled with woodworm and in danger of collapse. The problem for her is that although she can represent fragmentation (in words and symbols) when she is communicating with me, when she is alone she has no means of articulating her anxiety; it reverts to an overwhelming and nameless dread, and she is in such a state that she cannot think or use words but simply experiences psychic agony that is beyond communication. The loneliness and desolation of such a state of mind is complete. Her childhood was characterized by isolation, rejection, emotional coldness, and sexual abuse, perhaps combined with a temperament of ADHD that added to her tendency to fragment. Another feature of this patient is that on superficial meeting she can appear rather normal—intelligent, cultured, polite—but this is a personality veneer that covers her core of fragmentation and psychic agony.

Diverse selfobject functions in adult life

In Kohut's thinking, the selfobject functions provide the bulwark against fragmentation. The infant organizes its self around its selfobjects. This organization provides order, affect regulation (Schore, 1994), and emotional meaning—or (to put this in other language) facilitates "mentalization" (Fonagy, Gergely, Jurist, & Target, 2002). While the original selfobjects are the organizing functions provided by the child's care-givers, I suggest that in later life we tend to form organizations with a wide variety of linguistic, cultural, image-based, and behavioural selfobjects. These may include systems of knowledge and belief (political, scientific, or religious systems, including psychoanalysis), tribal affiliations (including professional affiliations), daily routines (the obsessional and autistic phenomena of everyday life), addictions of all kinds (behavioural and sexual as well as pharmacological) and all manner of compulsive seeking of stimulation. In all these diverse ways we may attempt to organize our inner states of mind by linking these to external sources of stimulation, soothing, and order. The problem for human beings, as Lacan pointed out, is that we are born prematurely (in order to accommodate the large brain) and are unable to coordinate our movements and maintain bodily homeostasis without continual intervention from the mother. Thus, we begin in a state of fragmentation and require an external source of organization. Even secure attachment is built on a substrate of the fragmented self, since it is, for any human baby, only the ministrations of the mother that hold back the threat of biopsychological disintegration. This is the background threat of annihilation, which I think corresponds to what the Kleinians viewed as the manifestation of the terrifying death instinct and the early paranoid–schizoid position.

The development of structure and the threat of loss of structure

I believe it may have been as a result of Kohut's discernment of states of fragmentation that he theorized about structures of the self: the "nuclear self", the "bipolar self", the "cohesive self", and so on. Such terms denote structures (of experience, agency, goals, and values) that can hold together or fall into fragmentation according to the availability of empathic care-givers. The bipolar self, containing the person's enduring ambitions and values, expresses an inherent tension, reaching into the past and leading into the future. It is developed through the selfobject functions provided by the object, but is not inherently concerned with the relationship with the object. Kohut was concerned with psychic problems rather different from those addressed by the Kleinians or the object relations school, or perhaps even the current relational schools of psychoanalysis in the USA. Nevertheless, the disturbances, tensions, and anxieties relating to the structure of the self may underpin disturbances in relation to others. Pathological structures or patterns of object-relating may be clung to because change may threaten fragmentation of the self. Psychic change is feared because it brings the threat of fragmentation. Thus, internal working models of relationships, as well as systems of belief (religious and political systems) may be tenaciously retained because these structure the person's experience. The emergence of the unknown authentic self may evoke dread as well as joy.

The fear of change can be observed sometimes at a physiological level. I have noticed on occasion with people who have been abused extensively in childhood that when attempting to process trauma with EMDR or EFT they show a particular resistance to allowing their level of arousal and distress to diminish beyond a certain level. One such patient experienced a severe panic attack when she attempted to listen to a relaxation tape; she realized that she was actually terrified of becoming relaxed. She and others seem to use their own musculature and physiological arousal as a means of bodily armour (Reich, 1949), holding the self together and protecting against a hostile world.

Kohut implied that even when a cohesive self has been established, the threat of fragmentation may remain, ever ready to invade the self when adverse psychological circumstances are encountered. He considered that persons suffering from psychoses, borderline, or schizoid states were not amenable to psychoanalysis because the underlying state of fragmentation might be exacerbated. Certainly, the phenomenology of many severely disturbed states of mind (such as hallucinatory voices and perceptual distortions) may be understood partly as an expression of the "disintegration products" of the fragmented mind.

Furthermore, Kohut indicated that fragmentation anxiety may emerge at crucial moments of psychic change, when an existing maladaptive selfobject organization is about to be given up. For example, in the case of Mr Z (Kohut, 1979), at the point when the patient was beginning to shift from the archaic tie to the mother and turn instead to a selfobject organization with the strong father (expressed in the transference and in his emerging positively-toned childhood memories of his father), he experienced

> a number of frightening, quasi-psychotic experiences in which he felt himself disintegrating and was beset by intense hypochondriacal concerns. At such times he dreamed of desolate landscapes, burned-out cities, and, most deeply upsetting, of heaps of piled up human bodies. [Kohut, 1979, p. 431]

In one of these dreams, Mr Z's mother appeared standing with her back to him. This was accompanied by "the deepest anxiety he had ever experienced" (ibid.), expressing his realization of her icy withdrawal from him when he attempted to assert his independence, and his emerging awareness that she had never presented a smiling mirroring face in response to his own developmental initiatives.

Wider perspectives on the fragmented body-self

The motif of the fragmented body-self occurs in the theorizing of many analysts. Kohut himself drew upon Freud's inference of an autoerotic stage of bodily incoherence prior to the stage of narcissism and the formation of the ego, as well as Glover's concept of "ego nuclei". In words similar to those used by Winnicott, who wrote of "unthinkable agonies", Kohut (1984, p. 8) wrote of "the unspeakable anxieties accompanying . . . a prepsychological state". Lacan, too, wrote of the stage of the "fragmented body image", prior to the engagement with images and language supplied by the prevailing culture. He postulated that the earliest experiences of the baby are of fragmentation due to the prematurity of birth in the human species, "a primordial Discord betrayed by the signs of uneasiness and motor uncoordination of the neo-natal months" (Lacan, 1949, p. 4). He believed that this infantile hell is displaced by illusions of coherence and completeness offered by an identification with the external image found in a mirror or in the sight of another child, and later in the images offered by pre-existing culture. These are Lacan's version of the selfobject. So, for Lacan, the ego, the illusory sense of a coherent self, is rooted in this alienating identification with external images, yet the threat of fragmentation is ever present, giving rise to what he called a "narcissistic passion"—"the passionate desire peculiar to man to impress his image in reality . . ." (Lacan, 1948, p. 22). Lacan pointed out that we all must construct our "identities" from the roles, images, and language available within the culture into which we are born—especially the microculture of our particular birth family. All human beings are born into a culture, but cultures are highly variable and plastic. The identities, the selves, that human beings prize and protect so vehemently are all illusory. Yet it is the threat of this illusion unravelling and exposing us to fragmentation and dread that can make us cling to it with such passion, as evidenced in fanatical religious and tribal conflicts throughout history. The wish to escape the terror of the disintegration of the illusory image gives rise, I suggest, to the ubiquitous human tendency to terrorize others and to impose an identity on them. Much of the distribution and economy of power in the world may depend upon who is most successful at imposing identity on the other (see Mollon, 2002a).

Drug induced fragmentation

We find examples of the breakdown of the illusory self in certain forms of reactions to excessive use of recreational drugs, such as marijuana. A young woman of nineteen, who had used marijuana extensively since the age of fourteen, described an occasion when she had smoked some particularly potent variety on her own. She had felt overwhelmed with utter dread and terror, believing that she was going to die, but feeling totally unable to communicate the nature of her anxiety. Since then she had often felt prone to anxiety and panic, as well as to chronic feelings of depersonalization. I suspect that such a state of mind, precipitated by marijuana poisoning, involves a partial decathexis of language—by which I mean language in the broadest sense of all the structures of symbol and meaning that underpin the organization of our phenomenal world. This decathexis means that the net of language and symbol that normally holds us, supporting our sense of self and identity, our location in a particular cultural, social, and familial matrix at a particular point in history, falls away, leaving the subject stranded ⁎ in an empty psychological space. Without words we cannot adequately reach out to others. Without words—the mother tongue given in lullabies of our earliest interactions—our experience becomes dumb and beyond the reach of empathy.

The artist's dilemma

The identities we take in from the available roles and images in the surrounding culture could be seen as our psychological clothes. Without them we feel naked, exposed, and vulnerable. This was brought home to me when talking with a young woman patient who is an artist. She attended art school and obtained a decent degree. However, her art is difficult to categorize, seeming to be somewhere in the area of conceptual and performance art. This has not been commercially successful. Sometimes she thinks she would like to do something very conventional. She told me of how she often feels anxious and self-conscious on leaving her house, as if naked, or wondering if she is inappropriately dressed. In some vague way she felt this was connected with her creativity. As she was speaking, it suddenly occurred to me that she was telling me of how it felt for her not to have any familiar or recognized social role and identity, that she felt unclothed without a category to place herself in and for others to place her in. This idea intrigued her and we went on to look at the dilemma of the artist. The creative urge leads to a suspension of the usual social categorizing of self, others and life as a whole, and yet this leaves the artist psychologically naked (without a semiotic covering) and exposed.

Kohut and Lacan

The combination of Kohut and Lacan (although these two are very different in style and culture) can be very fruitful. Both view the stage of the fragmented self as fundamental. Putting the two together, we can arrive at the following stark insight. All human beings are born into a state of disorganization and chaos—Lacan's "Primordial Discord"—because the infant is unable to coordinate and regulate its own body. The infant must form a system with the care-giver, the selfobject. Through the adequate availability of the empathic selfobject, the baby's mental and physiological being is organized, but the threat of chaos–fragmentation is ever-present. While the original selfobject is usually the mother, the need to form a system with an external organization remains throughout life. In addition to forming selfobject systems with significant other people, human beings also create organization through locking into/latching on to all manner of diverse structures and patterned phenomena. These include behavioural routines, addictions of all kinds, belief systems, identities (familial, tribal, racial, cultural, or professional), and all the linguistic and quasi-linguistic structures within which we find our place in the social world. Threats to these—for example, through confrontation with competing belief systems—bring the dread of disintegration anxiety.

The appeal of cults

As the traditional structures of society rapidly change in our "post-modern" world, there are increasing signs of disintegration anxiety, easily recognized in cultural and artistic expressions. Another striking symptom is the increasing appeal of fundamentalist and extremist religious organizations, including cults of all kinds. The contemporary cult tends to recruit from the emotionally vulnerable, offering a ready-made organization, with a set of clear beliefs and codes of behaviour, along with a nurturing group atmosphere to take care of attachment needs. Prior to joining, the individual may feel listless, lacking a sense of purpose, with clear goals and values—in Kohut's terms, suffering from an enfeebled or partially fragmented self—but after joining the cult he or she experiences all the sense of well-being that results from establishing a new self-object organization with an idealized object (the group, its beliefs, and its charismatic leader).

The addiction to familiar beliefs and organizing theories is profoundly true also of psychoanalysts, psychotherapists, and psychologists. Psychological practitioners of all kinds are, in my experience, often intensely loyal to their own theoretical beliefs, in such a way that may preclude openness to phenomena incompatible with those beliefs. We all look at clinical phenomena through a conceptual/theoretical lens and think we are seeing things as they really are, but this is not the case. Psychoanalysts and therapists are often deeply conservative in their thinking, despite the radical and revolutionary nature of the original psychoanalysis. While Freud was forging a truly new, independent, and lonely path, most of those who have come after have been , to some extent, followers, and each innovator has tended to spawn slavish adherents. Why is this so? There may be a number of contributory factors, but one could be the appeal of a seemingly powerful theory or scientific paradigm. This has an organizing function, analogous to that of a paranoid delusion that creates order out of the perceptual, cognitive, and emotional chaos of the psychotic state. Without an organizing theory of the world we are faced with potential fragmentation. The existence of phenomena incongruent with our theory of the way things are tends to evoke anxiety, as is very commonly the case in relation to EMDR.

Suicide as an organizing desire

Here is a brief vignette illustrating fragmentation. A woman of thirty presented with a relentless desire for suicide although she did not display any other psychiatric symptoms of depression. She appeared professionally competent and successful, as well as socially and sexually attractive. However, her childhood had been characterized by neglect and chaos at the hands of her alcoholic mother, followed by multiple foster homes. Her adult life had reinforced her general sense of disillusionment regarding the reliability of human beings. She was extremely intelligent and articulate and communicated vividly in psychotherapy, arguing vehemently regarding her right to take her own life. However, she complained that I was insufficiently responsive, did not give her clear guidance regarding solutions to her problems, and that psychotherapy took too long and would have an uncertain outcome. Her concern with control was a prominent feature, as she readily acknowledged. The therapy was characterized by an alternation between periods in which she allowed me to arrive at a deeper understanding and emotional contact with her, when she would indicate increased trust in me, and other periods when she would become hostile, combative, and would break off the therapy. A deep fear appeared to be of becoming trusting and vulnerable and of then being hurt and of feeling utterly helpless. Her failure to kill herself in two very serious suicide attempts left her distraught. On returning to see me after one of her periods of withdrawal, she reported having spent a couple of weeks in a psychotic state—not sleeping, feeling confused, "thinking every thought in the universe", hallucinating, experiencing paranoia, feeling overwhelmed with meaning and yet not understanding anything—a state she had never experienced before (at least not that she remembered). However, one day she had woken up and this state and her suicidal feelings were gone. She described feeling calmer and more positive. I talked to her about my thoughts regarding the stage of the fragmented self, and how the fear of fragmentation may have been particularly pronounced for her in view of her early experiences. This was meaningful to her and she acknowledged that during this period of confusion and disorder she had longed for the certainty of her previous clinging to her plan for suicide. I put to her that she had, as part of a healing process, relinquished her previous very rigid organization of her psyche and entered a spontaneous regression to the stage of the fragmented self from which she had eventually re-emerged in a new less rigid state of organization. She found this formulation extremely plausible and intriguing. I also had a vivid impression of how close she had been in her state of confusion to the possibility of reorganizing on a psychotic basis of delusional structures.

The false self

The subject's alienation in language, the paranoiac structure of identity emphasized by Lacan, can be viewed as the broader socio-cultural version of the alienation in false imported images that can occur within the personal relationships of the original family. Here we encounter the false self described by Winnicott—or the "alien self", as recently described by Fonagy, Gergely, Jurist, & Target (2002). Similarly, Kohut described many instances in which the child's natural exhibitionism had been hijacked by the mother's narcissism, her wish to have a child that mirrored *her* and fulfilled her ambitions. The authentic self—the child's own initiatives and his or her wishes to be mirrored and affirmed—is oppressed by an alien self based on the mother's narcissistic desires (Mollon, 1993). However, Kohut also argued that if the child's own exhibitionistic initiatives are responded to, and if his or her needs to idealize are accepted, then the lines of development of the bipolar self can progress. This move from the false self position of adaptation to the mother's desire evokes profound disintegration anxiety, as Kohut described in his case of Mr Z.

In optimum development, the mother provides selfobject functions of showing interest and pleasure in the child's natural exhibitionistic display. When this is not the case, the exhibitionism becomes a source of anxiety and shame, the flow of energy outwards is thrown into reverse and the subject is filled with painful tension (shown literally by the response of blushing); in place of the wish to exhibit there is an urgent wish to hide, to disappear. To be overwhelmed with shame is to be in a state of disorganization; the shame-filled person cannot function coherently.

Toxic shame

Even more profound is the *toxic shame* and fragmentation resulting from abuse by a care-giver (Mollon, 2002b). For the purpose of this

discussion, I define "abuse" as the deliberate and knowing withholding, distortion, or perversion of the normal selfobject responses
for reasons of the care-giver's own sadistic gratification—gratification that might include the projective evocation in the victim of
unwanted feelings and images belonging to the perpetrator. A
process of emotional violence that I have termed "imposed identity" (Mollon, 2001) is also an aspect of this abuse—the insistence
on viewing a person in a particular way irrespective of their own
subjective experience, thereby imposing an alien identity. This definition can incorporate physical, emotional, and sexual abuse. Toxic
shame resulting from abuse is worlds away from the normal shame,
embarrassment, chagrin, and disappointment in the self that we can
all experience from time to time. This toxic shame can be lethal,
poisoning the soul and corroding any vestige of self-esteem.

Abuse and fragmentation

Whereas mirroring and availability for idealization brings about the
emergence and firming of the bipolar self, abuse within a care-giver
relationship forces the child back into the state of the fragmented
self. In response, the child organizes his or her fragmented self
around the figure of the abuser—forming an aspect of the alien self.
This is a variant of identification with the aggressor. Challenge to
the perception of the self as bad and the abuser as good brings the
threat of fragmentation. The shame is structured within the personality—resulting in a part experienced as bad and unlovable, and
another part experienced as accusing and condemning.

Another possibility is that the child does become able to
perceive the abuser as bad, but then has to organize his or her self
around this denigrated figure. Then, in contrast with Kohut's
description of the idealizing position, in which the child feels "you
are perfect and I am part of you", the formula becomes "you are
bad and I am part of you". Again this means that shame pervades
the core experience of self.

Psychic murder syndrome

I have encountered other instances in which the patient has not suffered overt abuse in childhood, but the mother's rejection of the child's own communicative initiatives and his or her needs for understanding and empathy have been so profound that the potential authentic self is pervaded by shame and its development is ✳ blocked. In such instances the early environment was perceived as fundamentally opposed to the child's actual, authentic self and as intent on replacing it with a preferred alternative. I have written about this in a paper on "psychic murder syndrome", using the metaphor of a "Stepford Child", derived from the film *Stepford Wives*, in which the wives in a small respectable town were all killed and replaced with identical replicas that behaved in ways more to the liking of the husbands (Mollon, 2002b). In these circumstances the child may internalize the psychically murderous environment and the murder of the authentic self then continues internally throughout later life, the process being particularly activated whenever genuine emotional intimacy and attachment threatens. The maintenance of the psychically murderous structure is driven by disintegration anxiety.

In this outline so far, I have been describing ways in which the stage of the fragmented self—and the threat of regression to this state—are countered by the taking in of alien structures that are mistakenly perceived as "self". If offered a therapeutic environment, the patient may seek unconsciously the opportunity to return to the early unmet selfobject needs, discarding the false self structures, but risking a descent into irreversible fragmentation. Prior to the work of analysis, the patient knows neither self nor other. It is only by clearing away the transference effigies,[2] whereby both self and other in the consulting room are perceived in terms of imposed ✕ images, that the truly spontaneous and inherently unknown self can begin to emerge. This point of growth and change brings the terror of disintegration as familiar structures are relinquished.

Implications for EMDR work

Because EMDR and energy approaches tend to bring about processing very fast, disintegration anxiety naturally comes to the fore. Rapid change, even if positive, can be alarming. This is particularly the case if the person's ego, or psychological organization, is rigid or brittle, as it may be if a precocious independence and control had to be established because the childhood care-giving environment was inadequate, abusive, or unpredictable. EMDR will then come up against strong resistance, driven by disintegration anxiety. This would be the basis of a negative therapeutic reaction, or what the energy psychologists call "psychological reversal". To some degree the negative reaction to processing can be countered by addressing the disintegration anxiety itself with EMDR or EFT. Disintegration anxiety needs to be understood and explained.

Notes

1. A detailed discussion of the work of Kohut and his concept of the self-object can be found in Mollon (2001).
2. "The subjective medium is the transference effigy, that is, an invisible image of the object that is transposed between the analytic subject and the analyst, one that the subject cannot distinguish from the analyst without the analyst's interpretive intervention" (Grotstein, 1997, pp. 211–212).

CHAPTER SIX

EMDR treatment of a travel phobia with complex traumatic roots

(with Sid Singer)

The following account is an edited version of a talk by my colleague Sid Singer, concerning a patient he treated very successfully with EMDR in eleven sessions. It illustrates vividly the interweaving of past and present trauma in the development of anxiety, as well as the penetration of trauma from the previous generation. The structure of the patient's psychological difficulties was, schematically, as follows. A persisting phobia of travelling in a car (worse when a passenger) began eighteen years ago. This onset had followed the death from meningitis of the patient's young child. The crucial moment of onset had occurred while travelling with her husband on holiday following her son's death. On a mountain road, while her husband was driving, she had become overwhelmed with emotion and panic. Earlier contributors to her anxiety arose from her perception of her parents as providing insufficient care and protection. She recalled fear during childhood car journeys as her parents quarrelled and her mother expressed anxiety over her father's driving. A pervasive backdrop to her childhood experience was the silent reverberation of the fact of her parents being survivors of the holocaust. All these areas of trauma and emotional pain were processed rapidly and easily through EMDR.

Simone

Session one

Simone was a fifty-year-old woman who had lived in England for over thirty years. She was born in New York into a Jewish family. She is highly intelligent, very articulate, and dynamic—on the board of an international company. The presenting problem was a travel phobia. I saw her for a total of eleven sessions. She had been recommended to undertake EMDR by a friend in New York. Previously she had participated in many personal growth workshops and therapies of various kinds.

The presenting problem was that she has always been very anxious as a passenger in a car. She was able to identify the problem more clearly for the last eighteen years or so, but was aware this had been the case all her life. She did not experience anxiety when she was the driver. Her parents were also bad passengers in cars. The anxiety was experienced most strongly on motorway-type roads, or any sort of mountain road, where it would emerge as absolute panic. As a result, she could not participate in motoring holidays.

The problem started eighteen years previously, shortly after the death of her second child, a boy who was eighteen months old at the time. He contracted a very sudden and severe attack of meningitis, and died within days. She was naturally devastated. In an attempt at recuperation, a few months later the family decided to take a holiday in Italy. When travelling on a mountain road, just three months after the death of the child, she entered a state of panic that was so severe that she actually got out of car while it was still moving.

History

Both parents were holocaust survivors, having had spent many years in Auschwitz. Although Auschwitz was an extermination camp, many thousands of people did survive. Simone's mother was one such survivor; her father not only survived being in Auschwitz, but then survived a forced labour march—those were the marches during which most people just died on the way—and they both ended up in New York where they lived within a community of holocaust survivors. The communities of holocaust survivors in the United States, perhaps rather unlike those in Britain, not only commemorated the holocaust but relived it continually, talking about it, sending their children on annual holocaust summer-camps to learn about it, and this was the atmosphere in which she grew up.

Simone had two younger brothers. Her mother had died four years previously, but her father was still alive in New York. Academically she was extremely precocious as a child, skipping several grades, and graduating from university at the age of nineteen. She then visited Europe, and in Amsterdam met her future husband and shortly after married him and came to live in England. Simone's husband is a university professor. They have three surviving adult children.

Other traumas

Some years prior to this therapy, Simone had had a mastectomy and various further operations but was now healthy. Her pattern has been to deny her illnesses. She is a victim of the holocaust in the sense that she was the child who not only had to remember the holocaust but also had to be happy to compensate for the suffering. This may reflect a common reaction amongst parents of the holocaust—that their children have to be happy to compensate for their own suffering.

As a child, Simone presented much oppositional and other challenging behaviour expressing distress. At the age of seventeen she made a suicide attempt by taking a drug overdose in an attempt to demonstrate her unhappiness. This may be understood partly in relation to the reactions of the parents as holocaust survivors. Her mother particularly was over-anxious, worrying about everything, and experiencing continual panic and pessimism, while her father, by contrast, tended to use denial. Simone was constantly being made aware of her history as a child of holocaust survivors. All the children she associated with were children of holocaust survivors, and her holidays were summer camps for the children of holocaust survivors. So, at the age of seventeen she reacted against all this pressure, and was very unhappy. Following her suicide attempt, family therapy was recommended. They did start family therapy, apart from one brother, who declined to attend, but within a few sessions both parents had refused to participate. Their attitude was that it was her problem. So for four years she went to individual therapy, which she said helped her to understand a great deal, but did not change anything.

The phobia started when she felt her husband was driving too quickly on a mountain road. She became hysterical but he would not stop. Eventually she forced him to stop by actually getting out of the car while it was still moving. The problem had become so bad over the years that last time they planned a visit to the USA they had to cancel it; she refused to go because she would not travel in a car. Her father was quite ill, she wanted to pay him a visit, and they wanted to visit their daughter, so they decided shortly before coming to see me that they would go to the States in July and she was determined to try to overcome this problem before the holiday. This gave me a window of about six weeks to try to change this. Apart from a discussion of EMDR and what to expect and how we were going to do the treatment, that was the end of session one.

Session two

First we created a "safe place", which was her bedroom: in bed or alone in her room, watching TV, snuggled under her big white duvet with a soft pillow feeling cuddled and safe, and the word that would trigger this was "soft".

We clarified the EMDR protocol as follows.

1. The target problem is the passenger phobia, which started eighteen years ago.
2. The worst image is on the mountain road in Italy. In the passenger seat she could see nothing on the side of the road just the sheer drop; she became hysterical and started screaming so that her husband had to stop the car and she got out.
3. Negative cognition—"I am weak, I am stupid".
4. Positive cognition—"I am capable, relaxed, courageous".
5. Validity of Cognition (VOC): the validity of the positive cognition was somewhere between four and five (on the scale of 1–7).
6. The emotions associated with the scene on the mountain road were anger and disappointment with herself. This seemed to surprise her.

7. The SUD level (on the scale of 0–10) was quite low at this point, between three and four.

8. The bodily sensation was in her stomach, which felt "as though it were in a knot".

We went straight into eye movement, using the light bar in the standard way. Sets of eye movements were generally in the region of 40–60 saccade, with very little intervention on my part. In the transcription of the EMDR that follows, my interventions are enclosed by square brackets, and my explanatory notes are in italics.

EMDR

1. I'm feeling cut off.

2. It's not okay. *Abreaction.*

3. My son is dead, and I have to pretend to be on vacation.

4. I am angry.

[Where do you feel that?]

In my chest

5. I am angry with my husband but there's nothing that he could have done . . . but I just keep going back to that.

6. I'm very tired, I'm angry with my mother.

7. Like I'm being spun around, having to take care of everyone, I just want to get out. *Intense abreaction.*

8. Whatever I do . . . my son is still dead.

9. I wish I was stupid—then I could block it out.

10. It's my fault for being so smart.

11. I am being punished—but I don't know what I did.

12. There's a voice telling me I am too smart for my own good . . . I feel like a rat in a cage.

[Whose voice is it?]

It's my father's.

13. At seventeen . . . after I took the overdose . . . in family therapy . . . after a while my parents wouldn't come . . . they said I was sick, not them. My brother never came. *Intense abreaction.*

14. *Abreaction*. Unsafe . . . abandoned . . . they left me to do all that alone.

15. I just keep saying to my parents, I was never in the camps, I was never there.

16. They made my world so unsafe, I don't know why, just so unsafe.

17. I feel frantic, I'm running around from place to place, opening door after door looking for somewhere safe . . . frantic.

18. I'm stupid . . . it's stupid just running from place to place . . . I'm tired . . . I'm stupid . . . there is no safe place.

19. I'm not stupid . . . I can be strong, but I don't know how. *Intense abreaction*.

20. I'm confused.

21. All sorts of opposites . . . pulling me in different directions . . . but I'm only human.

22. Just a jumble.

[Return to target.]

It's understandable.

23. I took it all on myself to protect my family.

24. If I'm anxious all the time it will prevent things from going wrong.

[Where did you learn that?] From my mother.

25. Seeing my mother saying my father was too stupid to be afraid.

26. My father saying, "Just cut off", . . . but I can't. My father saying "You're too clever for your own good." (Laughter.)

27. *Return to safe place and close of the session.*

Session three

Simone reported feeling fine, but said she was stunned by how much emerged in the previous session, and how far back it went. She reported many vivid dreams about solving problems that were just out of reach. I asked her how she felt during the week and she said she felt all right. There had been a couple of significant events. She had to go to a funeral on the M25, her husband was driving, and they were a bit late. They were in a hurry and driving fast, but she felt totally relaxed in the car, with no problem whatsoever. She said she was stunned and could not believe this had happened. She described coming back from the funeral in the rain, which was an even worse situation, but with no problem. Another significant development was that she had started to talk to her husband about his experience of her behaviour, and she suddenly realized that she used him to relieve her anxiety—that she would provoke a fight and thereby feel relief from the anxiety and stress. She had other insights, one of which was a realization that her mother had tried to turn her into the sister (i.e. the mother's sister) who had perished in the holocaust. She talked at length, going over these issues that had come up the previous week; it was obviously a much lighter session and we prepared then for the following session the week after.

Session four

Simone told me that she had travelled in the car with her husband to pick somebody up at the airport, and that had not been a problem. Later it was raining, and she still felt fine. Then at some point her husband had got a bit impatient and hooted a driver in front, and she panicked again. She had become anxious, upset, and had asked him to stop. He didn't stop, kept on driving, and she had became hysterical, very angry, and then very afraid. Later on they talked about it and he recognized that it was his fault. He accepted that he could have driven slowly, but had just repeated the old pattern and he apologized for that.

When I asked her how she was feeling generally, she talked about feeling that she could not trust her husband to care for her; she believed that he wanted to be taken care of, and she thought he was resentful that she has had all these illnesses. This may again be a typical second generation holocaust reaction—the feeling that no one can be trusted. With regard to driving, she said she was more comfortable, and had even offered to give somebody a lift on the North Circular Road.

She had avoided thinking about other issues, but she had had a disturbing dream about going for a tattoo—a number—which clearly relates, of course, in some way to the numbers tattooed on the arms of holocaust victims. She felt that over the previous few days she had felt a lot more caring towards her father, and she had lots of memories about her father, some very pleasant and some not so pleasant. In particular she remembered when she was a child, four or five years old, and they got their first car. The family had started having weekend journeys out into the mountains, and she and her mother would always be anxious on these journeys. She recalled a particular place where her father would take a short cut over a bridge; her mother hated it and used to get angry and agitated about it. Her father would ignore her, and this was a cause of conflict between them. Simone remembered being very afraid on these journeys. She had another memory which came back to her: at the age of five driving through Harlem, which at that time was a particularly dangerous part of New York, and she remembered being very afraid.

She herself had been too fearful to drive until four years ago.

The EMDR process was focused upon her fear of being a passenger in a car, but targeting the image of being in the car with her parents in the mountains, when her mother was very frightened. Her body sensation was reported as anxiety in her stomach and chest.

EMDR

1. Fear . . . mountain road, high bridge, why don't they stop arguing?
Abreaction.

2. I want to put cotton-wool in my ears and block it out. My mother is scared and my father doesn't care.
The repetition is very obvious.

3. Very angry with my father.

[Where do you feel that?] In my chest. *Intense abreaction.*

4. I didn't exist, I wasn't entitled to be there.

5. Completely lost, I don't have anywhere to be with the memory.

6. A clear picture of being with my husband and wanting to pummel him and say, "I'm not okay".

7. Like a rat in a maze, everywhere I go there is a dead end. *Abreaction.*

8. I'm in a box . . . in one corner my crazy mother, in another corner my crazy father, in a third my dead son and in the fourth my cancer . . . and there is no way out of the pain. *Abreaction.*

9. I am five years old, and the only one who can take care of me is me. I am angry with my husband because he can't take care of that five-year-old. *Abreaction.*

10. *She talked at some length to the effect that she relates to her herself as the five-year-old* . . . and I don't like it and I don't like her, and I know the adult in me is strong enough to take control of the five-year-old. The five-year-old is like my mother and the adult part of me is like my father . . . my father is best in a crisis, in sickness.

Then it is as though she is talking to her self as a five-year-old. I'll make you a deal, I'll take care of you even if you're not sick.

11. Its weird . . . I am negotiating a contract with myself. *She outlined the terms of the contract, whereby she is going to look after the five-year-old and the five-year-old is going to allow her to be sick. This was too complex to note down in detail.*

12. If I sign that contract . . . but it's not two people, it's only one person.

13. It feels like I don't have to be a survivor. I've signed the contract, I'm scarred but not damaged.

14. I get to be like everyone else . . . when I need the skills of survival, they'll be there.

Session five

Simone reported having had a good week, and she felt very positive. During the week she had driven to Cambridge at seventy-five miles an hour and enjoyed it, and saw it as a great achievement. She was surprised at how easy it had felt and how much she had felt in control. She went over various issues and talked a lot about how she blames her husband for not caring for her, but recognized that it was not his fault, and that actually her complaint was more that her father had not cared for her in the right way. There were other insights regarding her experiences with her parents. I asked her how the target memory felt, and she said it was not particularly distressing and that it had become just a memory. She no longer had the expectation that she should somehow have been in control. We discussed where we would proceed with the therapy now—she wanted to continue the processing around the issue of trusting herself. The way she put this was: "Why I am so afraid that something dreadful will happen?", and of course this is fairly typical of children of holocaust survivors because something dreadful always did happen. The negative cognition for the next session was going to be "I don't deserve anything good". I asked her to put this into some sort of context with an example, and she brought up her son's death. At this point there had been no discussion as to whether we would process that particular trauma but she chose to bring that as an example of her not deserving anything good.

Session six

Simone was quite anxious because this was the day before the journey to the USA for three weeks. She reported having had some good experiences on motorways, both driving herself and with her husband driving. There had been no problems and she had been very pleased with the progress. I checked with her how she felt about proceeding with the work because it is not considered good practice to do an EMDR session before a break, but she insisted she could handle it.

We started to explore the negative cognition that she does not deserve anything good. She talked about being three years old when her brother was born, and told of trying to kill him by putting buttons in his mouth. Her mother heard him choking—he was eight days old at the time—and came in time to get the buttons out of his mouth. She remembered her mother being very angry with her, and denying that it was she who had done it. Then she recalled talking to an aunt about it, saying she had just wanted him to go away. She felt that life had never been good any more, and this week that particular memory had been very strong and she had felt very tearful. She also told of lots of other examples about how bad and naughty she was as a child.

EMDR

1. Mother shouting at me, saying, "Who do you think you are?"

2. I feel really angry with my mother. [Where do you feel that anger?] In my chest.

3. She put me down all the time, images of her humiliating me, putting me down, and telling me I was making her ill.

4. I could never do enough, my grades were never good enough, my behaviour was never good enough.

5. It's as though I never knew the rules, nothing was ever enough. [Can you give me an example?] I came home from school, I was eight years old, and I and called up from the street to my mother that I was one of six children to be chosen to skip a year . . . and all my mother said was, "Be quiet, you're disturbing the neighbours." *Abreaction*.

6. *Abreaction.* I was always in trouble for seeking attention. At about age nine I had a cough for a year, day and night, and mother told me to stop seeking attention.

7. At age ten I stole from my brother to get attention, and I see myself doing the same now—I get sick or break down to get attention. When everything is all right I don't get attention.

8. I tried to think of all the things I can do, but my mind won't stay with it. [What is coming up?] All the bad things [What sort of things?] All the illness—not my son's death. At age nine my brother had gastric flu,

and I had diarrhoea but my mother told me off for copying my brother to get attention . . . that has stayed with me forever. *Abreaction.*

9. Again I feel the split between the child and the adult. I'm angry at my mother . . . they made this world unsafe and gave me no protection . . . my brother was in a cocoon, he was protected.

10. Images of my mother, hysterical. And father like Homer Simpson, passive . . . and my brother in his corner . . . and me fighting off the world. The only time off was when I got sick—so I got sick. *Intense abreaction.*

11. I don't get colds or flu, I only get serious illnesses . . . back problems from the age of eight. I don't need to be talented or do anything, I deserve to get attention. *Abreaction.*

12. But I don't believe it . . . intellectually I know it's true . . . but why don't I believe it.

[Ask yourself that question and follow the lights]

13. If there was nobody else in the world there would be me to give myself attention. *Intense abreaction.*

14. There is enough of me to be good to myself.

[What do you mean by that?] My mother does not play much of a part now.

15. It's okay not to be perfect

End of the session

The following day she went to the States, and I saw her six weeks later.

Session seven

The trip to the States had been very successful and there had been very few problems in the driving. She had spent a lot of time talking to her brother about the family history, and her mother's anxiety when travelling in a car.

There had been only two instances of anxiety. One of these was when they were driving in downtown Buffalo and she had a panic attack— the place was very desolate and crime riddled. There was another time when they were with some friends who wanted them to see a new sculpture garden in Harlem, and she didn't want to go. She became anxious and felt unsafe, but was able to hide it and instead invented a headache as an excuse to go home.

We continued to discuss what the next target would be, and it was a negative cognition, "I am crazy, I am powerless, I have no control over acting crazy, and I have no choice". This related to the incident in Buffalo, because both the husband and the son, who had been in the car, were angry with her and she herself was scared by her own response. She recalled that her mother had behaved in exactly the same sort of way, and Simone had regarded her as crazy. When she and her husband are arguing he accuses her of being crazy.

Session eight

In this session she reported feeling a bit low. She had had a dream of a childhood friend who had died at the age of sixteen and had told her he had run out of excuses for being dead (or possibly excuses for *not* being dead) and she had connected this her to own situation. Driving was not a problem—even as a passenger she did not even think about it. However, she was aware of the panic of leaving home, which she had had all her life, and the fear of new places. She felt this related to her childhood insecurity. She recalled a summer camp at the age of sixteen, when she had gone home because she was in a panic and hysterical. She thought her mother was pregnant at the time. Being at home had been even worse, and she had gone back to the camp.

She talked about a constant low level of anxiety, and I asked her to recall her earliest memories of that. She said she recalled being very anxious in 1961, when her father had gone to Israel to visit his brother, who was dying. She was twelve at the time. At age seven she had learned that her father had a brother in Poland who had converted to Catholicism, and that her father had refused to sponsor him to come to the USA.

Again she referred to the incident at age three when her brother had been born, and she put buttons in his mouth. She recalled the screaming and shouting, and the aunt asking her what did she want to happen, and she said she just wanted him to go away. She had no recollection of being punished for it.

She brought up lots of memories of being treated unfairly, bullied in school at age ten; a teacher not believing her about something, some incidences of shoplifting—she had been caught and made to feel guilty but never actually punished. She reported feeling very angry with her husband lately without any apparent reason, and she was able to compare this to the way that her mother used to behave with her father.

I was trying to find where we were going, what would be the next target, but not wanting at this point to suggest a target of the death of her son, although this seemed to be the obvious one that she was avoiding; I felt it would be better to wait and see if this came from her rather than forcing the process. We seemed to be going round in circles a bit at this point. She then brought up issues about sexuality and intimacy, and not wanting to be touched. Her not wanting any sort of intimacy was causing a problem both for her and for her husband, but he was being very stoic about it. She mentioned a number of therapies she had had prior to the death of the child. At this point I decided to take the initiative and I asked her if might be a good time to work on the death of her son. She seemed quite relieved that I had actually suggested this and said that she did. She said she knew this would open up all sorts of issues but she wanted to do it.

Session nine

She started by saying that she had been quite depressed lately, she felt she had been feeling the grief like a tumour.

The EMDR process was focused on the sudden death of her son eighteen years previously from meningitis, the target memory being of leaving the hospital without him, the negative cognition of "I'll never be OK again", and the positive cognition of "I can be happy again" (VOC of 2), the main emotion of desolation (SUDS of 8), and the physical sensation of a lump in her throat.

EMDR

1. I'm completely alone.
2. A part of my heart was torn out. *Intense abreaction.*
3. How can I fix this?
4. Running from place to place, like there is no answer.
5. I have to take care of everyone . . . if I was alone I wouldn't have to feel anything. What did I do to deserve this? *Intense abreaction.*

6. *At this point I stopped trying to write anything down as Simone was in such distress that I didn't want to leave her and I just focused in on her. There was no way of finishing this adequately, so we decided exceptionally to continue the following day.*

Session ten

The following evening we continued from where we left off. I was not able to write any notes of the details since it was almost impossible to detach from her grief and from the processing. The issues coming up included many insights, lots of thoughts about the holocaust, themes connected with the parents and their treatment of her, and a great deal of intense abreaction. We did manage to reach a closure in that session.

Session eleven

We met the next week and Simone felt there had been an enormous change for the better, but she could not for the life of her remember exactly what we had talked about the previous week—and I had to admit that neither could I! She felt that a huge change had taken place. The week had been chaotic but now she felt much better. She felt light and reported a huge change in the relationship with her husband. During the week she had allowed him to become close, she had taken down the wall that existed between them since the death of the child, and he was able to respond to that and it was a very positive experience. She now felt very much closer to him, both physically and emotionally, than she ever did before. She felt that she no longer feared the eighteen-year-old son leaving home and leaving a vacuum, a prospect that had previously terrified her because he was due to go to college. She described how she no longer felt a victim. She felt that although the previous therapies had helped her to understand, they had not enabled her to change the way she felt, but this time she did feel differently. She felt that she could enjoy life and have fun without always having to work and justify her existence. She saw that it was her parents who were the survivors, not her.

Simone then recalled that previously she had brought up an image, and she reminded me of it, of her father on the death march, and how she had felt that she had to continue the march, but now she did not feel she had to do that any more. She gave an example of a change that had occurred: she had been participating in a personal growth course, and one of the tasks had been to develop a social action programme. She had created a brilliant programme, but the significant difference was that at one time she would have felt she had to do everything, whereas now she felt she could delegate and get others to do the work.

Simone said she felt she had reached the dark corners of her mind. I asked her how it felt when she talked and thought about the death of the child. She said she felt that she had carried the weight of the child on her shoulders for eighteen years, and now she could put it down. She gave another example: her daughter in California was getting married, and Simone had been very angry and resentful that the daughter had been planning it all herself and not involving her, and now she suddenly felt that this did not matter and she could just enjoy it. She very happy about it and could talk to her daughter about the details and plans. Moreover, she had made a decision to talk to her daughter about many things which they had never talked about before, including the death of her son. She felt this was a real opportunity now to start resolving unfinished business.

Simone concluded that a fundamental change had occurred that she could not explain or even describe. At that point we mutually decided this was as far as we needed to go, and we terminated the treatment.

Follow-up data

Follow-up at one year indicated that the gains achieved during the EMDR had been sustained.

Comment

Sid Singer's work with Simone covered a great deal of traumatic and psychodynamic ground in a short time. The results were clear in terms of resolution of the presenting phobia as well as other improvements in various aspects of life. After the trauma of the scene on the mountain road following her son's death had been processed, Simone was able to travel as a passenger without anxiety. The related childhood scene of the mountain road in her parent's car was then processed, along with much material to do with critical parental attitudes towards her. Her murderous rivalry towards her brother was processed. Eventually the core trauma of her son's death was addressed. Neither Simone nor the therapist could remember the content of this affectively intense session, perhaps reflecting the operation of appropriate repression, and indicating that positive change is not necessarily dependent on insight. The result was that Simone felt better, free of her disabling anxiety, and enjoying an improved relationship with her husband and daughter. She felt that a fundamental change had taken place, and it really did not matter that she could neither explain nor describe this!

CHAPTER SEVEN

Jane: EMDR and psychotherapy with a traumatized and abused woman

Jane was a thirty-five-year-old Dutch woman with a background of drug abuse and chaotic relationships involving violence from men. For a brief period her three young children had been taken into care, but were now living with her again. She had managed to establish a more settled way of life, free of drugs, but was still troubled by traumatic events of the past during the time when she lived in a crime-ridden area of Amsterdam. She felt fearful much of the time, and showed continuing symptoms of PTSD. Her childhood had involved some sexual abuse by her brother. She had felt close to her mother, but perceived her as needy and neglectful. Her relationship with her father had been distant, and her parents had separated when she was aged fifteen. Jane had undergone counselling previously, with some benefit. We agreed to proceed with a few sessions of EMDR, focused initially on the sexual abuse by her brother.

Overall narrative revealed by EMDR

Although the ensuing narrative is not simple and linear, the overall story of Jane's life emerges very clearly in these ten EMDR sessions.

Thus, she felt neglected and unprotected as a child, desperately wanting her mother's love, yet experiencing her mother as manipulative and "flighty". She experienced her father as violent and frightening. Her brother sexually abused her. Further abuse and trauma occurred in sexual relationships in her teens. She became cynical and promiscuous. Her emotional pain and traumatic stress were blocked with extensive use of alcohol and drugs. Rage at her mother is a recurrent theme in the EMDR sessions. She also manages to report (more directly than she ever had before, apparently) specific episodes of abuse and trauma—experiencing relief as the emotions are abreacted through the eye movements. Her awareness of the defensive function of her drug and alcohol abuse becomes clearer as a result of the EMDR.

Format of the session narratives

The client's verbatim speech is reported without quotation marks. Summaries of speech are in brackets (. . .). Direct speech by the therapist is in square brackets [. . .]

Session one

(As Jane tried to think of a "safe place" for the initial EMDR, she reported feeling relaxed by the eye movements, but also expressed sadness and tears. She said she had lost her sense of safety; the only safety she used to feel had been through drugs when she had no feelings. She spoke of having felt confused as a child, of having tried to be a "good child", feeling safe when near her mother, but feeling scared of her father. She recalled that her father would hit all three children rather than find out who had actually committed the misdemeanour, and described an occasion when he had "kicked me all the way down the street when I was aged six".)

Jane continued:

1. I'm feeling really angry. . . then really scared . . . I feel sick in my stomach . . . and ashamed and embarrassed . . . wanting to hide. . . like I've done something terrible . . . and some sadness.

2. I'm thinking "where's my mum?" I'm angry with her now . . . all I can remember is my dad being violent . . . why didn't he do it to my

sister? . . . I just feel it was wrong what he did . . . makes me angry . . .
I wish I could go back and say "Fuck off and get your hands off me"
. . . I didn't know what I'd done . . . he was just a bully.

3. I'm really angry . . . I remember going for a walk. . . blackberry picking . . . I was never special to him, but I was trying to pick loads of
blackberries to be noticed by him . . . but I never got his approval . . .
he preferred my sister.

4. I was remembering going to a wedding with my mum age about
twelve . . . getting drunk because my uncle kept buying me drinks . . .
I was wearing an outfit from Amsterdam Girl . . . then remembering
lying on a bed watching TV . . . not feeling cared for . . . then I was
thinking of dad giving my brother the cane . . . hearing him screaming
. . . feeling really scared and confused . . . standing outside the
bedroom.

5. I didn't want to be left without mum there . . . I cried if she wasn't
there . . . I would panic. I remember when my parents were away on
holiday . . . I was twelve . . . they'd left my brother in charge . . . he was
sixteen . . . he would frighten me . . . shout in my face and hit me . . .
always loads of my brother's and sister's friends around, drinking . . .
playing with a ouija board . . . a ghost said it would rape me in bed
. . . it was very frightening . . . a mad house . . . then it was like I never
went back to childhood after that . . . but I still feel like a child.

Commentary

Here Jane explores childhood trauma, relating to fears of her father's
violence, her wish to be special to him, and her feelings of being
unprotected and left in the care of her brother, who abused her.

Session two

1. I'm feeling in a state . . . I'm doing ok but I feel I don't live fully . . .
behind everything is fear . . . I feel angry . . . but I've also been feeling
a lot of joy this week and I've given up smoking. I've been feeling very
judgemental of people, but I've also felt more loving with my children,
especially with my son . . . I love being with them . . . I've felt more real
. . . and the fear of losing them has lessened . . . I feel I'm a better mum
. . . and feel a big bond with my son . . . I've never allowed it before.

2. I was feeling sad . . . then angry . . . like I'm a weak person . . . how
can I have let it all happen . . . especially with the kids . . . I feel so weak

and stupid. All through my life, if anyone has shown the slightest interest or attention I've trusted them . . . -makes me really weak . . . I've just
wanted to be wanted . . . -I've been a chameleon who would just fit in
. . . but I feel disappointment in my mother . . . she wasn't able to
provide me with love and protection . . . I'm more aware of my own
needs now . . . I'm trying to be so good after being so bad . . . I'm going
to the other extreme . . . but there's nothing that would work to stop the
fear now . . . no drugs, no person, no place . . . coming here is the last
hope . . . I'm scared to come here . . . what if it doesn't work? . . . I'm
needing to rediscover my sense of right and wrong.

3. It's bizarre . . . I was feeling I was missing my brother . . . I phoned
my sister and she mentioned my brother had visited . . . just then I had
this feeling of missing him . . . I can't understand it . . . I hate him . . . I
was wondering what he looks like . . . he was my first bully . . . I feel
sorry for him . . . I feel sorry for myself.

4. I feel really really sorry for him . . . I remember my mother kicking
him hard over the bonnet of a car because he'd lost a key or something
. . . but she would never stand up to him as he got older . . . it all seems
a bit sick . . . he manipulated her and she let him . . . I feel really angry
with my mum . . . my head and stomach are saying different things
. . . my head is saying she couldn't help it, she had her difficulties . . .
but she was really manipulative of us all . . . always these secrets . . .
"don't tell your father" . . . but I was also feeling sick about my brother.

5. (Anguished tears.) I feel sick . . . I can't open my eyes . . . like something bad will happen . . . I feel so embarrassed . . . I can't say it . . . I
feel sick . . . he's doing oral sex to me . . . I can't think about him making
me do it to him . . . making me wank him . . . I didn't understand why
it was wet.

6. I couldn't tell my mother . . . she would blame me . . . it's a feeling
I've done something bad . . . wanting to hide . . . feeling so ashamed
. . . so scared, ashamed and bad . . . there's nowhere to run . . . I'm going
to pass out . . . something bad is going to happen if I say it . . . he had
a toy gun . . . he was shooting plastic pellets up my bum . . . making me
do it to him . . . and he was trying to put his willy inside me but it
wasn't hard enough . . . it's all dark and cold . . . I hear him saying
"don't tell anyone" . . . I think he put his finger up me . . . asking if it
felt nice . . . making me wank him off . . .

7. (Relaxation.) I feel a bit sad . . . but hopeful . . . I feel relieved . . . I've
never been able to talk about it before . . . I would get to the beginning
of the memory and then would shut off . . . the roof hasn't collapsed
. . . you haven't run out screaming!

Commentary

Here Jane begins by speaking of her regrets about previous use of drugs and her longings for love and attention that led her to adopt a chameleon-like compromising of her integrity. From there she moves to thoughts of her brother, and then to a quite specific memory of his sexual abuse of her. After processing this memory she reports feeling sad, but relieved and hopeful.

Session three

(Jane reported that she had felt "really happy" after the previous session, more confident and assertive and with more feeling of self-worth, and less worries about rejection. However, she mentioned feelings of panic when she had encountered a somewhat threatening woman who reminded her of the kind of people she had associated with during her traumatic past.)

EMDR

1. [Just see what comes to mind]. I'm feeling angry . . . not about anything . . . just feeling it . . . in my stomach.

2. [Try asking yourself what you are angry about]. I am such a coward . . . angry at myself . . . scared to stand up for myself to anyone . . . just a wimp. Is it wrong not to like confrontation? Would it be normal to be afraid if you thought you would be hurt.

3. I'm afraid for my kids . . . it worries me so much if I think they might be hurt . . . I just want them to grow up healthy and confident, not like me . . . I long for them to have some mum and dad get-togethers . . . I'm frightened of something in myself . . . I don't know what.

4. I'm thinking of my mum . . . like I want to protect her . . . she's so weak . . . so stupid . . . she runs away. I let my dad bully me . . . and he bullies her . . . then she would take it out on me.

5. She's so selfish. I know she cares . . . but she can't care about us . . . she needs the attention, the love from us . . . she smothers us . . . I squirm when she gives me a kiss . . . she takes everything . . . she rejects, then smothers, then rejects . . . she blames everyone else . . . she won't take responsibility for anything.

6. She's a fucking snob . . . if I was ill she loved it . . . she would baby me, then reject me. Dad said he hated me because she babies me . . . she's a fucking victim. I can't feel angry with her because I feel sorry for her . . . she's so manipulating . . . I feel so torn because I still feel I want to look after her . . . I see her as a little girl that still needs look-ing after . . . I just wish she would fuck off . . . she just pretends to care. She could always look so good because my father was horrible. I would often sleep with my mother . . . but feel like I'm just a fucking toy for her to play with, and to put down when she finds some bloke. She can't face anything. I feel like I've done the same . . . let blokes have power over me. The more I try to do for my kids, the more I realize what she didn't do. I feel angry but torn . . . I still love her.

7. I'm frightened to get really angry. She throws these criticisms at me. She pretends to be the mum I want . . . but I can't bear it when she cuddles me . . . but part of me longs for a hug. She told me too much . . . treated me like an adult . . . I never got chance to be mothered.

8. (Laughs.) I was thinking of something dad said the other day . . . about my mother being very flighty. When I look at it now I feel OK. It's when I become a child who needs parenting that I feel pain. She's just like a child . . . I have to look after her. I so want her to be as I want her to be . . . but she's not.

Commentary

In this session, Jane speaks of her anger with her mother, feeling unprotected, manipulated, and exploited by her. She recognizes her longing for her mother's love. By the end of the session, after several sets of eye movements, her mood is lighter.

Session four

I talked to my mother . . . expressed a lot of anger . . . I tried to make her feel worthless . . . then we reconciled. I no longer feel damaged by the abuse . . . but I feel some shame about some things in my adult life . . . feeling sad about the way my life has gone . . . but am also appre-ciating the positive things . . . it's a strange new feeling . . . its unfamil-iar . . . I used to go to extremes, feeling either really good or really bad . . . -I used to have difficulty accepting how I feel without trying to change it . . . I suppose that's why I used drugs . . . it seems strange to feel these negative things, mainly sadness, as well as feeling OK. (She then talked of shame and guilt about having lost her children for a period.) I saw my son today, eating a sandwich, and I said to him "Oh I love you so much" . . . like I was seeing him for the first time. It's like it was someone else who lost the children . . . it's not who I am today . . . yet I have to take responsibility . . . but I am beginning to feel some compassion for myself about it . . . it was such a difficult time . . . I can see myself as someone who was really ill . . . I think all the time really I was wanting to be able to look after my children, but I couldn't. I saw my children go off with their grandmother today . . . I felt that . . . sadness (she gestures to her stomach) . . . I didn't use to realize that's what it was. (She talked of fears she might lose her children again, fears of doing something wrong, and fears that I might think she was not looking after her children adequately.)

EMDR

1. I'm thinking of Tom (ex-husband), their stepfather . . . anger at him . . . they sit in judgement, making me out to be so terrible . . . I'm wanting to be thought a good mum . . . feeling weak . . . scared not to have his approval . . . it's so easy for me to be the scapegoat . . . I notice I also say "sorry" a lot.

2. It's that feeling of being controlled and manipulated . . . how he is still doing that . . . I feel angry and feel sad . . . I miss having a husband . . . having another adult around. (She talked of being attracted to a particular man, of feeling vulnerable about this, of being afraid of losing Tom's approval and of losing this man's approval.)

3. I don't think I trust myself . . . so how can I trust anyone else? I feel really scared about this man. (She talked of anxieties about becoming involved with a new man, but she thought he seemed very nice. She expressed fears that I would disapprove and think she was not ready to have a boyfriend.)

Commentary

Jane reports having been able to express anger to her mother, which is followed by reconciliation between them. She describes increased feelings of love for her children, sadness regarding her earlier loss of them, and compassion for herself as having been a very troubled young woman. She speaks of having felt judged and controlled by her ex-husband and others (perhaps particularly associated with losing her children temporarily), and concludes with fears of the therapist's disapproval.

Session five

> (Jane reported that her life was going well. She felt more settled and generally much more free—"I feel it's OK to be me". She was still cautiously seeing her new boyfriend Paul, but was afraid of being hurt. She described an eruption of traumatic jealousy that had disturbed her.)

EMDR

> 1. The people I used to have in my life gave me nothing . . . just pain . . . now I have someone who is loving . . . he is worth the risk . . . but I feel sad . . . like a choice between being alone and safe or with someone and taking the risk.
>
> 2. I'm thinking of my daughter . . . she doesn't know people can have a good relationship . . . she doesn't have a concept of it. Whenever I meet someone I always look for the holes . . . my daughter does this too now . . . she always looks for the bad things men do . . . she doesn't understand that people live together. Do I want to show her that people don't have relationships? If I love someone else, do I love the children less?
>
> 3. I was so jealous of my dad . . . I wanted mum all to myself . . . it's like a fear of there not being enough love to go round . . . like my mother could only love one person at a time.
>
> 4. I feel angry towards my mum. (She described an episode when she was fifteen and living rough. The man her mother was living with would not let Jane visit and her mother did not insist—"she didn't care enough about me". She spoke of feeling very angry.)
>
> 5. I am too angry . . . I fucking hate her so much. (Jane spent some minutes expressing strong rage about her mother, before becoming calmer.) All I wanted was to be loved . . . it's all I ever wanted . . . it's not like that any more, but I still fear that no one can ever love me enough. I'm always looking to be mothered. It's this lack of protection . . . my mother left me in a caravan with Tony (violent man) when I was age fifteen. I feel really sad.
>
> 6. I'm so angry again . . . angry about my brother . . . so frightened of him . . . its like any man can do whatever they want to me . . . I've got

this feeling of indigestion . . . a stab of pain . . . I feel bad for feeling so angry at mum . . . it made me feel unlovable. I feel sad for her . . . I want things to be different.

Commentary

Jane begins by referring to her cautious embarking on a new relationship, contrasting the possibility of being loved with the pain and rejection she had experienced in the past. She speaks of her childhood jealousy, wanting her mother to herself. This mirrors the jealousy she reported in relation to her new boyfriend. She then goes on to express increasingly intense rage at her mother for not loving her and protecting her. This is interwoven with rage at her brother, who abused her, and her feeling that a man can do whatever he wants to her.

Session six

(Jane reported that she was still enjoying a good relationship with her boyfriend Paul and she felt there had been a big change in that she was more accepting of her feelings of jealousy. She spoke of increased intimacy and communication. She felt more able to acknowledge her own feelings and was experiencing more emotional freedom. She felt that letting go of her mother had allowed someone else to be in her life. At the same time she felt excited about talking with her father. She was feeling more adult and "good enough". On the other hand, she had decided to have nothing to do with her brother—she felt she would like a brother "but not that one!". She was pleased at being able to make such decisions. There was no EMDR in this session. It was agreed to end the therapy at this point, on the understanding that Jane could contact me if she found she was experiencing further difficulties; however, two months later she requested another appointment.)

Session seven

(Jane reported feelings of anxiety and panic regarding her relationship, which she felt were somehow to do with her daughter becoming age seven.)

EMDR

1. [Try asking yourself where this anxiety is coming from] I just got a feeling of panic.

2. I was thinking of when I was at infants' school—standing in the infants' school looking across the field to the junior school where I was going (i.e. she was remembering herself at age seven when she about to move to the junior school).

3. I've got a confused feeling . . . I'm embarrassed . . . I don't want to say . . . I remember being in the classroom . . . sex education . . . thinking "God the man wees in the woman!" . . . and remembering sitting in an old fashioned pram with my mother walking along.

4. I'm thinking of my mother going to the station . . . a big fear comes up then . . . there was a big playroom in the house . . . orange curtains . . . my mother going to the station . . . it was dark and wet [you were left behind?] think so . . .

5. Ballet clothes . . . sitting watching TV . . . brown shoes . . . I hated them . . . sitting there having tea . . . cold and dark . . . I just want to run . . . I feel confused.

6. My brother . . . his breath smelling . . . when that comes up it's like I don't want to know . . . I see his face . . . when I see his face I get scared . . . I don't remember being seven . . . I don't remember being eight . . . I don't really remember much.

7. (She appears very anxious and upset.) I remembered a friend, Sally, she had a brother . . . she said he tried to kiss her . . . I feel so frustrated . . .

8. I feel all over the place. When I was wanting to self-harm I was missing my brother . . . like I wanted to finish something . . . like I'd done something wrong . . .I feel anxious.

9. (Very tearful.) I want my mum. When I was sixteen with my boyfriend Tony, having sex, we'd split up . . . I'd had sex with one of his friends . . . we'd made up at a party and went back to his parent's place . . . he was being really nice to me . . . then he pulled a knife on me when we were having sex . . . I screamed . . . his dad came to the door . . . he said I was having nightmares . . . he put his hand over my mouth . . . just when I thought I was safe . . . I was so scared.

[So this is why you get frightened with your boyfriend now; when you feel safe it is a trigger for feeling upset. When you feel safe you expect it to be followed by feeling terrified, and linking back to feeling terrified of your brother.]

10. I jump out of my skin when he comes up behind me. I had quite a long marriage, but I was using drugs and alcohol to stop the anxiety . . . there was the relief of being able to shout at my partner, to get angry . . . he shouted back . . . but I've just got the memories of my husband trying to strangle me once . . . and another time sex with a man who was obsessed with holding amyl nitrate over me.

11. [Just remind yourself that these feelings are memories, it's not happening now.] I feel sad . . . it makes a lot of sense, especially the feeling about Tony . . . when I felt safe . . . With all the alcohol and drugs I must have spent many years with so many feelings suppressed. Sex is when I feel vulnerable . . . I can't keep it down.

Commentary

Jane begins with an unspecified feeling of panic in relation to her boyfriend, which she thinks is triggered by her daughter being age seven. Through the free-associative process of EMDR, she recalls her own feelings of vulnerability at that age, linking to abuse by her brother, and then proceeds to retrieve memories of later trauma at the hands of abusive men, These experiences make sense of her moments of fear in relation to her current boyfriend. She begins to understand more clearly her feelings of vulnerability associated with sex, and how she had resorted to drugs and alcohol in an attempt to suppress her chronic state of traumatic stress.

Session eight

(Jane reported that she had had a bad dream after the last session.)

Dream

I was in a big house . . . there were children on the terrace by the sea . . . there was a danger of them being washed away by waves . . . I kept saying to Paul that I had to get the kids, but I didn't . . . the water was flooding in . . . various people were getting in the way . . . I just kept thinking I've got to find my children . . . they might be washed away . . . dad was sitting in the way . . . then my kids were in a road playing, kicking a ball . . . then men made them bend over the bonnet of a car . . . I feel the fear . . . it was something to do with a tanker lorry . . . then their bodies were in the trees.

Associations

A memory of my mother beating my brother up over the bonnet of a
car, kicking him and hitting his head on the bonnet. A group I attended
for parenting ... there was a lot of anger about men abusers ... and
women were taking it out on partners.

(*Comment*. The dream clearly presents themes that derive from the
previous session: her sense of her child self having been overwhelmed
with the waves of abusive experiences and her fears for her own children now; her years of failing to protect her children; the lack of help
and protection during her childhood; her father being in the way rather
than functioning as a helpful and protective father; the allusion to her
mother beating her brother over the car bonnet; the image of the tanker
lorry, perhaps representing the huge phallus, as an erect penis would
appear to a child; the children's bodies in the trees perhaps indicating
the state of dissociation that she had resorted to during the abuse.)

EMDR

1. Anger ... and I was thinking I don't like men with curly hair ...
thinking of being thirteen ... coming back from the pub with one of my
brother's friends with curly hair ... snogging ... then he threw me on
the floor trying to do more.

2. I'm so angry I want to laugh, want to swear.

3. Loads of thoughts ... about my mum ... pathetic looking woman
... feeling really angry at her ... and angry at my dad ... but angry
with my mother for being so stupid. The man I went out with at fourteen ... he was twenty-six and married ... my mother knew.

4. [What do you think is the core of your anger with your mother?]
She's a fucking bitch ... she didn't give a shit what I did ... I can't
blame her for what I did though ... I think it's me I'm angry at.

5. [Can you feel the full extent of your anger towards your mother?] I
nearly did but I was frightened I was going to kick that over (waste
paper basket) ... I had to hold on to my foot.

6. I was feeling waves of sadness ... there was never anybody there
... nobody I could trust. Loads of thoughts about being a child ...
seeing myself as looking and not understanding ... but nothing made
sense ... I didn't know how to be, or what was expected of me, I've
just got to accept this ... that it's sad my mother couldn't parent me
... she gave me my view of men.

Commentary

Jane recalls more abusive and traumatic experiences with men, She expresses more anger towards her mother, again to do with not having been adequately protected.

Session nine

(Jane spoke of further feelings of anger and jealousy in relation to her partner.)

EMDR

1. [Where is the anger coming from?] I was seventeen or eighteen . . . I'd just got over the violent relationship, I was living in rented rooms, going with different men . . . I didn't care . . . using alcohol and drugs . . . feeling lost . . . everyone else seemed to have normal lives . . . I didn't know what normal was . . . like I was trying to live some else's life . . . I was unhappy but very cut off . . . I wanted to die, but I felt dead anyway . . . no self-worth.

2. I remember bumping into my ex-boyfriend, wanting to have sex with him, wanting to be back with him, like nothing else felt right . . . his girlfriend was having a baby . . . I used to meet him to have sex . . . he was nice to me because we weren't having a relationship . . . he said that after he'd had sex with me he would go home and make her have oral sex . . . that's probably what he used to do with me! I was so stupid! I'm not mad am I? [You think you were mad to go back to him?] It was like an obsession. I'd forgotten all that . . . but I can see it all as clear as day now. I was a cleaner at a house and there was a builder who paid me some attention, so I went off with him and had sex, but felt so empty afterwards. I just kept moving till I met my husband . . . I didn't really care who he was, he just seemed a nice bloke . . . I didn't think marriage would last. My wedding day was nice, a fantasy thing like normal people do . . . perhaps I distrust myself more than anybody else . . . like I didn't have any feelings. [You are afraid your boyfriend will behave like you did?] Yes, that he might cheat and lie like I did . . . I've got this distrust of him, but really it comes from me.

3. Mum used to have affairs . . . she would tell me the details . . . I was thirteen . . . she would be crying her eyes out, telling me about having sex.

[I'm wondering if one factor behind your anxiety is that you feel drawn back to the familiar pattern of experiencing cheating and abuse because it *is* familiar and it can be frightening to experience something different]. Yes I think so, because I really do love Paul

Commentary

With the aid of eye movements, Jane recalls vividly some of her desolate experiences with men, during which she had allowed herself to be used sexually, and how she, in turn, had adopted a cynical and exploitative attitude towards men. The conflict of trust versus cynicism is stirred up by her new relationship.

Session ten

(The light bar was broken, so this session took place with Jane wearing headphones providing continuous bilateral music.)

I felt very agitated after the last session . . . so much anger . . . full of feelings about my mother . . . I'm not used to feeling so much . . . all the lies and secrets of my childhood . . . my dad was so straight and honest and my mother was such a liar, always saying "don't tell dad". My mother is moving to Italy . . . I'm feeling abandoned . . . not wanted . . . not ever loved for me. I think my mother was like Munchausen's by Proxy, she used to revel in our being ill, she had a role and an identity then. I am able to do for myself what she wouldn't do . . . I am able to care for myself to some extent. I can accept that my father was emotionally inadequate . . . but I don't need it now. I can't reclaim what I didn't have then. I think it's all right. I think it will be nice when she is gone. The anger scared me, but it doesn't seem so bad now.

(Jane was clearly feeling calmer. With further discussion she concluded that the EMDR could end at this point. It was coming up to an August break and seemed an appropriate time to stop. She felt she had essentially processed her anger with her mother, the sexual abuse had been addressed, and she felt more at peace. These were the two main targets of the EMDR. It was agreed that no further appointments would be made at that point, but she could get in touch if she found that more work was required.)

Follow-up

A couple of months later, Jane did get in touch, requesting further help following a crisis provoked by a dispute over custody of her children. She was seen for a few more sessions, mainly consisting of conventional psychotherapy, working through some of the residual issues that had been highlighted during the EMDR. Jane continued to feel that the EMDR had been extremely helpful. Over the ensuing weeks she reported increased confidence and pleasure in herself, her relationships with her children, and her relationship with Paul.

Commentary

When Jane commenced treatment with EMDR she showed signs of chronic post traumatic stress, derived from both childhood abuse by her brother and violence from men in her adult life. During her late teens and twenties she had resorted to drugs and alcohol in order to numb her feelings. EMDR released a great deal of rage: towards her mother for being both needy and neglectful and failing to protect her; towards her brother for abusing her; towards other men who had threatened and abused her; and towards herself for letting the abuse take place. Jane recalled vivid details of abusive and traumatic experiences and felt much relief as these were processed. She acquired a new sense of self-worth and self-acceptance, became more open to her own feelings, and more able to love and be loved.

The therapeutic work based around EMDR proceeded far faster than would have been expected through conventional verbal psychotherapy. As is usually the case with EMDR, the transference relationship was of little significance, the main focus of the natural healing agenda being the processing of earlier trauma and psychodynamic conflicts.

CHAPTER EIGHT

Brief case illustrations

A wide variety of cases are described in the following pages, including rape trauma, phobia, depression and low self-esteem, sexual difficulties, the aftermath of divorce, obsessive-compulsive disorder, fetishism, and self-harm. Most involve the use of EMDR, some combine EMDR and EFT, and two are based entirely around EFT. The style of work does not always follow the original protocols for EMDR[1] (Shapiro, 2002a) or for EFT (as taught by Gary Craig, www.emofree.com), whereby the various elements of a trauma are accessed and desensitized until the subjective units of disturbance (SUDs) are reduced to zero. Instead, the EMDR is used as a general facilitation of free association and emotion-processing. It is used both to explore and to process the emerging emotions and psychodynamic conflicts. At times the emotional details and core psychodynamics elicited by EMDR are then "tapped" using EFT in order to bring about a more complete resolution. In every instance the content provided by the therapist is minimal. These methods facilitate the client's own healing process and require skill but little interpretative content from the therapist. Indeed anything more than an occasional interpretation from the therapist would obstruct the client's process. Perhaps partly because of this facilitating but unobtrusive stance from the therapist, phenomena of transference, while not absent, are not prominent and, certainly, transference is not the vehicle of treatment.

Outcome and follow-up data

All the clients described here were seen in routine clinical practice, representing a typical cross section of psychological problems, and were not part of a research programme. Follow-up data, therefore, are variable. All were sent letters asking for feedback at the time of writing this account, but only some replied. However, in most instances they had not sought further help from the mental health service; this in itself is suggestive of sustained improvement. Since EMDR and EFT tend to be brief forms of therapy, relative to traditional long-term psychoanalytic work, it is not claimed that they bring about comprehensive resolution of all the client's areas of psychopathology. The focus of the therapy is upon the presenting problem, even though this will usually link to thematically similar areas of earlier disturbance. Therefore, it is quite feasible that, having addressed some issues with EMDR or EFT, a client will seek further therapy at a later stage and, with some of the cases presented here, the illustrations should be regarded as snapshots of work in progress. It can also be the case that after years of conventional psychoanalytic therapy, a person may seek EMDR or EFT in order to resolve more fully the issues that have already been explored.

A note on the format of the clinical accounts

In most instances, the actual words used by the client during the EMDR processing are stated in the account. Where there is a summary of what is said, this is placed in brackets (. . .). Where there is an indication of a verbatim statement from the therapist, this is placed in square brackets [. . .]. For each session, the EMDR sets of eye movements are listed 1, 2, 3, etc. Each set consists of somewhere between twenty and 100 eye movements. After each set the patient is asked what comes to mind. In some cases the details of each set of eye movements and the client's response are summarized in a narrative, as in the first example of Alison.

Alison: EMDR treatment of recurrent depression following a rape

Alison was a twenty-eight-year-old woman who had been suffering with recurrent and quite severe depression following a rape by her boyfriend seven years previously. This trauma of the rape had never been addressed previously and Alison had not been fully aware of its role in her depression; in fact, for five years she had no conscious memories of the rape. Prior to this she had felt happy and confident. She described her childhood as essentially happy, although there had been a period of distress at age thirteen when various family stresses had coincided with the turmoil of her puberty. Alison was currently in a long-term relationship. She had her own highly successful business.

Alison was treated with two sessions of EMDR.

EMDR session one (two hours)

As Alison began to focus on the experience of being raped, she reported increasing distress, which then gradually began to lessen as she continued processing. She spoke more about the circumstances of the rape—her boyfriend had been drunk and it was the only occasion he had behaved in this way. He had raped her vaginally and anally. The next day she tried to carry on as normal and the episode was never mentioned between them until they eventually parted two years later. With further processing she began to recall "nice" features of the rape, such as the softness of the pillow and the comfort of the bed, and then also thought of positive qualities of her boyfriend.

She then focused on feelings of powerlessness and self-blame, feeling angry with herself for not having struggled more strongly against the rape. She referred to feeling generally not able to protect herself. Then her associations to feelings of powerlessness led to her recollections of childhood experiences with her father—not of experiences of abuse but of not having him sufficiently available to her. She talked of how special he had been to her (and still was) and how she has tried to emulate his qualities of energy and achievement, and her feelings of inadequacy in relation to him. She spoke of how she rarely saw him until she was thirteen—just brief moments of saying goodnight when she was in bed and he would return late from work. This had all changed when his business circumstances altered and he was at home much more. She recollected intense jealousy when he spent time listening to her friend who was ill while on holiday, her thought being "all these years you haven't had time to talk to me and now that you have you are already talking to my friend", and she spoke of the pain of feeling that she had not been his "top priority".

She then spoke of her feelings of anxiety and associated feelings of inadequacy, her thought being that although she was a high achieving professional woman, she could still be reduced to states of being like a frightened child during the night. As she continued processing, she concluded that the anxiety did stem from the time of the rape, and she decided that it reflected her fear of being attacked again.

Alison then recalled the feeling of strength and confidence that used to be characteristic for her prior to the rape. She remembered how she had felt strong in her body and comfortable with her sexuality. EMDR was used to enhance these feelings of confidence and security (focusing on kinaesthetic and somatic qualities of the experience, e.g. imagining how she would hold or move her body when she felt confident). By this point Alison was noticing a marked change in her experience and exclaimed, "Bloody hell—it works!"

This session then concluded with the acupressure emotional freedom technique, using this to process any remaining feelings relating to the rape and associated experiences. Alison reported strong inner reactions to this process, describing sensations that she recognized as similar to those experienced during therapeutic massage associated with the release of toxic energy.

EMDR session two

Alison reported feeling better since the previous session—less depressed, but with many more thoughts and reactions. She had become aware of further memories of physical pain during the rape, and she had also realized how fearful she had felt with her boyfriend for the rest of their relationship. Moreover, she had begun to reflect upon aspects of her current relationship that she experienced as abusive—feeling aware of her adrenaline shooting up when her partner comes home—and she spoke of times when he had been physically violent. She talked of giving herself time to consider whether she wanted to continue with the relationship or move on.

Although much positive processing was apparent, she went on to refer to her awareness of a continuing potential for depression, which she concluded was often evoked when she felt anxious or vulnerable.

As we continued the processing, she became aware of the extent of her general anxiety and how this relates to her depression, and she realized that she was continually afraid of being attacked. After associating to physical violence in her current relationship and also an attack in a park five years ago, she eventually concluded that the rape was in fact the earliest context for experiencing this kind of anxiety in relation to feeling very vulnerable. She recalled that as a child she would readily fight back if attacked in the playground and felt quite able to defend herself. By contrast, she recognized that the rape had been the first occasion when she had "lost the fight" and when she had felt real vulnerability.

With further processing, Alison became clearer about the sequence of her responses during the rape, and she became aware that it had been much more severe than she had previously recalled. Apparently her first reaction had been to fight, and then to surrender as her boyfriend overcame her, but then, when he began to rape her anally and she experienced intense pain, she had fought harder, before subsequently dissociating and surrendering. She realized that there was a definite gap in her memory of the event, which almost certainly corresponded to the period when she had dissociated.

We then spent some time focusing on her tendency to have blamed herself for not having fought hard enough during the rape. I introduced the idea that she had responded according to the biologically programmed strategies of fight, failed flight, surrender, and dissociation. With further processing she then began to revise her view of herself in relation to this episode, appreciating that she had responded as best she could.

Finally I explained to Alison the common pattern whereby the trauma of the rape had left her not only with anxiety specifically in relation to that incident, but also, due to the cracking of the illusion of invulnerability, she had been exposed to a massive influx of existential anxiety (Mollon, 2002a).

Alison had many cathartic reactions during this session. By the end she felt the issues to do with the rape had been satisfactorily processed and the work was concluded.

Follow-up

Alison was seen for a few more sessions looking at current issues in her life, particularly to do with her relationship with her partner. No further EMDR or EFT was undertaken. She continued to feel the rape trauma had been satisfactorily processed.

Commentary

Alison had been quite severely recurrently depressed for several years following the rape by her boyfriend, but for most of this time she had been unaware of the link between this event and how she was feeling, and had even banished the experience from her conscious memory for a considerable period. Through EMDR she became aware of the severity of the rape and recalled the pain. Her initial impression had been that she had surrendered to the rape without a vigorous struggle and she had felt distressed by this. However, this view turned out to be based upon her dissociation and defensive minimization of the trauma, and she began to appreciate her real feelings of vulnerability and helplessness. She realized that ever since the rape she had indeed felt vulnerable and fearful of being attacked again and that these feelings were associated with depression. As the experiences were processed Alison was able to revise, in a positive direction, her view of herself and of her responses at the time of the rape.

At an early stage of processing the rape, Alison's associations to feelings of helplessness led her to recollections of childhood inability to be her father's "top priority". What is interesting here is that although the associative link was surely valid and important, it was probably also defensive in that it took her away from the full intensity of feelings of helplessness and vulnerability in relation to the rape, which were not confronted until the second session.

Paula: treatment of self-harm relating to traumatic assault

This case describes the resolution in two sessions of a form of post traumatic stress disorder.

Paula was a twenty-one-year-old woman who presented with low mood and a number of recent episodes of self-harm, including overdoses, hitting her head, scratching, and burning. She did not know why she had begun behaving in this way, experiencing the impulses to harm herself as sudden and without apparent meaning. She had no previous psychiatric history, and indeed appeared to have been functioning well, with a job, a stable relationship, and a happy childhood.

As her background was explored, it emerged that while on holiday the previous year she had been assaulted by a man in a bar. The man had made sexual advances towards her but on being rebuffed had become suddenly and shockingly violent, punching her repeatedly in the face. She received medical treatment for various physical injuries but no psychological help. For a few weeks after the assault she had suffered nightmares relating to it and had felt anxious on leaving the house; however, she had forced herself to get on with her life, and her conscious preoccupations with the assault had faded. It was no doubt significant that the emergence of Paula's episodes of self-harm coincided with the time of year when she had suffered the assault.

Paula was initially unaware of a possible link between her psychological symptoms and the assault, although she accepted this as a plausible hypothesis when it was presented to her. It was apparent that her personality was characterized by strongly avoidant and dissociative features. She agreed to undertake a session of EMDR focused upon the assault.

EMDR session

1. (Paula chose home as her safe place.)

2. [Just think about the assault and see what comes to mind] I was just counting the eye movements that time.

3. I was remembering being hit on the head—punched—he was hitting me repeatedly . . . I couldn't get off my stool . . . there was loads of blood, and he looked so happy with what he had done to my face, he was laughing . . . then some English people took me back to the apartment . . . it was a nightmare, blood all over the sheets, my face such a mess . . . I had a broken nose and cheek bone.

4. [What was the worst part?] Seeing him laughing . . . laughing . . . his friend patted him on the back.

5. I remember thinking "Oh my God he's hitting me."

6. Then I was remembering feeling sick.

7. I was feeling how painful the injuries were . . . the injuries in my mouth . . . feeling stiff next day . . . black eyes . . . and like a golf ball lump on the top of my nose.

8. I remembered I initially laughed when I was hit . . . I thought it was a football . . . some kids were kicking a ball around and I thought I was going to pick up the football.

9. I was thinking how much I needed my mum.

10. I hate him . . . I would like to kill him . . . I would like him to *know* I was going to kill him . . . I thought he was going to kill *me* . . . I was afraid he would come back.

11. I was seeing myself killing him . . . I did think I was going to die.

12. I would want him to know that it was really going to hurt.

13. (Finish with relaxation.)

Second session

On meeting a week later, Paula reported that she had felt very depressed for part of the day following the EMDR, but by the evening this mood had lifted. She commented that she had not felt this depression before, and so its emergence seemed to be part of the emotional processing. Since then she had felt better. She had spoken to her boss and he had commented that it was the first time she had talked to him about the assault. However, she felt that the experience was not fully processed. She was reluctant to undertake further EMDR because of the strong feelings it might unleash. Therefore we used EFT, since it does not involve reliving the trauma in the way that EMDR tends to. Paula responded well to this, at one point bursting into a cathartic release of tears, after which she reported feeling much better. Similarly, during the EFT processing she reported a fleeting impulse to harm herself, which quickly passed. Paula was then able to speak and think about the assault without distress. She was happy to stop at that point and did not present again to the mental health service.

Follow-up

Follow-up at eleven months revealed that Paula was continuing to feel well. Her CORE questionnaire score had fallen well out of the clinical range. She rated the benefit of the therapy as "very much so".

Commentary

Prior to the EMDR, Paula had no conscious awareness that her low mood and impulses to harm herself were rooted in the traumatic experience a year previously. Her avoidant and dissociative tendencies meant that she did not think about the trauma, and thus her self-harm behaviour was, in effect, an implicit memory. Through EMDR she vividly recalled the experience, accompanied by intense affect. It became clear that the assault had been severe and that she had feared she was going to die (always an important feature of severe trauma). She became aware of her own rage and sadistic wishes for revenge, with conscious fantasies of killing her assailant. Paula's avoidant personality style meant that she was reluctant to engage in further EMDR, even though she felt the experience was not entirely processed. However, she responded well to EFT, with further cathartic release of affect. The trauma then appeared fully resolved and since Paula had not displayed significant psychopathology prior to the assault, there appeared no need for further psychological work.

Jessica: brief EMDR treatment of chronic depression and low self-esteem

Jessica was a thirty-five-year-old married woman, with two children, presenting with chronic depression and low self-esteem. She explained that although she was married to a wonderful man and had a nice home, she could not let go of experiences of the past involving her mother: "My mother thought I was useless". Her father had died when Jessica was aged six and her mother had quite irrationally, and perhaps sadistically, blamed her for his death. Her mother had died four years previously. She has a brother five years older.

First EMDR session

Jessica began by posing the question "Why did my mother hate me? What have I done?" She recalled her mother telling her that she was stupid and useless and that she would always fail. In particular she referred to her mother telling her it was her fault that her father had died, an accusation that in her six-year-old mind she had believed.

EMDR

1. (She chose "home in bed" as her safe place.)

2. (The target was the occasion when her mother had told her it was her fault that her father had died.) I remember her shouting "It's your fault". I'm scared. I want to run away.

(We derived the *negative cognition*: I must be bad.)

3. My brother hitting me . . . perhaps I was bad again.

4. I remember being put in the coal bunker by my brother . . . in the dark . . . he thought it was funny . . . he pushed me in head first . . . I told my mother . . . she said I was an attention-seeker. I was always black and blue with bruises from my brother. He would throw darts at me.

5. I tried to run away, age nine, he came after me.

6. I was thinking of convent school . . . bloody awful . . . the nuns didn't like me . . . I was bullied.

7. [Let's go back to the memory of your mother saying your father's death was your fault. Ask yourself if it really was your fault.] I was just a kid, it can't have been my fault. I like to think I am a good person, helpful.

(We derived the *positive cognition*: I am a good person. VOC 4.)

8. [Think that thought "I am a good person" (installation of the positive cognition).] It seemed strange telling myself that—quite calming—there's still a nagging doubt. If I was that good my life would be different (but then she acknowledges that her life *is* actually good apart from her belief that *she* is not good).

9. (We explored her disintegration anxiety relating to letting go of her core organizing belief that she is bad. Further eye movements led to her feeling more congruent about a view of herself as good.)

Session two

Jessica reported that she had given up her job. She felt unjustly criticized by her manager and had been "boiling with anger", which she had turned on herself depressively. She described feeling never good enough for her female manager, and we looked at the similarity with her experience of her mother. No EMDR was used in this session.

Session three

Jessica reported dreams about her mother telling her off. She spoke of regret that she could not prove her mother wrong (because she is dead).

EMDR

1. I was thinking of her voice . . . saying there's no point . . . I am useless . . . she makes me feel claustrophobic . . . I can't shake her out of my head.

2. [Ask yourself "Is it true that you are useless?"] She said I am, so I must be. I have this little voice in my head saying I have two gorgeous children I'm really proud of.

3. I was asking myself "Am I a good parent? Can I be better?" I worry all the time, like "Will I get them to school on time?" I get paranoid about my husband . . . will he leave me?

4. I'm arguing with my mother, but I was thinking that I miss her—I never thought I would admit that.

5. I was thinking of how she punished me because my Dad doted on me. (She talked more of how she was loved by her father and hated by her mother.)

Session four

Jessica reported feeling somewhat better but irritable, finding herself shouting at the children and the dog. She said she was feeling more positive, had enrolled in a college course, and was taking her motorbike test the next day.

EMDR

1. I was thinking that I let people down. I could do more to get a job. It's this expectation of failure.

2. I sometimes hear somebody calling my name when there is no one there. Originally it was a voice saying I was useless. When my mother

died I used to "see" her laughing at me and telling me I was useless, telling me to do them all a favour and die.

3. [Are you ready to let go of your mother?] Maybe I can't let go. She's made me who I am today. Maybe she is my crutch. Would I be lost without her? If someone has been there a long time, even if in a negative way, in a way you miss them. The day she died I felt free for the first time, then I felt guilty.

4. Can I let her go? Maybe I don't want to. I've got to learn to let her go. Maybe that's my problem—that I blame her and don't take responsibility for my own actions. She's dead but there are questions I want to ask her: why did she hate me so much?; why did she treat me the way she did?

5. My Nan came to mind. She looked after me. She was everything I wanted my mother to be. She was my guardian angel. I had the relationship with her that I would love to have had with my mother.

6. [OK—think of the feeling of being loved by your Nan] I miss her so much.

7. [Perhaps you can hang on to your Nan rather than your mother.] I feel quite calm.

Session five

Jessica reported that she was feeling "pretty good"—she had passed her motorbike test and had obtained a distinction in her college assignment. She felt that these real achievements countered her feeling put down by her mother. Crucially, she reported feeling that she was no longer thinking of her mother in the same way. She also noted that she had been less clumsy in the kitchen, no longer dropping things so much. Her son had remarked that she was singing more. She said she was feeling "normal" for the first time.

Jessica went on to describe how she had twice visited the cemetery where her Nan was buried—she said she would not have been able to do that before the EMDR.

EMDR

[Focus on the realistic positive messages from your Nan] I can hear her! She would have been proud of me!

As measured on a widely used routine clinical outcome questionnaire (CORE), Jessica was no longer suffering any clinical symptoms. It was agreed to end the therapy at that point.

Follow-up

At a three month follow-up using a feedback questionnaire, Jessica rated her improvement compared to when she first sought help as "very much so" and wrote "I feel a lot more positive about my life".

Commentary

Jessica's difficulties were rooted in her experiences of relentless criticism from her mother. Her mother's scornful and critical voice was vividly present in her mind—and sometimes actually hallucinated. Jessica had organized her sense of self around her belief that she was "bad" and "not good enough". Under the stimulation of EMDR she realized that her mother probably resented the way that her father doted on her, and thus that being loved by a man was associated with the expectation of hostility from her mother. As the EMDR proceeded she began to recognize her resistance to relinquishing the dysfunctional attachment to her internalized critical mother, a prospect associated with disintegration anxiety. However, she then began to recall the much more positive and loving experiences with her grandmother. She was able to shift from a focus on the negative and critical messages of her mother to a new appreciation of the positive and realistic messages of her grandmother. This is an interesting variant on the usual process whereby EMDR results in a shift from the negative cognition deriving from the injurious experiences to a more realistic positive cognition. Most of the therapeutic work was accomplished in just three EMDR sessions.

Kelly: brief treatment of sexual inhibitions in relationships

Kelly was a thirty-five-year-old woman who presented with recurrent difficulties in her relationships with men. After an initial sexual involvement with a man she would rapidly lose interest in sex and, in fact, she commented "The more I like someone the more I want to avoid sex". She did not know why, but she felt this problem was ruining her chances of a lasting relationship. She also was inclined to feel anxious.

Kelly told me that she had been sexually abused by two older boys when she was aged about eleven. Her parents had separated when she was aged nine and her mother needed to work. Kelly would spend time with a "rough family" down the road, where one of the sons and his friend would engage in sexual activities with her, including intercourse. She said she used to blame herself for this, but more recently had come to see that it had not been her fault because she had been so young. The abuse had gone on for a year or so, until she and her mother moved away.

During her first few years of life Kelly had lived in France with her parents, but her father had been largely absent. She had no brothers or sisters.

Kelly agreed to explore these problems with EMDR.

EMDR session one

1. I want to stop dreaming about my ex-boyfriend . . . I think about him, but I don't love him . . . he hurt me very badly . . . he slept with someone else and made her pregnant . . . we had a fight and he bruised my face . . . it was a lucky escape . . . I didn't want sex so he went elsewhere. [What are your feelings about sex?] If you want a relationship it's something you have to put up with.

2. Am I always going to be like this? It's not worth going into a new relationship.

3. [Where does the problem come from?] It's the way my mother is . . . I can't talk to her about it . . . my mother and stepfather's beds were always apart.

4. [So when these boys were raping you, you wouldn't have been able to tell your mother?] No, I should have done, but they said I would be taken away and then I wouldn't be able to see my Nan—and I loved my Nan.

5. I need to talk to my mum, but I don't want her to know anything about me . . . I don't think she would open up to me.

(It was agreed that next time we would focus on the childhood sexual abuse trauma.)

EMDR session two

Kelly reported that she was feeling stressed; she was worried about her Nan who was very old and ill, and also worried about a boyfriend coming to stay.

1. I had some really angry thoughts about Mum . . . I've been doing so much rushing around after Nan . . . thinking Mum is not a good mother, then felt terrible for thinking that. As a young child in France, seven years old, I would go out on my bike at night looking for her . . . she'd be drinking in a bar . . . I would wake up in the night and she wouldn't be there. Now my mother is lonely . . . but I can't go round looking after everyone . . . I feel everyone wants a piece of me.

2. There's too much going through my head.

3. I want to speed my life up, get it all out of the way so I can move on.

4. [Do you want to think about the rape as a child?] I wonder what their lives are like now . . . whether they are fine and happy and settled down . . . and how it has left me. [You feel angry?] Yes. (She talks of anxiety about her anger, andwhether she should bury it.)

5. I want to let it go . . . maybe I'm angry at my family for not being there for me . . . but they couldn't have been because they didn't know . . . I think my anger all came out when I rebelled.

6. [Can you bring to mind what happened when you were raped?] It was my twelfth birthday . . . they knocked at my door and asked me to babysit at their house . . . they took me down to the cemetery . . . it happened there . . . that's why I never celebrate my birthday . . . it went on until the pubs shut . . . there were two of them . . . one had intercourse and the other couldn't manage it . . . I remember feeling cold . . . I wanted my Mum . . . I didn't want it to be happening . . . I felt cheap . . . they called me a slut . . . they said if you tell your mum you'll be taken away . . . they blackmailed me . . . they would threaten to tell so they could go on doing it . . . then eventually I just got used to it . . . I showed no emotion.

7. That wasn't the first time I was raped. The first time they got me round at their house . . . they said they were babysitting . . . it was only one that raped me that time . . . they egged each other on . . . but it started before that with making me put my hand down his trousers. . . he would say all girls did that.

8. I remember thinking afterwards "Well that's it, I'm grown up now, this is what grown-ups do." (We then spent some time unravelling the cognitive distortions associated with the abuse, her feelings of

self-blame, especially since she may have felt aroused by the experience, and her feelings of guilt, shame, and confusion.)

9. I was thinking about how they called me a slut . . . and how I've got to change my way of thinking . . . to stop thinking that about myself.

10. (She located very strong feelings of shame and the thought that sex is bad and does not belong in a relationship of love.)

Session three

This session involved a little EMDR to facilitate processing, but there was much conventional psychotherapeutic exploration. Kelly talked more about her pattern of backing away from long-term relationships with men—how she preferred friendships rather than intimate sexual relationships. She wanted to be a "free spirit", and felt she did not need relationships where there is "someone tagging along". She thought her mother was like this, too, and then associated to childhood experiences in France when her young mother would be out socializing and Kelly would be looking for her. We began to see how she had originally been the "someone tagging along", the needy child in search of her mother. It was then possible for Kelly painfully to recognize the (hitherto unconscious) element of compulsive rejection and humiliation of men, whereby she projectively placed them in the position of being the discarded needy one and avoided experiencing further rejection herself.

Session four

Kelly talked further about her pattern of going off men. She felt this would often occur after she noticed a particular kind of negative character attribute. It occurred to her that this negative quality always concerned some indication of self-centredness. We could see then that in this way too she was compulsively seeking to avoid re-encountering the abandoning and self-centred aspects of her mother as she had experienced her in childhood.

By this point Kelly felt ready to end her therapy and continue exploring these emotional themes in the course of ordinary life and relationships.

Follow-up

No follow-up data were available. Kelly did not seek further help from the mental health service.

Commentary

Kelly's presenting problem of withdrawing sexually and emotionally from men turned out to have two main roots, the first being in
her childhood experience of rape and other sexual abuse by older
boys, and the second being her childhood feelings of being
neglected and rejected by her mother. She began to see that in relation to men she compulsively turned the tables on the childhood
situation, so that she took up the role of her mother in wanting to
discard the "someone tagging along". Unconsciously she had been
very afraid of becoming emotionally attached and vulnerable and
of being rejected again. She became more aware of anger towards
her mother. Moreover, she identified that the triggers to her withdrawal from men were any perceptions (perhaps unconscious) of
indicators of self-centredness that reminded her of her childhood
experience of her mother.

Ashok: treatment of obsessional anxieties and rituals

Ashok was an eighteen-year-old man who presented with obsessional anxieties and rituals, focused mainly upon worries about the
safety of others. He feared that if he did not perform certain actions
or movements of his body then harm would come to a member of
his family. There was much typical magical thinking in his fantasies.
Apparently he had always tended to be anxious and sensitive. The
family—pillars of the local Asian community—appeared close and
caring. His parents appeared understanding of his need to pursue a
Western lifestyle that conflicted with traditional Asian customs;
nevertheless, he clearly felt some conflict about this cultural tension.
Ashok's OCD had interfered with his education and his employ-
ment. An underlying theme that emerged in the preliminary discussion was Ashok's separation anxiety and fear of change. He was able
to recognize the existential anxiety that lay behind his illusions of
being able to control the world magically through his rituals.

First session

> During this initial EMDR, Ashok associated to anxieties about the
> welfare of various members of his family, e.g. his fears that one of them

might have an accident. He mentioned a fear that if he focused his thought on any particular worry he might thereby make it happen. After six sets of eye movements, Ashok remarked that whenever he feels angry he is compelled to perform a ritual, which led to some exploration of his general feeling that anger or hostility cannot be expressed in the family. He spoke of worries about upsetting his mother. More generally he conveyed fears of moving away from the family and the Asian community.

Second session

Ashok began by referring to some increased anxiety because his parents were going away for the weekend, and some worries about his mother's health. He had felt compelled to perform some rituals for her safety. He then spoke of negative views of himself concerning the fact that he was not working and, unlike his peers, did not feel capable of going to university because of his anxiety. While making the eye movements he was asked to imagine going to university to notice what came to mind. He reported feeling that he would miss home too much. Further processing led him to speak of ambitions to travel, which were in conflict with his anxiety about leaving home.

I then changed therapeutic tack and invited Ashok to consider a possible future time when he might feel ready to go to university. With further eye movements he selected a university of his choice—in a quiet town—and was encouraged to imagine this with sensory detail. As Ashok continued the processing he was able to consider many attractive features of being at university. Then he commented, "It sounds great and I would like to do it, but it seems so permanent!" However, he was able to feel more comfortable by imagining that he could go home at the weekends. By the end of the session, Ashok appeared much calmer as he imagined going to university, although he still expressed the fear that it was all too big an undertaking for him at that point.

Third session

Ashok talked of having obtained a part-time job and also of having met a nice girl in a pub. He expressed worries that if she rejects him it may be because he had not performed a ritual adequately. Initial EMDR processing led him to express social anxieties and feelings of insecurity concerning how he might be viewed by his peers. He then spoke of his mother's car having been vandalized and expressed feelings of anger about this, as well as worries about his mother being vulnerable, sensitive, and easily hurt. Further eye movements produced thoughts about when he feels down in his mood, which he then linked to having heard that the girl in the pub already had a boyfriend, and it then became clear that this had been the trigger for the upsurge of his social anxieties and feelings of inadequacy. Finally, the theme changed with the emergence of strongly negative attitudes and his assertion that he would not get any better. However, he was then able to acknowledge the protective function of his cynicism and negative self-image, shielding him from disappointment and the dangers of being "overconfident or arrogant".

Fourth session

Ashok reported that although he was still performing his rituals he was not feeling so worried as previously. He then talked about two recent experiences with girls, and how these had not worked out. Humorously he commented on the fact that his rituals had clearly not worked! He said he had begun to see how his rituals were an activity he performed when he was anxious and were like an addiction. Then he spoke of how it had been the first time ever that he had got angry with a girl for finishing with him. He described feeling "led on". His feelings of anger in such circumstances were a new experience for him and he had felt guilty. He had expressed his anger towards the girl "passively" but had talked to his friends about how he felt. A friend had commented that he always tended to blame himself rather than becoming outwardly angry, and Ashok acknowledged this was true. I pointed out to Ashok that he seemed to transform any potential anger into an excessive worry about the other person's welfare.

EMDR then proceeded as described below.

1. My anger didn't help with that girl because I'm still not completely over it. [But at least your anger is a normal and appropriate response, as your friends tell you.] I suppose so, yes.

2. I'm quite nervous about going to work tomorrow. [Any particular worries?] It's like social situations when I'm under pressure . . . but there I have to be totally on display . . . but its weird . . . I haven't really done many rituals about it . . . maybe because I know I can always leave the job. [Maybe also it is because you are beginning to realize that

the rituals don't make any difference one way or another.] Except that part of me still believes it . . . I'm not convinced . . . like it's two different parts of my mind . . . logically I can see that the rituals can't do anything . . . I can see that it is very unlikely that they will work.

3. I was thinking how I haven't really done many rituals recently but that thought suddenly made me think I should do one, so I quickly did one (a certain bodily movement).

4. I was wishing I was back in my old job . . . I've never liked change.

Fifth session

Ashok talked about feeling stressed: his parents were going away on holiday to India, he had a new girlfriend who is lovely but has family problems, but he had not been performing rituals very much. He remarked, "In fact I'm too stressed even to think of doing rituals!" As he talked about his girlfriend it occurred to him that he was channelling his worries about her welfare into realistic and practical help rather than resorting to rituals. An overall impression was that he was now experiencing more directly the state of stress that previously would have been held in check by rituals.

EMDR

1. I was thinking about my girlfriend and her family problems. I told her about my OCD but I downplayed it—I didn't want to worry her—I keep trying to think if there is any way I can help her.

2. I was thinking of the work I was doing in the pub . . . it's like I don't feel built for the adult world . . . I feel childlike . . . I get too stressed if I'm criticized . . . I crave comfort.

3. I find it very hard to confront issues, to bring them out in the open . . . it's the fear that it makes it more likely to happen. [Is there an example?] Well, like if Dad was taking a plane trip, I couldn't tell him I thought he was going to crash in case that made it happen.

4. When my parents were booking a holiday they asked me how I felt about flying. I told them there was no way I could go on a plane but I wouldn't want to stop them . . . but I would be worried about them.

5. I was thinking of how I worry if I am not worrying . . . like I feel it is dangerous to relax . . . I mustn't let my guard down.

Sixth session

Ashok reported that he had been away to Dublin with his girlfriend for a weekend; it had been the first time he had been away without his parents and it had been OK, his anxieties had been much reduced. He remarked that it was strange how little he had been worrying recently. The relationship with his girlfriend was going well. He also mentioned that although he had been prescribed Seroxat some months previously he had not been taking it.

EMDR

1. My girlfriend will be travelling for her gap year before university . . . I try to take each day as it comes and not get my hopes up . . . I'm not very good at reading how someone feels . . . I don't want to seem too intense . . . I suppose I have a low opinion of myself . . . my experience of relationships going sour . . . she may get bored with me . . . but generally I feel less anxious in this relationship than in others before.

2. My girlfriend is worried about her A levels . . . she has to concentrate on revising so I suggested she see me just once a week, but she said she would be worrying about me and about not seeing me.

3. Next year will be the first time I have not had a group of friends. Most of them will be away. It takes me a while to make good friends . . . but my best friend John might be staying here.

(I put to Ashok that all the anxieties he was expressing were quite normal concerns that a young person might have, e.g. worries about his relationship with his girlfriend, whether the relationship would last, whether she will get bored with him, how he can best help her, how he will feel when his friends move away, and so on. Ashok agreed with this. He indicated that his rituals were now relatively infrequent. Moreover, he was now able to contemplate going to university himself. His remaining concern was that he might suffer a relapse of his anxiety. However, he was agreeable to stopping the work at that point, on the understanding that he could come back if he needed to.)

Follow-up

At six month follow-up, Ashok reported that he was continuing to do well, with much lessened anxiety and compulsion to perform rituals. On the feedback questionnaire he rated the benefit of the therapy as "quite a lot".

Commentary

EMDR quickly revealed some of the underlying anxieties and conflicts behind Ashok's OCD. His compulsive rituals served to restore an illusory sense of control and safety. His sense of danger arose not only from general existential anxiety concerning human vulnerability in an unpredictable world, but more specifically reflected anxieties over anger and separation. Secondary feelings of low self-esteem and social anxieties resulted from his awareness of inhibitions in engaging the normal pursuits of his peer group. Ashok quickly worked through these anxieties in just a few sessions, so that he was able to acknowledge feelings of anger, feel relaxed going away with his girlfriend, and look forward to going to university. His faith in the efficacy of his rituals diminished and he resorted to them much less frequently.

Zoe: three-session treatment of a vomit phobia

Zoe was a twenty-five-year-old woman who presented with a phobia of vomiting, which appeared very pervasive and greatly restricting, leading to states of panic and avoidance of many everyday situations in case she encountered a person being sick. She had been troubled by these anxieties since the age of five. She was not aware of any original precipitating trauma. Zoe has a sister three years younger.

We proceeded with EMDR as described below.

EMDR session one

1. [Safe place] On a beach with my boyfriend.

2. I was thinking of my boyfriend being ill two months ago . . . fear he was going to vomit.

3. I was thinking of a friend being sick in front of me, she threw up all over the carpet. But I feel safe here so I don't feel anxious . . . but what happens is I build it up in my mind . . . like recently I couldn't get on a train in case there was some drunk who had vomited.

4. I was thinking about being on an aeroplane, sitting next to someone being sick.

5. I was thinking of pubs and clubs where it might happen.

6. I was trying to tell myself "that's not going to hurt me". I feel calmer when I'm with someone else.

7. My sister used to be sick in the car when we were little.

8. I was suddenly feeling anger with people . . . I used to get angry with my sister and shout at her. It's strange . . . when I'm angry I don't feel so panicky.

Commentary

Zoe's responses were fairly bland during most of this session—various thoughts about different situations where she would feel anxious—but then the process sprang into psychodynamic life at the end, with the sudden emergence of recollections of anger towards her sister.

Session two

Zoe reported having felt slightly calmer and spoke of having been able to watch someone vomiting on television.

EMDR

1. [Perhaps continue your thoughts about your sister.] We shared a room. We had bunk beds, she slept on top. One time she complained of feeling ill and was asking me to get mum, and then I heard her being sick . . . I ran out in panic.

2. I was thinking of being on an aeroplane, my sister feeling sick. I was also thinking of wanting to sit in the front of the car to get away from my sister being sick . . . my parents telling me I was being stupid.

3. I'm trying to calm myself down, stop myself feeling upset.

4. I was thinking of being told off for making a fuss.

5. I was wanting to cry.

6. I was thinking it is a shame my mum is not with me today when I'm upset—she was the one who told me to come here.

7. I was thinking of my mum, what I would say to her if she asks me how it has been here today. My mum went back to work when I was born, but she gave up work when my sister was born!

8. Why is it so upsetting to think of telling my mother something? Probably when I think of someone being sick I think of being told off . . . probably what I wanted was to be given a cuddle.

9. Maybe that is the reason I have the problem . . . if she had been different maybe I would have been OK . . . I'm wondering what I can tell her . . . I don't want to upset her.

10. I used never to be embarrassed talking about the problems about vomiting, but now if this is what it is about then it seems more personal . . . its embarrassing that it is different from what I thought.

11. Why am I just thinking of mum rather than dad? Dad used to tell me off more . . . but maybe I wanted cuddles more from mum.

[You wanted more cuddles from your mother than you got?]

She wasn't overly affectionate—I would not have kissed her.

12. I'm trying to remember times when she was affectionate . . . but I'm not a particularly affectionate person . . . but I would have preferred to be cuddled rather than told off.

13. I did have a feeling of being loved when I was young . . . I think of comfort when I think of mum. My dad's mum had Alzheimer's . . . she wasn't very nice . . . she was aggressive . . . my mum said she was always like that towards my father . . . she wasn't very affectionate.

14. [Can you try to imagine someone vomiting now?] It's hard to imagine it now.

Session three

Zoe reported that she had felt upset after the previous session, but gave the impression of having felt less anxious. She spoke of worries that her boyfriend would come home drunk and would vomit.

EMDR

1. [Focus on worries about boyfriend vomiting.] Why do I get so paranoid about that?

2. I get angry with myself for feeling that.

3. I'm thinking of going on holiday with my boyfriend . . . the hotel room might be small . . . I'm worried about being trapped if he is ill.

4. I was thinking I wouldn't know how not to react like that . . . I've always reacted that way . . . why can't I stay calm? I can't think of what other way I could react.

5. I'm thinking of when I came out of a nightclub . . . a friend saw a girl drunk, looking like she might be sick . . . she said to me "don't look" . . . my friends expect me to react like that . . . to cry. Do I expect myself to? (She then talked about the idea that just as she had developed a reputation for having a vomit phobia amongst her friends, similarly she had created a kind of internal reputation within her own mind so that she expected herself to react with anxiety and distress.) After all, someone being sick is not a terrible thing . . . do I really need to react like that?

6. I was thinking about how people expect me to be anxious and in a way encourage me. (She describes how friends/family/boyfriend in effect reinforce her anxiety and prevent her from arriving at a more realistic response.)

7. (More about how others have encouraged her to feel anxious.) [It is like you have hypnotized yourself—and others have hypnotized you—so that you think you will be anxious.]

8. I feel a bit confused. Is that why I stayed anxious for so long? (We discuss how her anxiety has become a habit of mind, reinforced by avoidance.)

9. (She talks of her realization that vomit is *not* terrifying but merely unpleasant.)

10. I was telling myself that I need to calm myself rather than reacting the way I have done until now.

[How true is the thought "Vomit is not terrifying but merely unpleasant"?] VOC 5 (out of 7).

11. I was thinking it is like a fairground ride, taking the plunge, then realizing it is not so terrifying. I need to tell myself that it is OK, I can stay calm if someone is ill.

12. I must convince myself that I can stay calm . . . I *want* to feel that.

13. Yes, I've just got to tell myself that I don't need to react that way.

Follow-up

At six month follow-up Zoe reported that she had maintained her improvement and rated the benefits of therapy as "quite a lot".

Commentary

Zoe's vomit phobia turned out to have roots in childhood conflicts involving sibling rivalry—her anger towards her sister, who would be sick in the car. She recalled painful feelings of rejection over being told off by her mother rather than being given the affection and reassurance she craved. The impression is that Zoe had felt full of anger that potentially could explode, that the presence of her sister made her "sick", and she would have liked to expel her sister. After some processing of this material, Zoe began to realize that her anxieties may have been maintained as behavioural habits (or habits of mind) reinforced by the collusion of friends and family (in accord with basic behavioural principles of anxiety learning). She had become imprisoned by an external and internal "reputation" as a person with a vomit phobia, and with this realization she felt she could relinquish the anxiety.

Caroline: EMDR treatment of sexual inhibitions and relationship difficulties

Caroline was a forty-year-old woman who presented with recurrent problems in her relationships with men. She experienced sexual anxieties and inhibitions, which she believed resulted in relationships ending. Because of this pattern she would at times become depressed and entertain thoughts of suicide. She sought help following the ending of another relationship.

> Caroline described her varied sexual responses and behaviours. At times she had been promiscuous, while at other times she did not want sex at all. She could become angry and aggressive during sex. A consistent problem was an inhibition over orgasm, often experiencing a shutting down of her feelings as a climax approached.
>
> Caroline expressed the hope that therapy would help her to express anger, to feel sexual pleasure, and to like herself as a woman.
>
> Preliminary exploration at assessment revealed that Caroline had experienced her mother as both very controlling and very disapproving of sex. She recalled her mother calling her a "whore" during her teenage years and telling her that sex was dirty. She also reported that her

mother did not allow her to be angry. Caroline's relationship with her father seems to have been less problematic. A crucial point emerging in this initial enquiry was the idea that Caroline had felt her body and sexuality belonged to her mother, and that during sexual activity she would have a fantasy of her mother watching and disapproving.

Caroline agreed to explore these issues further with EMDR.

First EMDR session

1. The dots of light (she was following the light bar) made me think of approaching my mother and then being pushed back . . . her rejection . . . then she would be all jokey and approving . . . she could be all lovely, accepting and warm. Bill (previous boyfriend) could be like that too . . . he swept me of my feet and then I felt suffocated . . . then he would be rejecting and critical. My mother called me a whore for sleeping with my boyfriends at the age of twenty-four, and my Dad didn't defend me.

2. I was remembering sleeping in the bedroom with my Mum and Dad when I was age nine or ten . . . sounds of them having sex . . . I would put my head under the pillow . . . I didn't like the sounds my mother was making . . . like it was hurting her. Then I remember playing on the floor, looking up at mother . . . she had no clothes on top . . . her breasts hanging down . . . standing at the window . . . I felt uncomfortable . . . then I remember finding a condom wrapper under their pillow, thinking it was absolutely disgusting, they were too old to be having sex. My mother used to go on and on about periods . . . every week she would ask me about my periods. I don't want to talk about my mother any more, she gets too much attention.

3. I'm feeling hungry . . . thinking about food . . . then I'm thinking of the lights (the light bar), penises, and eggs. (Then she spoke of realizing that she is very sexually hungry. Recently a man had sat next to her at some social event and she had felt very strong sexual chemistry and desire for him, and realized that she wanted to have sex with him and noticed a pleasurable experience of sexual desire.)

4. (She spoke of her sudden realization that her own disapproval of "tarty" women was like her mother's attitude. She described her increased awareness of her own intense sexual desires and also her aggression. She talked of her liking for "rough sex". However, she feared being called "a whore" as her mother had called her.)

5. (She spoke of her fear of being called "a slapper".)

Session two

Caroline began by remarking, "After last session I realized that when I thought that all men wanted was to have sex, it was really *me* that wanted sex!", and she spoke of enjoying her new awareness of sexual desire. Moreover, she also spoke of what we came to formulate as her desire to evoke men's desire.

She then mentioned a nightmare, the details of which were unclear, but she felt it was to do with being "used and abused" by members of her family and feeling angry about this.

EMDR

1. [Think about the dream.] I'm feeling suffocated . . . angry then apologizing . . . like in my last relationship with Bill.

2. I was thinking of how I take up the mother role in relationships . . . they all come to see me as a mother . . . also thinking of how I have sex whether I want to or not . . . as if I will have sex with anyone who gives me attention.

3. I was thinking of sex with Bill . . . but I have to accept that he is back with his old girlfriend. (Then she spoke of how her mother had recently enquired about her cat's sex life.)

4. I am starting to feel angry . . . thinking of my sister saying "How can you go to bed with someone you have just met?" . . . it's like my attitude has been "open your legs and let them do what they want" . . . and thinking of medical examinations (she described repeated internal examinations from age nineteen to her late twenties in connection with a medical condition. She had found these very humiliating and learned to dissociate during the experiences.)

5. I want to have children . . . I have sex to have children . . . I want an orgasm and children!

6. I don't know how I'm supposed to behave in relation to men . . . I want to eat men up, then feel bad about it.

Session three

Caroline reported that she was feeling "wonderful"—Bill had reappeared and her sexual inhibitions had diminished. She said she was now accepting that she has a high sex drive and she had been enjoying sex and had been able to relax. She had not been using contraception and it had been her fertile period—she wanted to have a baby. However, she expressed disappointment that she was still unable to have an orgasm through intercourse.

EMDR

1. [Try asking yourself the question "What stops me having an orgasm?"] I think it is the need to have one! (She then described how the focus of her attention moved during the eye movements from her head to her lower body.)

2. (She spoke of a flashback of sexual experience at age sixteen; it had not involved intercourse but had been very enjoyable.)

3. (She spoke of how she tends compulsively to look after the other person even when in bed, neglecting her own desires.)

Session four (one month later)

Caroline appeared at ease with herself, albeit relatively low-key. She had ended her relationship with Bill because he could not commit to her.

We reviewed her progress in achieving her goals for therapy. She spoke of feeling more accepting of herself as a woman and less resentful of other women; she was making more effort with her appearance and felt more feminine. She found that she was noticing and enjoying attention from men and, crucially, she felt she now had permission to enjoy sex. We concluded that her goals had been reached and no further work was required at that point.

Follow-up

No follow-up data was available. Caroline had not sought further help from the service.

Commentary

The EMDR work with Caroline revealed a complex and multi-layered psychodynamic web underlying her sexual inhibitions and relationship difficulties. Her initial associations were to her conflictual relationship with her mother—how her mother would be alternately accepting and then rejecting and critical—and her mother's disapproval of her sexual interests. She then thought about the "primal scene" (childhood experiences of being exposed to the parental intercourse), states of overstimulation and anxiety, with fantasies that sex was damaging to her mother, followed by further material expressing her discomfort with her parents" sexuality. Her realization of her own sexual desires then emerged strongly—expressed orally, with thoughts of food and penises—but was followed by ideas of her mother's disapproval, of being called "a whore" and "a slapper".

In the subsequent session, Caroline reported a sustained pleasurable awareness of her own sexual desires (previously projected on to men), recognizing her own high sex drive. She then, via a dream, went on to associate to feelings of being used sexually and recollections of distressing and humiliating internal medical examinations, from which she had dissociated. Then she returned to feelings of hunger, for men, sex, orgasms, and babies.

In the third session, Caroline reported greater enjoyment of sex and reduced inhibitions. However she was still disappointed not to be able to reach an orgasm through intercourse alone. During EMDR she asked herself what was stopping her from reaching an orgasm, and her answer was that her concern with a need to reach a climax was interfering with her sexual response. She recalled a very pleasurable sexual experience from age sixteen.

By the fourth session she had taken the initiative to end the relationship with Bill because he could not commit to her and she chose not to feel further abused. She reported feeling much happier with herself as a woman and felt she now had permission to enjoy sex. Her therapeutic goals had been reached.

Thus, the themes woven into Caroline's sexual conflicts appeared to include the following: anxieties about her mother's rejections, and particularly her mother's disapproval of her sexuality; anxiety and overstimulation associated with the primal scene; feelings of being used and abused as a result of her wishes for affection and attention. Behind her inhibitions there was revealed to be a strong sexual appetite.

Although Caroline still experienced some difficulty in reaching an orgasm through intercourse, a clear result of the therapy was that she felt she now had permission to enjoy sex. It is perhaps important to note that this "permission" was not given by the therapist since his own input in terms of content was minimal; it was Caroline who gave herself permission through the EMDR.

Helen: coming to terms with life after divorce

Helen was a forty-five-year-old fitness instructor, a mother of two young children, who sought help for feelings of depression following a divorce. She had decided to leave her husband because of his chronic emotional unavailability. Helen described a general pattern in her life whereby she felt she was always trying to please others. She reported a happy childhood, but mentioned having been in hospital for several weeks at age five; she was uncertain of the reasons for this but her mother reported that she had been suffering with severe diarrhoea and vomiting. It was agreed to explore these problems using EMDR.

What emerged was a core psychodynamic pattern in which she compulsively attends to the needs of others, her fear being that otherwise she will be abandoned. Her anxiety about being left alone linked to the childhood experience of being in hospital at age five, when she may have indeed been left alone and without food for long periods. She recalled her feeling that she had been abandoned because she had done something wrong and her thought that she must try to be like the more active and happy girl in the next bed. An associated theme was her unrequited longing for her father's affection.

EMDR session one

1. (Helen experienced difficulty in thinking of a safe place.)

The feelings inside me prevent me feeling safe . . . feeling stressed.

2. I just feel really sad . . . my marriage . . . everything I did wasn't right for him, but I can't cope without him . . . I just feel a failure . . . I'm not doing very well . . . I want to be strong again . . . I want to be contented.

3. I'm thinking how I please others before myself.

4. I like making other people happy, but then people overstep . . . they are not giving, they are taking . . . I let it happen.

5. I want to be able still to give, but to receive in return . . . I don't receive well.

6. I would like to feel strong inside myself . . . not feel that people say one thing and mean another.

7. Why does everything *else* have to be important . . . why can't what *I* think about be important?

8. *I* should be important in my life, instead of what anyone else thinks . . . it's important what happens to *me* . . . why do I let people insult me?

9. I let people treat me like this, I'm not strong enough.

10. [Can you think of the first instance of this?] I went to lots of different schools . . . trying to please people . . . then with my first boyfriend . . . he would come and go as he pleased.

11. I want to be more in control of my own life, but how?

12. I don't want to stop caring for people . . . I need to be around people.

13. (During this next sequence there was some dialogue during the eye movements.) I must be giving all the time. [Why?] Because then I'm in control. [And what happens if you are not in control?] Well how would anything get done, and how would I know what was going on? Giving is easier. I've always been stronger than my mother . . . she gives too much . . . but no affection from my father . . . I would like to receive affection but would feel it wasn't true . . . I can't receive it so I will give it instead . . . it's too hard to let people in . . . they hurt you. [So who has hurt you?] My dad and my husband. (Helen then reported blocking on feelings of pain about the lack of affection from her father.)

Session two

(Helen reported feeling slightly better. She said she had been able to think more and had been realizing how much she tries to be in control.)

1. I've always felt I needed to be in control. When I was eighteen I had anorexia—not severe, but it was my way of keeping control.

2. I was congratulating myself that I managed to come out of anorexia by myself.

3. I was wondering if I had ever been happy with myself . . . having children was nice . . . they needed me.

4. I want to feel much better about myself, but I don't know how to do it.

5. [So what is your basic view of yourself?] I want to please everybody all the time . . . doing something that upsets someone is not acceptable . . . everything to do with me is not there, it has to be about other people . . . the fear that they won't like me.

6. [So why won't they like you?] My dad . . . but it can't all be his fault . . . maybe I felt he never said anything I did was good.

7. I wanted affection, a squeeze or a hug . . . I felt not good enough.

8. I like affection, I want affection, I want approval . . . I'm happy if I'm pleasing others . . . but why can't I be happy with myself? . . . because I don't have self-beliefs, I gauge myself from the way other people see me.

(At this point we clarified the core negative cognition: "My role in life is to please others—I should be a perfect wife, mother etc.—and I have to be in control or it all falls apart") I don't want to continue like this, but I can't stop myself saying "yes" all the time for fear of upsetting them.

9. [What would be so terrible about saying "no"?] They might not like me, then I won't get the emotional support . . . [Like you didn't get from your father?] Oh yeah—wow!

10. I've got lots of friends who do offer emotional support, but it needs to come from within.

11. If I don't keep pleasing people everyone will hate me and I will be left all on my own.

Session three

(Helen spoke of being preoccupied with the question of how to stop being constantly at other people's beck and call, and feeling guilty if she says "no". She thought she needed to value herself more.)

1. [What stops you valuing yourself more?] Other people have a lot to offer, but I don't . . . other people are more important to me than I am to them.

2. I pretend I am coping—that I am OK (she describes an almost automatic concealment of her inner feelings) . . . I don't find it easy to cry . . . if I did, people would know how I feel . . . I would not be in control . . . I can be hurt . . . people let me down, especially men, so I keep my thoughts and feelings to myself.

3. I feel unhappy about needing all these people . . . I want these people in my life but not to need them . . . I've never had *one* best friend . . . I

need people to speak to every day . . . I have four close friends, two men and two women.

4. [Can you think of how you would like to be?] To be able to say what I wanted to say without apology.

5. [So what stops you?] I might be abandoned.

6. [Who first abandoned you?] I was in hospital age five . . . I had no food . . . injections in my bum three times a day . . . and visits were restricted.

7. I feel really sad.

8. I didn't want to be in that bed on my own.

9. It really hurts . . . I feel so lonely . . . it's a feeling like maybe I've done something wrong . . . maybe if I'm good I won't be on my own.

Session four

(Helen reported feelings of panic at the idea of loneliness and abandonment.)

1. Panic at being alone—the idea of being alone for hours.

2. Why am I looking at it from a lonely let-down position? Why not welcome the time? Why not appreciate the contacts I do have?

3. I'm still feeling like the five-year-old girl in hospital.

4. I'm going round in circles . . . I'm not strong enough.

5. [What stops you being stronger?] I need to be with the people who love me . . . but then I'm cross that I can't be strong.

6. [Is it so bad to be alone for periods of time?] It's bad to be alone . . . if people don't want to be with you it must mean they don't love you . . . so I try to please so people will love me . . . so I won't be on my own.

7. I was thinking of the girl in hospital . . . the girl in the next bed *was allowed* food . . . I feel panic thinking of that . . .

8. I wasn't allowed out of bed.

9. I've got this shaky feeling.

10. The other little girl seemed happier—she got more attention. I was trying to avoid thinking about me then . . . I wanted the lights to stop because I didn't want to think about me.

11. I was not meant to be upset when my parents visited, but I was lonely when they were not there, and bored. (She then described the child's terror of overwhelming boredom.)

12. I don't want to be bored and lonely . . . the other girl seemed happier . . . she got more attention . . . so maybe I have to be active and happy all the time to get attention.

13. Not being active definitely seems lonely and boring . . . the other little girl's bed seems lighter and brighter.

Session five

(Helen reported that she had spoken to her mother about the period in hospital. Apparently she had been very ill and visiting was restricted to evenings. Helen would cry every time her parents left. She went on to speak of having been enjoying the weekend, but had then felt very guilty on seeing her ex-husband upset. She talked of her feeling that she damages other people in pursuing her own life.)

1. [Perhaps think of the question of whether you have the right to pursue your own needs and happiness.] Yes I do—but then I'm always hurting somebody.

2. I'm thinking about all the people I'm trying not to hurt . . . but I can't change the way they feel . . . I feel I should be able to help them . . . like it's my fault . . .I should be able to help them.

3. I don't want other people to feel unhappy or lonely, because then they wouldn't like me . . . everything I do is wrong by somebody . . . always doing wrong to somebody.

4. Life is such a struggle . . . why do I care so much what people think?

5. My head spins with how much I care about other people. How do I get a balance between caring for myself and caring for other people?

6. I feel guilty when I do what I want—but wanting to make people happy doesn't make me happy.

Sesssion six

(Helen reported feeling somewhat better and said she was coping with being alone more, although she still found loneliness frightening. She said she was now less troubled when she thought of the memory of being in hospital. She wanted to be able to relinquish her pattern of compulsively attending to the needs of others.)

(The following material emerged during continual EMDR.)

[Can you try thinking of ways in which you can take account of your own needs?] I can't think of ways because that would upset people and they wouldn't be happy. (Helen then spoke of sudden feelings of fear.) [Fear of what?] Of not being in control. When I'm in control I know what is going to happen. I wasn't in control in the hospital . . . injections . . . and I couldn't have jelly and ice cream (this was said with much sudden anger—she explained that she had been given a choice of jelly *or* ice cream, but she had wanted both) . . . I was happy about the idea of soothing jelly and ice cream, but then they took it away! If you leave it to other people you don't get what you want . . . but I'm actually hurting myself by not letting myself receive. (She talked more about her difficulties in asserting herself and her feelings of guilt if she says "no".)

Session seven

(Helen spoke of having felt better since the previous session. She realized that, in part, she was experiencing an inevitable post-separation depression, after twenty years of marriage. We saw that the fact of it being her choice to leave her husband may have obscured the sense of loss that she nevertheless felt. She felt that being on her own was beginning to feel more tolerable, although she yearned for stimulation and excitement and preferred being sociable. No EMDR was used in this session.)

Session eight

(Helen reported that she was having more "good days" than "bad days". She acknowledged loneliness but was continuing with a new relationship that was a good friendship. She missed the practical help her husband used to provide, but affirmed her experience that he was emotionally unavailable. She still wanted to achieve a greater sense of control over her life, but felt inevitably constrained in how much attention she could give to herself when she was a mother of small children. Most of the dissatisfactions Helen described at this point related to real aspects of her circumstances, and we agreed that enough psychological work had been done and that it was time to stop. The "Clinical Outcomes in Routine Evaluation" questionnaire [CORE] indicated that Helen's level of distress was within the normal range—a marked improvement on her score prior to beginning therapy. On her feedback questionnaire she rated her the overall helpfulness of the therapy as "quite a lot", a score of four out of a possible five.)

Follow-up

No follow-up data were available. Helen did not seek further help from the mental health service.

Fiona: *brief EMDR treatment of a pattern of self-harm*

This case describes how the dynamics, structure and origin of a pattern of self-harm was explored and resolved in a single EMDR session.

Fiona was a twenty-five-year-old single woman with a history of self-harm, mainly involving hitting herself repeatedly with a hammer and also cutting. This had begun at age seventeen when girls at the gym said she was fat. There had been episodes of bullying about her weight later at college. Difficulties in expressing anger were apparent from her account of childhood. She described her parents as strict and physically punitive, not tolerating any expression of her own anger towards them. Fiona agreed to undertake a session of EMDR focused on these difficulties with anger.

EMDR session

1. (Fiona selected "my friend's house" as her safe place.)

2. [Just think about your problems in expressing anger.] I was thinking of when I self-harm—the feeling of determination to carry it through.

3. I'm wondering why I do it—and whether I would ever go any further.

4. I'm thinking of my boss at work . . . how annoying he is . . . he ignores me but talks to others.

5. I'm remembering hearing my sister cry when I was four or five. We were being babysat by my cousin who was twenty . . . he pushed me out of the room and locked the door . . . then he sexually abused my sister (aged eight) . . . I heard her crying . . . I was going to tell my parents but I forgot when they bought me an ice-cream . . . I forgot until I was nineteen.

6. I was thinking of the anger I still feel about that—I should have said something.

7. My real Dad would beat up my mother . . . my sister saw this . . . he had wanted a boy when I was born . . . he doted on my sister but never touched me . . . he would say "I'm never taking that brat out—she's not mine" . . . he never came to see me.

8. I never got to know friends at school because my mother wanted me to go home for lunch . . . this made me an easy target for bullying . . . I would get picked on.

9. There was this boy called Mick at college . . . he really pushed me over the edge, made me feel I was scum . . . he was always very quick-witted, taunting me about my weight, making comments in front of others . . . I tried to act as if I didn't care . . . but then I started hitting myself.

10. [Can you try to imagine your anger flowing towards Mick?] I couldn't imagine hitting anyone . . . [except yourself] I'm afraid of being angry . . . [why?] the last time I hit someone I knocked them out . . . I'm quite strong . . . I'm afraid of not being able to stop . . . I feel it is safer to do it to me.

11. (With further eye movements Fiona experienced increasing calm when thinking about her own anger.)

When seen four weeks later, Fiona reported that she had stopped self-harming. She was feeling much better and had acquired a new job. After some further discussion of her plans to lose weight, we concluded that no further psychological work was required at that point.

Follow-up

No follow-up data were available. Fiona did not seek further help from the service.

Commentary

As Fiona moved through the EMDR session, the experiences and psychodynamics behind her pattern of self-harm were rapidly revealed. Beginning with a focus on her feelings of wanting to harm herself, she then raised the question of why she felt this. After then thinking of her anger at her boss who ignores her, she associated to sexual abuse of her sister and her anger and guilt that she had not reported this incident to her parents. She then thought of her biological father who, like her current boss, ignored her (but doted on her sister). Next she thought about being bullied at school and how she was vulnerable to this because of her mother's insistence that she go home for lunch. Then she thought of experiences of being bullied later at college, this being the context for her beginning the pattern of self-harm. When prompted to imagine expressing her anger outwardly towards its true target, Fiona quickly became aware of her fear of losing control in attacking another person, and recalled an earlier incident of knocking someone out. Thus the thematic thread of bullying flowed through all her associations; a subsidiary theme was of being ignored (by father and by boss).

John: brief EMDR treatment of a man with a fetish

John was a twenty-eight-year-old man who sought help after losing his job in personnel management as a result of his addictive pursuit of certain fetish images on the Internet. These images had to be either of a woman smoking or of a particular woman's haircut. John would spend large amounts of time in these searches. His wife was unhappy about his addiction.

John described his childhood as happy, with a good relationship with both his parents. However, he described his mother as the "boss" and said she "ruled the roost", while his father was more laid back. He mentioned that his mother smokes but his father does not. One memory seemed particularly significant—that on one occasion his mother had her hair done differently and he could not bring himself to talk to her. In association to this, he spoke of how he used to be frightened to have his hair cut, but later this became a source of pleasurable excitement for him. However, he would also insist that his hair be cut by a woman.

John was treated with a single EMDR session, which he found helpful. By comparison with a conventional psychoanalytic style of work the therapist's interpretations might appear somewhat intellectual, but in the context of EMDR these seemed to facilitate John's free associations and understanding.

EMDR session

[Just think about the fetish images.] I'm thinking about hairdressers ... various images of hair in rollers ... the hair images seem more special than the other images of women smoking.

(John seemed happy to continue with more or less continuous eye movements following the light bar, while he gave a running commentary on his thoughts, with just occasional pauses from the eye movements.)

(He associated to the fact that his mother had been a smoker and also her change of hairstyle.)

I'm thinking of my mother smiling ... in a pub ... I don't like to look at my mother smoking ... she had breast cancer ... I worry about her getting ill ... I'm scared of becoming aroused as I think about the images.

I'm remembering age seven when my mother changed her hairstyle ... my fear of her ... like looking at a stranger.

Once my sister put curling tongs in my father's hair ... made it look curly ... he was a very placid man ... I felt embarrassment.

My mother was the boss ... I think I am placid like my father.

[Perhaps you were experiencing a fear of the dominant mother with a phallus—the woman with a cigarette—who might take away your father's and your masculinity.]

I'm thinking of how I missed my father—he died of a heart attack ... I was ten ... my grandmother died the same year.

[Perhaps your father dying contributed to an image of him as weak and vulnerable in comparison with your mother.]

I am aware of a countdown to being as old as my father. I used to worry about my mother dying and being left an orphan.

(Then he recalled that it was around this time that the fetish preoccupations had begun. He had drawn an image of a woman smoking, but then he would change the images of the woman's hair by pasting parts of other images on top; in this way he could "change the image".)

[Perhaps you are describing here a feeling of having omnipotent control over the image—being able to change it as you wanted—and perhaps in this way being able to defend yourself against the fear of further loss, the fear of losing your mother.]

(John agreed with this formulation. He began to recognize how he has been inclined to resort to a preoccupation with images when faced with loss or loneliness.)

(John then spoke again of how he used to be afraid of having his hair cut.)

[This perhaps relates to your fear of the image of the dominant mother—the woman with the cigarette phallus—and your impression of your father as weak and passive, and your own similar view of yourself, a fear of losing your masculinity—of losing your phallus—represented in your fear of having your hair cut. This is reflected, then, in your image of the woman smoking and the reassurance of being able to change the image at will and in that way to deny that any permanent loss is possible: the image of the woman with a cigarette is like a woman with a penis, an image that works to deny that women do not have a penis and so reassures you that there is nothing to lose.]

(John indicated that this made a great deal of sense to him. He expressed appreciation, indicating that none of the doctors and counsellors that he had seen before had given him any kind of understanding of what might lie behind his fetish preoccupations.)

Follow-up

John was seen for a follow-up a month later. He reported having felt much relieved, calmer, and less preoccupied with the fetishist interests since the EMDR. The session was spent clarifying and elaborating the insights arrived at during the EMDR.

No additional follow-up data were available. John did not seek further help from the mental health service.

Commentary

A complex web of anxieties and phantasies were revealed to lie behind John's fetishist interest in very particular images of women. The idea of the woman smoking a cigarette was closely congruent with Freud's (1940e) formulation of the meaning of the fetish as a denial of castration, in his paper on splitting of the ego. John's perception of his mother as dominant—perhaps "wearing the pants"—and his view of his father as weak and passive (exacerbated by his father's death) clearly played into his fears for the integrity and strength of his masculinity and his anxieties about the danger of castration (expressed vividly in his fear of having his hair cut). This fear of the dominant and potentially castrating mother would be expressed in the image of woman with the cigarette-phallus, but in addition this image would be reassuring because it would function as a denial of the possibility of castration. However, there were obviously also more fundamental anxieties relating to the painful shock of the death of his father and his fears of losing his mother and becoming an orphan. These fears, along with his feelings of loneliness after his father's death, provided the context in which John turned to drawing and collecting images. These images, especially in the way that John would add or remove features, functioned to deny loss. Moreover, the images were able to function at different levels simultaneously, denying both the danger of losing his penis and that of losing a parent. This under-lying structure of John's fetish would almost certainly have taken a considerable time to unravel in conventional psychoanalytic ther-apy, but emerged rapidly through EMDR.

Gillian: treatment of obsessional anxiety in a single EMDR session

This case describes how the underlying dynamics and structure of obsessional anxieties were revealed and processed in a single EMDR session.

Gillian was a thirty-year-old woman, in a long term relation-ship, who presented with obsessional anxieties regarding mess and dirt. These interfered with her sexual relationship. She spoke of her dislike of bodily fluids and of wet patches in the bed, and she found that some of her partner's sexual desires disgusted her. In an initial discussion, Gillian recalled her mother's strong prohibition against sex before marriage—she and her partner were not married. She particularly remembered her mother's reaction of threatening to disown her when it came to light that she had had intercourse with her boyfriend at age seventeen.

EMDR session

Gillian was asked to think about her anxieties regarding mess and disorder. She associated to crumbs in the bed. and then to thoughts of the house being untidy and of washing up not being done, and of the carpets needing vacuuming, and of orange juice spilt on the bed, and of one of her toddler children wiping faeces, and of sexual mess.

Then, to her astonishment, as she thought more about the crumbs in the bed, she began to imagine *more* crumbs and felt a strange *wish* for there to be more crumbs and more mess. This was followed by feelings of desire for sex, and then of feelings of wanting to swallow her partner's ejaculation—desires that she had not been conscious of before. She then imagined kissing her partner passionately and becoming aroused, but this was followed by a sense of shutting down sexually.

With further eye movements, she imagined her partner wanting to give her oral sex, thinking that first she would resist this but then would begin to enjoy it. She then thought of her toddler son picking at his "pooey bottom" and smearing faeces on the pillow, and she imagined just turning the pillow over. As she thought of this, she exclaimed, "That's not me at all!"

She then recalled a teenage phase of looking at "dog poo" and thinking how attractive it looked, and wanting to eat it (although she had never actually done so), and of associating to chocolate.

Then she thought of her fears of other people hearing her having sex, or of hotel staff finding some evidence of sexual activity. However, she then recalled that at university she used to find the idea of being over-heard at her moment of climax very exciting.

Gillian subsequently reported that she had found this EMDR session very helpful and illuminating. She did not require any further psycho-logical therapy.

Follow-up

No follow-up data were available. Gillian did not seek further help from the mental health service.

Commentary

This example illustrates a fundamental psychoanalytic principle that exaggerated conscious attitudes may function as a defence/disguise against opposite desires. Prior to the EMDR session, Gillian believed she strongly disliked mess, and particularly sexual mess. On engaging with eye movements she rapidly discovered her pleasure in sex and mess. Oral, anal, genital, and exhibitionist

impulses were all vividly expressed in her bilateral free associations. It seemed clear that part of the reason for the repression
of (and reaction-formation against) these impulses was Gillian's
experience of her mother's disapproval of sexual and bodily
pleasure.

Priscilla: a young woman with low self-esteem and feelings of shame

This account describes very brief EMDR treatment of feelings of
shame, low self-esteem, and negative self-image, associated with
the patient's mother's alcoholism.

Priscilla was a twenty-five-year-old woman, presenting with
low self-esteem, feelings of embarrassed self-consciousness, and
"paranoid" expectations of being criticized by others. At the time of
referral these problems had become sufficiently acute that she was
off work because of her anxieties. She spoke of feeling generally not
good enough. Although she had in the past had boyfriends, these
relationships did not prosper; she described how she would alternate between being too trusting and feeling "paranoid". She
worked in a repetitive factory job, although she believed she would
be capable of a more challenging job if she could be more confident.

Priscilla was asked her thoughts regarding the origin of these
problems. She referred to repeated geographical moves as a child,
explaining that her parents worked in a field associated with the
military, which meant they would stay in different places for just a
few months at a time. Her parents had split up when Priscilla was
in her early teens and she had stayed with her mother and, subsequently, her stepfather, although she had felt closer to her father. At
times her mother had taken to drinking heavily. Priscilla felt that in
certain ways she had been treated without respect by her mother.
She mentioned feelings of shame regarding her mother's drunken
behaviour. In addition she spoke of bullying at school, at one time
being repeatedly called "ugly", and she described how she came to
believe this was true.

Priscilla said her hope regarding therapy was that she might
come to feel more confident and not worry so much about what
people might be thinking of her. She thought that if she were more

confident she would be more outgoing and would be able to think of getting a different job.

Priscilla was treated with two sessions of EMDR, using eye movements, after which she felt confident to proceed with her life.

EMDR session one

1. (Priscilla selected "sitting on the wall by the ocean" as her safe place.)

2. (Next she was asked to think of the statement "I am a worthwhile person" while she made the eye movements. Although it was clear that she would not at this point be able to accept such a thought as true, its introduction here was intended to reveal some of the obstacles to a positive self-image. After the eye movements Priscilla reported feeling sad "because it's not how I see myself". We then established that the view of herself that she did hold—the negative cognition—was "I am unhappy, I am not good enough", and she described this as a "very upsetting thought".)

The session continued.

3. [Ask yourself "Is it true that I am not good enough?"] I kept saying no . . . fighting myself . . . and this time it was like someone else was saying "you *are* good enough" . . . it felt more right that time.

4. It felt a lot more determined that time . . . but I've got a pain in my chest . . . I'm not sure what it is.

5. [Just notice that pain in your chest.] It felt like anxiety then . . . like I might feel in a crowded place.

6. [Just go with that.] It's like I'm scared of thinking I might be good enough . . . like it would be a change if I started thinking differently.

7. [Just go with that.] It wasn't as strong that time . . . deep down I suppose it is a shock to start thinking something different.

8. [Just go with that.] It's speeding up again.

9. [OK—go back to your safe place now (it was time to stop).] It's slowing down now.

Second session (two weeks later)

Priscilla reported feeling much better—"unburdened and lighter"—since the first EMDR. She said she had tried to go back to work, but when it came to it had felt too anxious; she thought she would go back part-time initially. In addition she referred to continuing feelings of shame.

EMDR

1. [Think about these feelings of shame.]

I still feel responsible for the way my Mum acts . . . I shouldn't think that way about my parents . . . so I feel guilty and give her a cuddle . . . it's her laziness and her drinking . . . I make comparisons with other Mums . . . I feel I'm walking on eggshells the whole time with her.

2. It's not really my problem . . . I've got to get on with my life . . . she's not me . . . maybe I'm afraid of ending up like that . . . but it's her problem not mine . . . if I can let go of that it would be a big step. I spoke to Dad and he said he'd noticed I had no confidence. I need to lighten up, not take things so seriously.

3. I'm not responsible for other people's actions, I'm responsible for my own life . . . I'm thinking I am good enough . . .I felt it that time . . . it felt natural . . . I'm starting to believe it.

4. I was just saying to myself "Don't feel ashamed of yourself, be proud of yourself" . . . it didn't feel upsetting saying it then . . . it's getting stronger . . . feel more determined . . . it's not just a little voice saying it.

5. I'm still saying I *am* good enough, but there's a niggling doubt, as if not quite 100%.

6. [Ask yourself why you can't feel good enough.] I am afraid . . . I don't know what of.

7. [Ask what you're afraid of.] I'm afraid that it's not true.

8. [Why might it not be true?] I don't know. [Could it be just a habit of mind?] Yes, I've got into the habit of saying it to myself . . . I don't think there is anything really.

9. I'm feeling angry now . . . I think I am good enough . . . I'm angry with myself for doubting it . . . I'm feeling more determined . . . there's no reason why I should put myself down.

10. I *am* good enough . . . I believe it now . . . I don't feel there's anything holding me back . . . I don't feel upset or afraid about saying it.

11. I'm not ashamed of myself . . . it does feel comfortable saying that.

12. [Try imagining yourself in the future.]

I feel happy, confident, smiling . . . but I'm not usually a smiley person.

13. [Try thinking about going back to work.] I feel happy to see my friends again, also I don't feel ashamed about having taken time off . . . anyone can have a problem, it's part of life . . . I don't feel ashamed . . . I can go back and say this is me . . . that was the main thing I was worried about in going back . . . I want to go back and start socializing.

14. I'm feeling happy . . . going back to work and seeing friends . . . I'm not feeling paranoid anymore.

Follow-up

Priscilla did go back to work. She felt better. However, when followed up by telephone some months later, she reported that she had suffered a partial relapse after abruptly stopping her anti-depressant medication, thinking that she did not need it. She vividly recalled in detail the positive movement of her thoughts and feelings during these two sessions and agreed to further EMDR to build on this achievement.

Commentary

The two sessions with Priscilla focused upon her self-image and self-esteem. There was no discrete trauma to process. Instead, the work had concerned Priscilla's feelings of shame about having a mother who drank alcohol excessively. As is often the case, the processing towards a more positive self-image proceeded rapidly. At one point Priscilla expressed the common fear of change, but once identified, this soon passed.

Amanda: treatment of an unhappy young woman using the emotional freedom techniques (EFT)

Amanda was a twenty-five-year-old married woman, referred because of chronic feelings of depression. During the initial consultation, after stating that she loved her husband very much, it gradually became apparent that she really felt very dissatisfied with her marriage, feeling controlled and oppressed by her husband and eventually acknowledging the shocking thought that she had made a mistake in marrying him one year previously. A more general pattern emerged in which she felt compelled to try to fit in with others' expectations of her, but would then feel secretly resentful. This had been the case in her relationship with her parents, but particularly her mother, and now in her relationship with her husband. She felt that her whole persona was false; for example, she felt that people (including her husband) expected her to conform to an image of being timid and dowdy, but really she wanted to be flamboyant and wear miniskirts. There was a deep mood of schizoid despair in much of Amanda's discourse, expressing her sense that no one really knew her. Chronic feelings of depersonalization and derealization were apparent. One interpretation offered in this initial consultation was that early in her life she had developed a split between a part of her that would participate in relationships with others and another, more hidden and secret part, that would always seek to be alone. This formulation seemed very meaningful to Amanda and she spoke of how she felt that part of her was married, while another part rebelliously wanted to run away and be alone. As these issues were explored, Amanda became increasingly aware of the extent of her pattern of outward compliance, with hidden resentment and rebellion, and how this was expressed in her chronic depression. Amanda agreed to therapy using EFT.

Session using EFT

> Amanda reported that she had had a big row with her husband. He had accused her of looking like "a tart" because she had worn a miniskirt. She felt he blamed her for all the problems in their relationship. She spoke of feeling numb.
>
> The rest of the session involved the use of EFT tapping, focused on each emerging issue. The overall aim was to explore and resolve the factors underlying her depression. Although the standard protocol for EFT involves tapping on each emotional issue until the SUDs rating falls to zero, a different approach was used here, allowing the tapping to facilitate the emergence and rapid processing of emotional experience and its meaning.
>
> [Tapping on "feeling numb".] I feel energized.
>
> I felt about to burst into tears, then I felt like smiling.
>
> I feel more optimistic . . . not so heavy . . . a nice feeling.

[As you tap, ask yourself "Why am I depressed?"] I feel exhausted—sad and lonely.

[Tap on "sad and lonely".] I feel more sad and lonely. I've just got to look after myself.

[Ask yourself when you have felt this before.] Since I was a little girl . . . I felt unhappy but I couldn't tell anyone . . . I felt like crying inside but couldn't show that to anyone . . . I knew my parents weren't happy with each other.

I'm not a little girl any more, I am in control of my own life . . . I should be in control of my life but I am not . . . I've got to live *my* life to be happy and not live for somebody else . . . I worry about others too much.

I shouldn't have to worry about my parents the way I did . . . I wasn't responsible for them . . . they were adults, they were responsible for me . . . if they had been more keyed in to their children I wouldn't have felt so responsible for myself.

I can choose to live my life for myself . . . I feel quite happy . . . excited.

The negative feelings come back . . . I can't do those things . . . I never know what I want . . . I never make the right decision, so I end up not doing anything.

[Tap on "I never know what I want".] I am angry with myself . . . I've never done anything that has really challenged me . . . I have a "can't be bothered" sort of attitude.

[Could it be that if you did what you wanted your mother would undermine you?] Yes, my parents would make fun of me. (She described pervasive feelings of shame and spoke of how she had felt her parents were never interested in her academic achievements.)

[Tap on "parents put me down".] They've no right to put me down . . . I've done many things in my life that they should be proud of but they are not . . . they took the piss out of me . . . out of everything I did or said.

[Tap on "my parents took the piss out of me".] (Tearful.) That's how I feel . . . David (husband) is now doing the same . . . rejecting me . . . he is not letting me be what I want to be, so I don't know who I am . . . I chose someone who rejects me, even though I went out with other people who did not . . . I've just gone from my parents to my husband . . . with my husband I do act like a child . . . I act like I wanted to act with my parents but didn't dare . . . I didn't act like that with them because they would not have put up with it.

[Tap on "I'm very angry with my parents".] I feel quite angry . . . like I want to punch the wall.

I do feel very angry . . . but like I don't know if it is safe to be.

I desperately want a good relationship with my parents now . . . I want to be close to my mother . . . there is nobody that I can confide in . . . I don't trust anyone.

[Perhaps your early experiences with your parents lead you to feel you cannot trust anyone because they would hurt you?] Yes . . . it's within my behaviour . . . my husband says I don't trust anyone, but it's not conscious.

[Tap on "don't trust anyone".] I have lots of friends but I don't talk about me, it seems too much hassle.

[Is it possible that your early experiences led you to give up trying to communicate how you felt, because you learned that your mother didn't understand you?] Yes, she didn't understand . . . there wasn't anyone.

[Tap on "mother didn't understand me".] I feel quite upset . . . if I couldn't have that relationship with my mother, how can I have a close relationship with anyone else?

[Tap on "I'm upset because my mother could not understand me".] I feel relieved . . . I don't feel it so strongly . . . I don't think any more that it is because I'd done something wrong . . . I don't think its because she didn't like me, but because she couldn't understand me.

[Tap on "I choose to recover from the problems of the past"] I feel quite uplifted and optimistic.

Session three

Amanda was seen again three weeks later. She reported feeling much better and said that the previous session had helped a lot. She had talked to her husband and they had managed to sort out a number of issues and were now getting on very well.

She then reported two dreams. In one dream, her sister had died. In the other, everyone at work was saying they hated her. Her associations were to worries about work, and her relationship with her sister, who was eight years younger. Apparently, her sister had had a row with her mother the previous weekend and Amanda had been concerned enough to text her sister later to ask if she was OK. I suggested to Amanda that both dreams expressed the idea of a hostile environment, like the one she had experienced in childhood, and that perhaps the sister in the dream represented a part of herself that "died" in that hostile environment of childhood. Amanda replied that she felt she was indeed very sensitive to hostile emotional atmospheres, and that she had always felt very aware that she did not want her siblings to experience what she had gone through, and she had tried to support them. Amanda did not appear particularly disturbed by these dreams, which seemed to be an expression of unconscious elaboration of the work done in the EFT session.

Amanda went on to speak of feeling generally more settled and appreciative of her marriage. She commented, "I feel I did marry the right man", and described how her new sense of greater freedom was allowing her to feel much closer to her husband. She added that she felt the best she had for a long time—no longer lonely, more active and enthusiastic, and more level headed and sane. Her responses to a routine questionnaire indicated that she was no longer experiencing a clinical level of distress and she was happy to stop at that point.

Follow-up

Follow-up at one month revealed that Amanda was still feeling happy. She rated the helpfulness of the therapy as "very much so". Her CORE questionnaire score had fallen from eighty-four (a mean of 2.5, a high score indicating a significant level of clinical distress) prior to therapy, to ten (a mean of 0.3, a very low score).

Concluding comments

Amanda presented with chronic depression and schizoid despair. Behind this was revealed a split between a part of her that related compliantly to others, and a more hidden part that she felt must remain detached and protected. Considerable resentment of her husband, perceived as controlling and rejecting, emerged initially, but it was only through the EFT tapping that the extent of her childhood feelings of humiliation and shame in relation to her parents became apparent. After this was processed, she felt much more positive and was able to talk to her husband and once again feel happy to be married to him.

Depression and PTSD: three-session treatment using the emotional freedom techniques (EFT)

Mrs Z was referred in connection with depression and anxiety following a distressing episode when her brain-damaged adolescent daughter had become disturbed and violent. She spoke of panic associated with the hospital where the incident had taken place when her daughter, Louise, had needed treatment at A&E. In addition, she described feeling sad, suicidal, frightened all the time, sometimes numb, suffering nightmares and sleep disturbance, and said she felt a complete failure. Her sense of failure was linked to feeling she had not coped adequately with her daughter's disturbance. Mrs Z described her childhood as unhappy, including physical and sexual abuse. The latter, which had stopped short of intercourse, had taken place between the ages of seven and sixteen, and had ceased when she stood up to her father. She had subsequently forgiven her father, although she said she did not love him, but did love her mother. Mrs Z had sought help for a previous episode of depression just once before, after separating from her first husband fifteen years ago; since then she had remarried.

Mrs Z agreed to proceed with EFT, addressing both the sexual abuse in childhood and the more recent trauma involving her daughter.

First EFT session

> Mrs Z reported the following feelings and thoughts associated with the memories of sexual abuse.

> Feeling sick; feeling afraid; never enjoyed it; I used to send myself somewhere else, like a robot, with no feeling.

> She was asked to think of a specific episode and she chose one when she was aged sixteen. EFT tapping was used free-associatively, as Mrs Z was asked what came to mind with each round of tapping.

1. I was feeling I wanted to stick up for myself.

2. I tried to run out of the locked bathroom . . . my father hit me in the stomach (tears).

3. Why? Why did he do it?

4. Why did I keep quiet?

5. I am angry with myself. I should have spoken out. I did try to speak to different people—my grandmother and my GP.

6. I went on a school trip to Holland and a Dutch teacher asked if I had problems—he could see I was troubled—but I said "No, not really". It was so pathetic!

7. [Are you still angry with yourself?] No, not really—what else could I have done?

After this series of EFT tapping, Mrs Z reported feeling calm about her experiences of sexual abuse in childhood.

We then addressed the more recent trauma involving her daughter. Mrs Z gave a narrative account of what happened, including her thoughts and feelings, and EFT was used for each segment of this. Her daughter had taken an overdose and had then jumped out of an upstairs window.

1. I thought she was dead.

2. I knew she wasn't dead.

3. I was completely bewildered.

4. Watching my daughter so distressed. I couldn't get through to her. I felt helpless (tears).

5. I was frightened of my daughter. She was so strong and aggressive.

6. I shouldn't be frightened of my daughter.

7. I feel a bit kinder towards myself.

Session two

Mrs Z reported feeling less anxious and more sad, but she added that she was no longer feeling devastated in the way that she had been. She spoke of feeling sad that Louise was no longer living with her, but she said she was blaming herself less since she believed that Louise had been so disturbed that it would not have made any difference whatever she had done to try to calm her. However, she was still not sleeping well, although she had not been troubled by further nightmares of

Louise jumping out of a window. She was feeling she wanted to go back to work. We proceeded with EFT.

1. I feel sad about Louise.

2. Louise self-harmed badly last week, cutting her arm—I worry about her.

3. I still have a tremor (since the traumatic episode with Louise).

4. I'm trembly all over—digging at my nails.

5. My legs feel tingly.

6. My legs feel floaty.

7. My left hand feels more shaky than the other.

8. I feel calm, but tired.

However, Mrs Z reported continuing feelings of tension in her body. These were released using the energy method called EmoTrance (Hartmann, 2003b). She was asked to focus on the physical sensation, with the thought that this is energy that can soften and flow, and to observe what it then does. Mrs Z described a sensation of tension then flowing from her stomach, along her arm, and out of her body—a process which took about a minute. She was startled by this effect, remarking, "That's amazing!"

Session three

Mrs Z reported that she had been feeling "quite well" since the last session. In particular, she was pleased that she had been able to sleep through the night since this made a big difference to how she felt. She said she was no longer troubled by intrusive images of the trauma with Louise, and that her attitude now was one of "Well, that's happened—it's OK, it doesn't frighten me." She added, "I've been anxious for so long, but I feel quite calm now—I don't know what's happened!" In addition, she said she had been applying the tapping method on her own and had found this beneficial.

Mrs Z then went on to talk of her conflicts about going back to her work in the field of education. "How can I help other kids when my own daughter's life is in such disarray? I wanted so much to sort out my own child's life."

The session then continued with EFT tapping.

1. I should spend more time with Louise.

2. I'm feeling really sad . . . I miss her . . . I'm sad about her being bullied at school.

3. I've just got to learn to accept that it doesn't matter what I did or could have done, it doesn't change anything.

4. I think I have been hard on myself.

5. I don't feel quite so sad.

6. I feel tired.

7. (Sadness—SUDs 1).

8. [How are you feeling about going back to work?] I have mixed feelings, but I am leaning more towards going back to work.

9. I still feel this ache about Louise.

10. I feel calmer now.

Session four

Mrs Z reported that she was "feeling good—a lot happier" and that she had gone back to work. She said Louise had come to stay for one night and this had been good and she had felt more accepting of the problems. She then added an interesting and important observation:

"I feel I really like myself—and I've never felt that before. I feel this is me and it's OK."

She also spoke of feeling she was more assertive. She had used EFT tapping on her own, regarding return to work, and said people there had commented that she looked better than ever.

I drew Mrs Z's attention to her account of how she had felt prior to the therapy with EFT. She remarked, "I remember how bad I felt, but I am not feeling it now. I can't understand how I feel like this now when I felt like that then—it sounds like another person."

She then added that she felt the turning point in the work had been the very brief intervention with EmoTrance, which she felt had left her body significantly calmer so that she had been able to sleep subsequently.

The work was ended at this point.

Follow-up

In her feedback questionnaire after one month, Mrs. Z reported that she was continuing to feel well. She rated the helpfulness of the therapy as "Very much so".

Commentary

As is often the case in brief treatments using EFT or EMDR, relatively little was known or explored regarding Mrs Z's life and development. She presented the two issues that needed to be addressed: the childhood sexual abuse and the more recent trauma involving her brain-damaged daughter. These somewhat thematically linked experiences were processed rapidly, moving through feelings of helplessness, inadequacy, self-blame, and sadness, and Mrs Z arrived at a state of peaceful acceptance in relation to both. All her symptoms of depression and PTSD were resolved. No interpretative content or cognitive interweave was offered by the therapist. The therapy simply facilitated Mrs Z's own healing process. Interestingly, Mrs Z reported feeling better than ever afterwards, with improvement in her self-esteem. She attributed particular benefit to the calming of her body, using EmoTrance, which allowed her to sleep. This method has some similarities to strategies of mindfulness (Segal, Williams, & Teasdale, 2002) and involves attention to bodily sensation, as in EMDR. Again the facilitation from the therapist is content-free, except for the idea of letting the energy flow.

Brief EFT treatment for a combination of rape trauma, medical trauma, and loss of future babies

This case study is included partly because it illustrates in detail the use of EFT acupressure tapping following the standard format as taught by the Association for Meridian Energy Therapy.

Mrs D, a thirty-five-year-old married woman, presented with feelings of depression and anxiety following an ectopic pregnancy that had been misdiagnosed three months earlier. She felt she had been mistreated by the hospital. This event had also triggered flashback memories of a violent rape at the age of fourteen, the rapist being a seventeen-year-old boy. Following this rape she had developed marked post traumatic stress disorder and had become a very disturbed teenager, self-harming and attempting suicide. She had not told anyone about the rape at the time because of feelings of shame, and also because she had reacted by dissociating from the whole experience. Mrs D's earlier childhood had been happy. She was an only child. She reported a supportive relationship with both parents until the undisclosed experience of rape had destroyed her security. As an adult, Mrs D had become more settled and had established a successful career as a music teacher. She was happily married with one five-year-old son.

First session

During the first session, the above history was taken and the possibilities of therapy using EFT were discussed. Mrs D was keen to proceed. She had a favourable impression of acupuncture and so the idea of a therapy based on similar principles appealed to her. The most prominent emotional target was her constellation of feelings about the hospital. The aspects were as follows:

Main situation: hospital error over ectopic pregnancy.
Aspects: overwhelmed with anger (SUD 10)
because of lies (SUD 8);
they tried to cover up mistakes (SUD 8);
nobody said sorry (SUD 7);
I was misdiagnosed (SUD 8);
they nearly killed me and showed a blatant disregard for my life (SUD 10).

These aspects were not identified initially; they emerged as the EFT proceeded. Thus, we began with the general feeling of anger. After this was tapped, the various aspects emerged. Each reduced to SUDs of zero after just a few rounds of tapping, but the strongest affect was associated with the thought that "they showed a blatant disregard for my life". Mrs D left the session appearing much relieved. We agreed to address the rape trauma next time.

Session two

Mrs D reported that she had been feeling rather better, although she experienced some renewed agitation about the hospital having looked at her records. This agitation was relieved with a brief round of EFT.

We then proceeded to the rape trauma. She was not initially able to identify feelings about it now, other than "a feeling in my throat" and "panic".

Rape trauma

Initial aspects: feeling in my throat (SUD 5);
panic (SUD 7).

These two rapidly reduced to zero with a couple of rounds of EFT (beginning with the set-up "even though I have this feeling . . . etc."). However, she revealed her state of dissociation by saying it felt as if it had happened to someone else. Therefore, I asked her to think about the fact that it was actually she who had been raped. We then tapped again. She then reported the following aspects:

Further aspects: No one would believe me (SUD 8; VOC 8);
I feel all alone with it (SUD 7);
I feel sorry for myself (SUD 7);
I am tired of it being in my head (SUD 8);
I feel overwhelmed (SUD 10).

These aspects were all tapped to zero, needing just a few rounds each. Mrs D was tearful but then reported feeling more relaxed. She then added that it was still difficult for her to accept that it was she who had been raped. Therefore, I asked her to make the statement: "I was raped". In response she reported a "sickened feeling" and that it was "horrible".

Further aspects: Sickened feeling (SUD 9);
It was horrible (SUD 9).

After tapping these to zero, Mrs D then reported some residual feelings of panic. She decided these were to do with the feeling at the time of the rape that she did not know what was going on.

Further aspect: Not knowing what was going on (SUD 10).

After this was tapped to zero, Mrs D reported feeling relaxed, but then detected a "cold feeling inside", which she then elaborated as "not sure if I would live—I thought I was going to die". This was, of course, a very important aspect of the rape trauma, and a key contributor to her PTSD. It also echoed the more recent trauma in which she felt her life had been in danger at the hospital.

Further aspect: I thought I was going to die (SUD 10).

As this was tapped, the following aspects rapidly emerged. Since these tumbled out together we did not take SUDs for each. This part of the session took the form partly of the story method.

Further aspects: Very scared—I wanted my mum;
Feel very upset;
Empty feeling;
Numbness;
Frozen feeling;
Struggling feeling.

We kept on tapping as these various feelings and thoughts emerged, not stopping to take SUDs—just keeping on tapping until she reported feeling calm. This part took about 5–10 minutes. She described the feelings as "fading".

Testing

Mrs D was now able to recall the entire episode without distress. She was also able to state "I was raped" without emotion.

Summary of target and aspects in session two

Target: rape at fourteen.

Aspects: Feeling in throat
Panic
No-one would believe me
I feel alone with it
I feel sorry for myself
I'm tired of it being in my head
I feel overwhelmed
A sickened feeling
Horrible
Thought I was going to die
Very scared—want my mum
Empty feeling
Numbness
Frozen feeling
Struggling feeling

Third session (three weeks later)

Mrs D reported feeling better after the last session, but her mood had dropped just recently because she and her husband had been looking into the possibility of *in vivo* fertilization. She could not have more children through normal means as a result of the ectopic pregnancy. However, she had concluded that the IVF procedure seemed so alien and clinical—"like growing babies in dishes"—that she could not face this prospect. As a result she was "facing the fact that I cannot have more babies".

Mrs D agreed to use EFT to address her feelings about not being able to have more babies. Tapping on the idea that she could not have more babies simply led to her feeling "numb". However, when I asked her to consider the future without more babies, she reported feeling "empty".

First aspect: Feeling empty (SUD 9).

First round of EFT: SUD 5.

Second round of EFT: SUD 2.

Third round of EFT: SUD 0.

I asked her how she now felt about the future without more babies. She reported feeling sad.

Second aspect: feeling sad (SUD 7).

First round of EFT: SUD 0.

Mrs D reported that now she did not feel sad, but felt "low".

Third aspect: feeling low (SUD 4).

First round of EFT: SUD 1.

Second round of EFT: SUD 0.

Mrs D then spoke of feeling numb and tired. EFT for these feelings resulted in her feeling "more lifted". However, she said it was still hard to accept that she would have no more babies. After a further round of EFT directed at this she reported feeling "a bit lighter". With yet another round of tapping she said "it just feels all right now".

Testing

I asked her to imagine the future with no babies. She said she felt "nothing". I asked if it was painful to think of the future without more babies; she said it did not feel painful.

Summary of target and aspects in session three

Target problem: facing the fact of not having more babies.

Main aspects: Feeling empty
Feeling sad
Feeling low

Follow-up session

Mrs D was seen for a follow-up two weeks later. She reported a continuing improvement in her mood, and described feeling much calmer. No longer term follow-up data are available.

Summary of the case

Mrs D had experienced a violent rape at the age of fourteen. Prior to this her childhood had been secure and happy. Her state of shock and dissociation following the rape contributed to her feeling that she could not tell her parents, or indeed any adult about what had happened to her. She developed PTSD and became a disturbed adolescent. In adult life she became more settled, but the adolescent trauma was re-evoked by the thematically similar experience of feeling abused in a life-threatening manner by the hospital. The resulting inability to have further babies was a further source of distress. All three areas of emotional pain were addressed using EFT. As might be expected, the rape was the experience associated with the most intense and most varied pain.

*A note on the "apex effect" and other negative
responses to rapid improvement*

Roger Callahan has drawn attention to an interesting an important phenomenon often found in responses to successful and rapid treatment with energy methods. Because the person is bewildered by the sudden change in their experience, and because this does not fit pre-existing expectations, the previous state of distress may be denied, or spurious explanations may be given for the improvement. Callahan (2001) called this the "Apex Problem" (drawing upon a related idea of Arthur Koestler), because at such moments the mind is functioning below its apex.

The following case illustrates this. Louise presented with traumatic stress symptoms, associated with disturbing events at work, which had linked with childhood trauma. She was seen for a single assessment and energy treatment session, during which her subjective distress relating to both the recent and childhood traumas subsided to zero. At followup a month later she remained symptom free. She was sent a routine feedback form. Her responses to this were interesting. She rated her improvement at maximum, but rated the value of the therapy at the lowest point on the scale. She had also added a comment that she thought she should have seen the therapist for longer. In view of this intriguingly paradoxical rating, I telephoned Louise to enquire further. She explained that she was feeling completely well, was happily back at work, and her colleagues had remarked that she seemed better than ever. However, she felt puzzled by her recovery—"I feel a bit of a fraud ... maybe I was making it all up". When asked about her comment that she should have seen the therapist for longer, she replied " Well I thought I would have needed to talk to you about all my anxieties and nightmares and have counselling for months, and I didn't see how that tapping could have helped." When I explained the apex effect to Louise, indicating that it was a common reaction, she agreed that she had found her sudden relief of symptoms bewildering and confusing because she had found the therapy utterly implausible, and this had led her to doubt her previous state of stress. She was greatly relieved by our brief telephone discussion because she then no longer needed to invalidate either the therapy or her previous state of traumatic stress. Since this experience with Louise I have found it useful to warn patients of the potential apex effect.

A related phenomenon is that, because energy methods and EMDR are effective and rapid therapies, a patient's resistance to recovery may become much more apparent than it would be if slower, talk-based methods are used. Some patients are highly resistant to engaging with such therapies, despite their conscious protestations of wanting relief from psychological problems and distress. Often this may reveal an unconscious agenda, not of recovering from psychological illness, but of settling into a long-term "therapeutic" relationship for the gratifications and reassurance inherent in that. This misuse of the therapeutic relationship, in the service of remaining sick rather than recovering, is less likely to be apparent when the therapy offered is long-term.

Another form of resistance is similar to Freud's (1923b, pp 49–50) account of the negative therapeutic reaction, based on wishes to suffer, perhaps associated with feelings of guilt. Gillian was referred following complex grief reactions following the death by suicide of her sister a couple of years previously. When an energy method was described to her, Gillian replied that she was willing to "try anything". However, it was apparent that she did not want actually to start the work, since every time the therapist invited her to begin she would find something else to speak of. When this was pointed out to her, she expressed feelings of guilt that she had not been sufficiently aware of her sister's state of mind, and clear feelings emerged that she should suffer in sympathy with her sister. Once these feelings of guilt had been articulated Gillian was ready to begin the energy therapy and responded rapidly to this.

Note

1. Shapiro (2002a) describes a clear eight stage protocol for EMDR. These stages are:
    (1) history taking;
    (2) establishing rapport and client preparation;
    (3) assessment;
    (4) desensitization through bilateral stimulation;
    (5) installation of the positive cognition;
    (6) body scan, checking for feelings of bodily disturbance when the original trauma is held in mind;
    (7) closure and debriefing, explaining to the client that further processing may take place after the session;
    (8) re-evaluation in a follow-up session, enquiring what other memories, thoughts, and emotions have emerged.

CHAPTER NINE

Using EMDR and energy methods in practice

"My excursion into EMDR was considerably briefer than my experience in psychoanalysis, but in certain respects it took me to places I had never reached with psychoanalysis alone"

(Wachtel, 2002, p. 131)

B oth EMDR and energy methods are effective—considerably more so, for many problems, than conventional psychotherapeutic methods. However, this efficiency does not mean that the work is necessarily simple. The treatment of simple PTSD (resulting from a single trauma), which was the starting point for EMDR, is structurally simple. Essentially, the traumatic memories are processed and the patient then feels better. However, when used with structurally more complex psychopathology involving multiple developmental layers of emotional conflict and emotional pain, with psychological defences deeply structured into the personality, then the work is inevitably complex. In order to make good use of EMDR or an energy method in complex cases, the psychotherapist will need to have an adequate understanding of psychodynamics ✂ as revealed by psychoanalysis, as well as an awareness of the deep cognitive structures of the mind, and an appreciation of relevant areas of neurobiology. These areas of knowledge and understanding must be combined in an awareness of the overall interactive functioning of the psychosomatic system (Damasio, 1994).

Combining EMDR or energy psychology with a psychoanalytic perspective

For the seasoned psychotherapist, used to conventional psychoanalytic work based on the assumption that interpretation of the transference is the essential vehicle of healing, EMDR might seem a most odd and unwieldy method to introduce. Similarly, a patient who has become used to seeing his or her analyst for years would probably be puzzled and alarmed at the sudden suggestion of using any kind of "technique", especially one as weird sounding as EMDR or EFT. This would certainly have been my own view at one time, both as an analyst and as a patient. The psychoanalytic stance is one of caution regarding modifications of the frame and procedure of the therapy, alert to unconscious motivations of the psychotherapist and to the unconscious meanings for the patient. Thus, the introduction of EMDR or EFT into what had previously been conventional verbal psychotherapy could reflect some kind of manic move on the part of the therapist—perhaps a denial of despair and hopelessness—and might be perceived as such, consciously or unconsciously, by the patient. However, this is less likely to be the case if the possibility of using EMDR or EFT, and the meaning of doing so, is considered carefully over a period of time, thereby avoiding a manic flight by either therapist or patient. What is much easier is if the possibility of sometimes using EMDR or EFT is introduced as part of the frame at the very beginning.

Obviously some kind of explanation for the patient of such a strange-sounding method is required, just as Freud would originally have been obliged to justify his theory and eccentric new method of free association on a couch. My own brief explanations of EMDR are usually in terms of the capacity of bilateral stimulation to facilitate emotional processing, the tendency for trauma to block processing, and I may also make links with the rapid eye movement stages of sleep and the function of dreams in "digesting" emotional information. In the case of energy methods, I outline the theory of bodily meridians and make links with acupuncture and acupressure, pointing out that while the assumptions of these frameworks are outside conventional western medical science, there is nevertheless a genre of rational enquiry and research that has a bearing on such methods. However, I do not seek to persuade clients of the truth or validity of these models and analogies, but simply to provide some rudimentary rationale that will render the method sensible rather than bizarre. It is not necessary for the client to "believe in" EMDR, or energy methods, in order for them to be effective. The client's belief is fairly irrelevant, except that without some kind of rationale he or she is unlikely to agree to use the method. This irrelevance of the client's belief is also true of psycho-analysis, unless, similarly, the belief system prevents the client from embarking on the therapy at all. Interestingly, the most popular and highly hyped contemporary therapy—cognitive therapy—does appear to depend upon the client being socialized into the "cogni-tive model" and accepting this. Part of the appeal of the cognitive approach often seems to be its seeming plausibility and face valid-ity; it is very easy for clients to grasp. Thus, cognitive therapy may involve much more of an element of suggestion than psychoanaly-sis, EMDR, or energy methods. Typically, clients will express scep-ticism about EMDR or energy methods, even if willing to "give it a go", but then express utter astonishment later on discovering how remarkably it has worked. People do not expect that following a therapist's moving finger or a moving light, or listening to alter-nating clicks in each ear, or tapping parts of the body, are going to help; for most of us, such methods are simply implausible. This lack of plausibility or face validity indicates that suggestion may not be a significant factor in the success of EMDR and energy methods.

The extent to which EMDR is central to my therapeutic work depends on the nature of the presenting problem and the desires and expectations of the client. In a National Health Service (NHS) setting, particularly, clients do not necessarily expect to be taken on for long-term psychotherapy lasting for years. They may want a cure for their disabling anxiety or problematic behaviour as quickly and efficiently as possible. For such people, EMDR or related methods may be the primary treatment of choice, especially if there has been an identifiable trauma, or if the presenting symptom is anxiety or phobia. On the other hand, some people, perhaps more so in private practice, may be explicitly seeking long-term psychotherapy or psychoanalysis, on an informed basis, because they see this as the route to self-understanding, self-knowledge, and personality development. EMDR or an energy method may have less relevance in such cases. However, wherever effectiveness and efficiency of the therapeutic work is a consideration, the selective inclusion of EMDR or EFT may be of help.

Psychotherapists who would experience most difficulty in feeling comfortable using EMDR are likely to include those who follow the contemporary British psychoanalytic fashion for restricting the analyst's remarks solely to interpretation of the "here-and-now" negative transference. According to the (in my view erroneous) assumptions underlying this stance, all of the patient's communications can be taken as unconsciously referring to the relationship with the analyst. The incorporation of a method such as EMDR would be regarded as hopelessly compromising the therapeutic frame, rendering true psychoanalytic work impossible.

By contrast, those psychotherapists and analysts who hold to a more classical view of the coexistence of the transference relationship and the real relationship, and who do not consider that interpretation of the negative transference is the "be all and end all" of analytic work, may be more able to envisage how an adjunctive technique may comfortably be incorporated. It is a matter of loosening one's grip on a fixed idea of the form of psychoanalytic work, so as to see other ways in which the principles of trauma, developmental experience, and psychodynamic conflict may be addressed. Although many analysts would tend to view attention to the transference as almost defining psychoanalytic technique, the transference need not be regarded as an inherent core of the psychoanalytic approach. Freud discovered the psychodynamic mind, with its conflicts, its methods of symptom-formation and dream-formation, its unconscious modes of thought and representation. He thought dreams were the "royal road" to the unconscious, but these days, for many analysts, the understanding of dreams has been hijacked by the near-exclusive preoccupation with transference (Loden, 2003). Freed from this obsession with the patient's unconscious relationship with the analyst, it becomes much easier to introduce, from time to time, different ways of working, without this detracting from the overall ongoing analytic process. If the rationale of EMDR is presented at the beginning, it can often be useful to use bilateral audio-stimulation throughout the sessions, thereby greatly facilitating the emergence and processing of psychodynamic material. Psychoanalytically orientated practitioners who are comfortable incorporating EMDR into their work include Grand (1998, 2001), Manfield (1998) and Wachtel (2002), while a Jungian perspective is presented by Magliano (2003).

Of course, it is still important to be alert to the meanings and implications, both conscious and unconscious, of introducing EMDR or an energy method. These will vary from patient to patient. Similarly, the therapist must monitor his or her own motivations. For example, a defensive flight from anxiety, despair, or negative transference obviously would not be a sound basis for introducing EMDR. As in every other area of therapeutic work, a thoughtful and enquiring stance is appropriate. Once a patient has experienced the value of EMDR or an energy method, he or she is likely to want to use it again and may well ask for it.

Incorporating EFT into a conventional psychotherapy session

With some clients it is very helpful to incorporate a method such as EFT, within otherwise conventional psychotherapy, in order more easily and rapidly to process the emerging insights. It is not always appreciated fully that, although some insights can be relieving, others can be distinctly traumatic, provoking resistance, depression, and feelings of helplessness. Typically, the actual EFT may take only a minute or two at the end, but may greatly enhance the value of the preceding work.

For example, a woman spent most of her session talking of her puzzlement and distress at the way that she had been reacting with anger and depression in response to a lessening of her partner's previously somewhat abusive behaviour towards her. She reported a dream: she was at her children's school; she had forgotten to give them money for an after school activity; the school turned into a stately country home; she worried what the teachers might think of her; she then faced a steep staircase and was worried how far she might fall. When she woke up her mind was full of thoughts about her mother's snobbish and embarrassing behaviour—how she had actually been a very neglectful mother but had presented herself as rather posh and conscientious. Eventually, it was possible to arrive at the following understanding. When her partner used to behave somewhat abusively towards her, she had been able to occupy the moral high ground and feel superior. Her partner had functioned as the container for her projected feelings of inadequacy. However, as his behaviour had become less abusive, she was deprived of a container for this projected and disowned part of her self—hence her mood of depression and anger. In these dynamics she had been behaving like her mother, who had similarly tried to present herself as superior and to denigrate others. Her dream had expressed this by portraying *her* as a neglectful mother, swanning about a rather grand country house school, preoccupied with what others thought of her, but fearful of falling from her lofty manic height. This insight was highly shocking and disturbing for her—i.e. it was *traumatic*, as insights often can be. Her view of her self was fundamentally challenged. However, a few rounds of EFT not only relieved her shock and distress, but also led to deepening insight. She recalled, with great embarrassment, further instances of her own behaviour in which she had talked in ways designed to interest and impress others, just like her mother. Her overwhelming embarrassment was then rapidly processed with more EFT. Thus, the addition of an energy method allowed the emerging insight to be much more easily integrated than otherwise, reducing the shock effect that in itself constituted a trauma.

Titrating the emotional intensity

EMDR and related methods work best if the client is sufficiently in touch with an area of emotional distress that the thought field is appropriately "tuned", yet not so much so that an unmanageable level of traumatic experience floods the psyche. Too little or too much tuning to trauma will render the method ineffective or, in the case of affect overload, may be actually harmful. As van der Kolk comments, "In the language of neuroscience, the challenge is determining how to process trauma so that it is *quenched* rather than *rekindled*" (2002, p. 66).

When there is too much affect

A common occurrence with an inexperienced clinician is for bilateral stimulation to take the client rapidly into uncontrolled reliving of a severe trauma that does not lessen in subjective severity throughout the session. The client is left feeling worse than ever and refuses to engage in further EMDR, and the clinician is left feeling shaken and guilty. Similar problems arise if there has been repeated childhood trauma: this will inevitably tend to be re-evoked if it is linked thematically to a more recent trauma that is the initial target for EMDR.

The following modifications and adjustments can be considered.

1. One possibility is that any form of bilateral stimulation is contraindicated. The client simply does not have sufficient ego strength to tolerate processing trauma. Supportive or cognitive therapy may be more appropriate.

2. EMDR could be undertaken in an inpatient setting (Courtois & Bloom, 2000; Melbeck, 2003). Although elective admissions are unusual within mental health services, they are possible if the purpose is carefully agreed with patient and clinical team. Such an arrangement can allow the opportunity for the patient to obtain support from nursing staff and experience the safety of the ward when potentially overwhelmed with affect and experiencing impulses towards self-harm. If the work is planned thoughtfully, with much prior discussion, the patient may be able to put areas of disturbance into what is experienced as a compartment of the mind, knowing that at an agreed time they can be taken out and addressed. An example is given below.

3. Discrete areas and episodes of trauma should be processed in manageable chunks. Although it is always preferable to focus EMDR or energy methods on particular discrete experiences, this may be even more important where there has been extensive trauma. Paradoxically, it is in such cases of very large areas of repeated trauma that there can be a tendency to be drawn into rather generalized and unfocused targeting. What is more useful is to focus on discrete experiences and then to allow these to generalize. A discrete trauma can itself be further "fractionated" into more tolerable sections, processing

the episode bit by bit. In the case of EFT, a commonly used method is to ask the client to tell the story of the trauma, using a tapping sequence at each step in the narrative wherever there is indication of distress.

4. The bilateral stimulation can be used to induce pleasurable feelings of relaxation. For some very traumatized clients this in itself provides valuable relief from PTSD symptoms. A prolonged period of such use may precede work on processing trauma.

5. Instead of attempting to process the actual trauma, the focus can be instead upon its meanings, particularly the client's self-related thoughts (self-image and self-esteem) that have resulted from the trauma. Often, if the trauma has involved rape or abuse, the self-related thoughts are of being worthless, rubbish, disgusting, dirty, fundamentally flawed and bad, and so on. These may not alter easily, but continued bilateral stimulation whilst the client is tuned to these thoughts often does eventually lead to some re-evaluation. The client may be guided to ask herself the question "Is it true that I am dirty/pathetic/flawed, that it is my fault that I was abused?" during the bilateral stimulation and to note the answers that appear in her mind. It is important to note that the therapist does not need to try to persuade the client that her cognitions are unrealistic or invalid; the client's own processing leads to the change. By focusing on the trauma-derived cognitions rather than the trauma itself, the damaged self-image and self-esteem are addressed while avoiding a potentially overwhelming reliving of the original experience.

6. Attention can be given to accessing or installing positive mental resources (Korn & Leeds, 2002; Leeds & Shapiro, 2000; Omaha, 2004).[1] During bilateral stimulation, the client may be asked to think of previous experiences of coping successfully, and to notice the pleasurable feelings and sensations associated with these. For example, a man who was overwhelmingly anxious about the prospect of processing a severe road traffic trauma was enabled to recall many experiences of success and skill in many areas of life, including driving. This led him to a lifting of his depressed mood and an upsurge of feelings of confidence, allowing him then to proceed to the target trauma. However, sometimes a client may be unable to think of any

prior experiences of successful coping. In such instances, he or she can be asked to think of a person who does cope well and to imagine how this would feel. Often it is better to draw upon an image of a person who manages a situation with a normal level of competence rather than a very high level that would be felt by the client to be an unrealistic standard to aim for. By using bilateral stimulation, with the thought field tuned to this imagined behaviour and experience, the client can gradually install the sensory and affective components of successful coping with whatever is the problematic situation. Kinaesthetic imagery can also be incorporated here, asking the client to assume or imagine a body posture congruent with feeling calm, assertive, fluent, or whatever the desired state might be (Kinowski, 2003). In EFT, positive resources can be installed with the "Choices" method (Carrington, 2001).

7. The periods of eye movements or other bilateral stimulation can be made very short—perhaps ten or less—so that the client is repeatedly brought back to the safety of the present room. This short and therefore more manageable exposure helps to build up a sense of mastery. The helpful effect may be enhanced if the client is encouraged to look around the room carefully in order to be grounded perceptually in the present. Another strategy can be to make the eye movements extremely short or extremely slow, or both. The original method of a moving finger may enable the clinician to be more sensitively responsive to the client's state than is possible using the various technology of bilateral stimulation.

8. The periods of bilateral stimulation may be interspersed by relatively long periods of conversation. Also, although normally it is preferable for the therapist to say as little as possible during the processing, so as not to interfere with the client's innate healing agenda, in some cases, where the client is experiencing a very high and unmanageable level of distress, it is helpful to engage in some degree of related conversation while the client revisits the trauma in order to help him or her remain partially grounded in the present.

9. Although, in its purest form, the EMDR process allows the client's own brain to assimilate traumatic experience and move spontaneously towards its resolution with minimal content

from the therapist, there are occasions when it is appropriate to introduce new information or ways of thinking that were not already present. Shapiro termed such interventions the "cognitive interweave", perhaps implying a "weaving in" of new information. However, they may also at times correspond to what would, within a psychoanalytic framework, be termed interpretations. These can sometimes help a person to perceive their role in a traumatic event somewhat differently, allowing a revision of self-image and initiating a resumption of processing.

10. Some forms of bilateral stimulation are more calming than others—and clients may differ in their preferences. Bilateral music, or hand taps, or mechanical tactile stimulators may be more soothing than eye movements.

11. An energy technique, such as EFT or TFT may often be far less distressing than EMDR since it does not involve conscious processing of the trauma. These can be considered if they are acceptable to the client. Often an energy technique may usefully be included at the end of an EMDR session to bring about a deeper state of relaxation.

12. When using an energy method, the client's experienced distance from the target trauma may be increased by using a more neutral phrase, or code word, which is agreed upon as a signifier, e.g. this "yellow experience", or this "number 5 feeling". Such an approach builds upon the natural dissociation that tends to occur in response to trauma. It is often surprisingly effective, allowing the troubling emotion to be processed without intense conscious experience of it.

13. Instead of engaging with the emotional meanings of an experience, the bodily sensations of the emotion may be released using the energy method called EmoTrance (Hartmann, 2003). This is often extremely helpful because when the physiological and energetic dimension of emotional experience is released and the body is calm, then the painful emotion is much more tolerable. Since it is the physical experience of emotion that is addressed, framed as "just a form of energy", rather than its meaning, this method can be of value when the full raw emotional experience is intolerable. For example, a patient who had experienced extensive sexual abuse throughout her childhood became overwhelmed with feelings of anger, greatly alarming

her; she experienced the emotion as like red lava bubbling inside her body, later shifting into a fiery ball in her abdomen. She was unable to process this any further, continuing to express terror of the intensity of her anger. The clue to the problem arose when she commented that she could not let go of the fiery ball because it was symbolic of her anger, which it would not be safe to release. The therapist reminded her to focus on the *sensation and image* of the energy rather than any symbolic meaning, and the ball of energy then rapidly dispersed, leaving her feeling immediately calmer. EmoTrance can be of particular value with patients who are inclined to self-harm as a means of releasing bodily tension. When the body is calm the urge to cut may be greatly reduced. This energy method may be considered a form of "mindfulness", a meditation that attends to experience while not being captured by it.

14. If an EMDR session has to be brought to a close before a target traumatic experience has been adequately processed, an energy method may help to calm an agitated client. The "touch and breathe" modification of EFT, introduced by John Diepold, whereby the client lightly presses each of the acupressure points while taking a deep and gentle complete breath inspiration and exhalation, may be more calming than the tapping technique (Diepold, 2002; also see article at www.emofree.com)

15. EMDR facilitates association. For most clients this is likely to be helpful. However, some patients with schizophrenic tendencies already suffer from an excess of association and are unable adequately to organise, focus, and evaluate their thoughts (De Masi, 2003). Therefore, there is a risk that EMDR could lead to a worsening of such a patient's condition. On the other hand, if the excessive association is in essence a manic flight from unmetabolized traumatic experience, then processing the trauma could result in an improvement in the patient's mental state. An energy method, such as EFT, may be safer since it has less propensity to stimulate association.

When there is too little affect

The opposite problem in EMDR work is that of the client insufficiently engaging with emotion processing. Although apparently thinking about the target problem, he or she reports a lack of emotion or distress. He or she may comment that it is impossible to think of the problem while making the eye movements, or may say, "Well, I was just looking at the lights [on the light bar]." The following ways of addressing this can be considered.

1. Often continued application of the bilateral stimulation will eventually lead to emotion processing, sometimes occurring rather suddenly. Sometimes altering the direction or form of eye movement may initiate processing, and sometimes switching to another sensory modality of bilateral stimulation may be what is required. Experimentation is important.

2. An absence of emotion when the client is supposedly thinking about a distressing experience may indicate that he or she has dissociated and therefore is detached from emotion and from bodily experience. Asking the client to notice all the sensory modalities of the experience, and particularly to be aware of these in the body, may often help him or her become engaged with affect.

3. It may be important to focus the processing on a particular experience. An unfocused or generalized idea or image may fail to engender appropriate affect. The resulting failure of emotional engagement may be analogous to the attempt to undo a rusty nut on a car using a spanner that grips only loosely. Clients with avoidant and phobic tendencies may be very inclined to stay in an unfocused position unless this is addressed by the therapist. Of course this may also occur in long-term conventional psychotherapy.

4. In the case of EFT, it is best if the phrase held in mind during the tapping sequence is derived from vivid emotional or metaphorical language, perhaps using bodily imagery, and possibly quite crude terms. More abstract or refined language may be less useful. The client may be asked to come up with a phrase that captures the experience. For example, a patient had been very disturbed by an internal medical examination that had evoked physical sensations similar to those of sexual abuse during her childhood. While tapping to the phrase "internal examination" had very little effect, her expression "being stretched to breaking point" was more potent.

5. The target experience selected might not necessarily be the most severe episode of trauma or anxiety, but could be the most recent related event—one that is thereby nearest to the client's consciousness.

6. The failure to process might be due to the phenomenon of "psychological reversal", identified originally by Diamond, Callahan, Craig, and other energy therapists. While this may be the result of a variety of psychological factors, and is no doubt related to what is termed a negative therapeutic reaction within psychoanalysis, the effect is that processing and healing, of any kind, cannot take place. The energy cannot flow in a positive direction. Although the underlying psychological conflicts, anxieties (including disintegration anxiety), and secondary gains can be explored, the immediate correction of the psychological reversal can be made through stimulation of the "karate point" or the "sore spot" combined with an affirmation of self-acceptance. The correction of more pervasive "massive reversal" and "neurological disorganization" may be helped by additional techniques from kinesiology, such as Cook's hook-ups, cross crawl and figure of eight movements, or collarbone breathing (Feinstein, 2004; Gallo, 1999; Grudermeyer, 2003).

7. Regular excessive intake of alcohol may, in some cases, substantially interfere with the processing of emotion.[2] EMDR or energy methods may simply not work at all until the client stops drinking. In this respect, alcohol may fall into the category of an "energy toxin" (Callahan & Callahan, 1996).

When processing does not take place

Although both EMDR and energy methods are generally extremely facilitating of psychosomatic change, there are occasions when neither seems to lead to the expected processing of emotional experience. In such cases, deeper sources of psychological reversal (resistance) may need to be investigated. These may involve fears of the consequences of loss of symptoms, such as fears of being vulnerable and in danger if anxiety is relinquished, or fears of being abandoned and expected to be independent and responsible if disabling symptoms are resolved, or feelings of not deserving to be released from distress, or concerns that a more positive experience of self is incompatible with a core feature of identity. Disintegration anxiety is commonly a deeply rooted source of resistance and psychological reversal.

Neurological disorganization is a further factor to be considered (Feinstein, 2004; Gallo, 2000; Krebs, 1998; Walther, 1988). When this is present, the person's experience will often be characterized by states of confusion (including left–right confusion), disorientation, indecision, and perhaps a lack of clear thematic themes in the therapeutic discourse. It is a state in which the brain subtly works against itself, rather as if generating conflicting signals and impulses that cancel one another out. To some extent, the eye movements of EMDR may have a brain balancing effect, and this may be enhanced if they are conducted as figure of eight movements. In addition, the various corrections for neurological disorganization, outlined in energy psychology literature (derived from applied kinesiology), may be considered.

A common psychoanalytic stance is to leave the patient in a blocked, resistive, or otherwise unproductive state of mind, attempting to resolve this only by means of interpretation, and basically waiting for the blocks in the free-associative process to be released. However, from the perspective of EMDR and energy methods, there seems little merit in such a passive approach if the problem is basically psychological reversal or neurological disorganization.

Energy work with the deeper structures of the personality

Many emotional aspects of traumatic experience and psychodynamic conflict can be processed relatively easily. These are identified, an energy technique is applied, and they are rapidly resolved. This is the case for most emotional content that might be addressed using an energy method. However, there are some aspects that will not resolve until a deeper cognitive-emotional structure is addressed.

For example, an energy method was used with a woman who had suffered extensive abuse during both childhood and adult life. As she addressed an abusive adult relationship, she rapidly processed a number of emotional aspects. However, the feeling of being "worthless" did not alter in its intensity. Muscle testing revealed that she felt it not safe to modify this view of herself. In further exploration, she explained that this self-image formed a core organizing construct whereby she made sense of self in the world. All her experiences of abuse had led to her conclusion that she was worthless. She remarked, vividly, "If I stopped thinking of myself as worthless, then it would be like meeting a stranger in my own body, who had the same face as me but was not me." This belief had to be addressed before it was possible for her to modify her view of herself as worthless.

In another example, an intelligent and talented woman presented with chronic incapacitating anxiety. Consciously she wished to be free of this so that she could get on with fulfilling her undoubted potential. However, muscle testing revealed that she believed it was not safe for her to be free of her anxiety. Later in the session, after many areas of experience and belief relating to her anxiety had been processed, the possibility of feeling secure was addressed. At that point her state of calm was disrupted by what she reported as the onset of panic. It was then apparent that a sense of safety or security was for her, paradoxically, a trigger for anxiety. The underlying belief was then identified as "If I let my guard down, I will be in great danger". A further related belief was "If I let myself function independently I will be abandoned". As these beliefs and associated anxieties were processed she was able to feel more deeply and fully calm.

The experienced clinician becomes able to identify during general free-associative enquiry core beliefs, fantasies, and self-defining anxieties, as well as the associated protective and defensive strategies.[3] These are the areas to target for processing in order to bring about deep and pervasive changes within the personality.

Example of an elective admission for therapy using EMDR and EFT

Janet was a twenty-five-year-old woman with recurrent suicidal preoccupations, and a history of self-harm associated with a very negative self-image ("a worthless piece of shit") and low self-esteem.

She reported a childhood characterized by extensive sexual and other abuse from her uncle and aunt, with whom she had lived after her being abandoned at birth by her drug-addicted mother. She had never known her father. EMDR, or indeed any form of psychological therapy, on an outpatient basis, was not feasible since she would become overwhelmed with uncontrollable impulses to cut herself or take an overdose in the wake of any enquiry into her internal world. However, Janet was motivated to engage in therapy using EMDR combined with EFT, and this prospect provided some motivation for her to establish a period of stability in preparation for a planned three-week admission to a general psychiatric ward. The ward staff and the rest of the care team understood that the purpose of the admission was to provide a safe and containing setting in which EMDR and EFT would be feasible. It was agreed that Janet could seek the support of nursing staff if she felt this necessary after each session. The therapy took place each day. Much of the work used the EFT acupressure format rather than EMDR because of its lesser tendency to evoke flooding with unmanageable affect, which was a major hazard in working with Janet.

The following summary does not detail each sequence of EMDR or EFT tapping, but these were used continually, with the result that emotional information emerged rapidly. As Janet reported various emotions she was asked where and how these were experienced in her body, and then these were processed with EMDR or EFT. At certain points, long, slow eye movements with the light bar were calming. EMDR was also more useful when enquiring about the thoughts behind a particular view or self-image held by Janet. For insight, EMDR is somewhat more helpful than EFT, but the latter can enable easier processing of affect.

The elective admission formed a component of ongoing psychotherapy and psychiatric care. None of Janet's narratives of childhood experiences took the form of "recovered memories" and she did not describe any period of amnesia for the abusive experiences she reported.

Day one

We began with a focus on Janet's negative self-image and self-esteem. She expressed the thought that she was "a worthless piece of shit". This derived from her view that her uncle had not loved her and had abused her. However, as the processing continued she shifted to thoughts about having been abandoned by her mother. She was surprised by these thoughts and feelings, saying that she did not usually think much about her mother.

Day two

Janet said she had continued to think about her mother. She had not met her until the age of thirteen, and this had been a disappointing encounter for Janet since her mother had shown little curiosity about her. The effect had been to confirm Janet's belief that her mother had never cared about her and that she was therefore worthless and unlovable. Each birthday her despair had deepened as her hope that her mother would send her a card expressing some love and care was repeatedly dashed. She said she would have liked to ask her mother certain questions: what was it I had done that was so wrong?; was I that terrible? Janet proceeded with EFT tapping, tuned to the thought that her mother was not interested in her. She reported feelings of sadness, which then shifted to anger and hatred towards her mother, followed by guilt at having such feelings. Janet then described "churned up" feelings in her stomach. She said she was struggling to control her feelings. In particular, she was endeavouring not to cry. She reported feelings of anger, associated with struggles against the impulse to cry. She wanted to hurt herself "to take control of how I am feeling", and emphasized that she would rather hurt herself than cry. I asked Janet what was so awful about crying; she said she had always been taught that it was wrong to cry and she would be punished for doing so: "the more you cry, the more you get hurt". She also said she was afraid of how much she might cry once she started. Her impulse to harm herself was very high.

Day three

Janet reported that she had felt unsettled after the previous session, but had slept better. She had found some relief by vomiting. We explored further her feeling that it is wrong to cry. She described how her aunt would sadistically make her cry and then punish her more for crying. After discussion, and some rounds of tapping, Janet said she felt nearer to believing that it was OK to cry. However, she described still feeling that she must have done something wrong in order for her aunt and uncle to want to hurt her. This then led to her speaking of feelings of "respect" for her aunt "because she brought me up—she took me in when no-one else wanted me", and expressed the view that no one can love her. She spoke of feeling "dirty and horrible", and this feeling did not diminish with further attempts at processing.

Day four

Janet said she had been thinking more about her aunt and how she would punish her for crying. This led her to tell me more about her aunt's bizarre behaviour—how Janet would be punished for the slightest untidiness or neglect of a task, and how her aunt would wake her up in the middle of the night in order to beat her for some alleged misdemeanour. It began to appear that the aunt had regarded Janet as the scapegoat for anything that was wrong. I put to Janet that her aunt had developed what amounted to a delusional fantasy that she was the cause of all dissatisfaction in the family, and that Janet had come to share this delusion. Janet found this idea intriguing and challenging. We looked a various alternatives to Janet's assumption that the reason her aunt had punished her was because she was a terrible and worthless child.

Day five

We continued exploring Janet's relationship with her aunt and identified a circular piece of reasoning: although she believed that her aunt was a nasty person, she felt respect for her aunt because she did at least take Janet into her home and bring her up; the aunt deserved respect for taking her in when she is such "a worthless piece of shit"; the reason she must be "a worthless piece of shit" was that this could be the only explanation of why her aunt punished her so repeatedly. As Janet continued processing these thoughts, she articulated the feeling that she was "dirty and horrible". Her reason for this feeling about herself was to do with sexual activities with her uncle, and particularly the pleasure she may have found in these at times—the enjoyment of the attention and affection, as well as sensual pleasure. It became apparent that this was a very difficult area for her, associated with intense feelings of shame, guilt, and self-hatred. We did not make much progress in processing these. However, we were able to understand more about her childhood dilemma: she may have feared that her aunt knew about the sexual activities with her uncle and this may have contributed to her hostility and sadism, but if she tried to avoid her aunt's disapproval by rejecting the sexual activities with her uncle, then she would invoke her uncle's disapproval.

Day six

She reported that she had cut herself over the weekend. This had related to increasing tension and anger building inside her in relation to her uncle. She had begun to feel very angry towards him because of his abuse of her, but this anger had given rise to feelings of guilt, resulting in her turning her anger on herself and cutting herself. She spoke of feeling she had let her uncle down by talking of his abuse of her when she was "not supposed to". She described how her uncle had made her promise not to tell anyone, that he would hurt her more if she did, and that if she were to tell she would probably lose him, and this would be disastrous for her because he was the only person who would ever love her. We targeted a specific memory of her uncle making her promise not to tell. This was an occasion when she had become extremely distressed after her uncle's penetration of her had made her bleed. She then disclosed that in addition to raping her, her uncle had thrust a broom handle into her and it was this that had made her bleed. She remained extremely agitated with this memory and it was very difficult to process. She reported strong impulses to harm herself. These were associated with fears of not being in control of her emotions. She spoke of how vomiting can have the same function as self-harm, but with less injury to herself. With continued processing it was possible to reduce the intensity of aspects of her distress experienced within her body.

Day seven

What then emerged was that the urge to harm herself was to a large extent driven by her experience of a hallucinatory voice of a kind often associated with histories of extensive childhood abuse. Although she believed that the voice must in some way be an expression of her own thoughts, the phenomenology was that she experienced it as a distinct and separate voice that addressed her in the second person ("you)". She explained that the voice is always present in her experience, although its intensity and loudness varied. The voice had first appeared when she was aged twelve, telling her that she was worthless and must harm herself. Its agenda appeared to be suicide. With further processing using eye movements, we clarified that the content of the voice was essentially the same as remarks made repeatedly by her aunt—that she was worthless, horrible, and unlovable. She referred to a specific memory of an argument with her aunt about whether or not her uncle loved her. She had told her aunt that her uncle did love her, but her aunt had retorted that he did not love her but simply put up with her. Janet described how the more her aunt repeated this the more she came to believe it. As she talked of this experience she reported a pain in the area of her heart, which with further processing became calm. Janet also revealed more about the origins of her desires to hurt herself "so that I could not be hurt so much when I was punished by my aunt". By hurting herself more she felt she was taking control of the experience of being hurt. Inconsistencies were apparent in the messages of her internal voice. For example, the voice agreed with her uncle (that he loved her and expressed this sexually towards her), with her aunt (that she was not lovable and that her uncle did not love her), while also claiming that she was worthless, as demonstrated by the way she was treated by her uncle and aunt. As I pointed out these inconsistencies she reported that the voice was saying that I was trying to confuse her. Since it is usually therapeutically unproductive to attempt to process the experience of an internal voice directly, the main focus was upon continuing to process aspects of the traumatic experience that was fuelling the voice, particularly the wounds inflicted by her uncle's abuse and her aunt's cruel words.

Day eight

By the following day, Janet reported some reduction in the intensity of feelings about the memory of her uncle assaulting her with the broom handle. As processing continued she described a shift from feelings predominantly of anxiety to feelings of anger. Initially this took the form of anger towards herself for having failed to prevent her uncle abusing her, but gradually this moved in the direction of anger towards her uncle.

Day nine

Janet described experiencing "mixed-up feelings", which we clarified as anger, guilt, sadness, and anxiety. Each of these feelings was processed in turn, using EFT. We then identified a paradoxical reaction to relaxation: becoming more relaxed evoked her anxiety. She acknowledged that she did not like to relax or experience a loss of the familiar patterns of tension and anxiety. As we explored this it was apparent that her fears were twofold: of letting down her guard against a hostile world, and of disintegration anxiety if the rigid structures of her mind began to change. This use of the musculature and physiological arousal, as a kind of bodily armour, seems not uncommon amongst people who have experienced extensive interpersonal trauma in childhood. It does mean a powerful resistance to therapeutic change, a formidable form of "psychological reversal", as the energy psychologists term it. Later in the day Janet still felt very agitated, and articulated feelings of anger and frustration. She was not sure of the target of her anger. Long, slow eye movements using the light bar were used to explore these feelings. Janet thought she was angry at people who had let her down—her uncle, her aunt, and herself. She was angry with herself for not being strong enough to cope with her experiences. As the processing continued, she reported feeling physically calmer but described angry thoughts about the way she had been treated.

Day ten

Janet said she had been crying more. She said she realized it had been necessary to cry but had felt very anxious about doing so. However, she alluded to disappointment that her negative self-image was still present. I talked to her about the inevitability that she would have organized her self around the faulty information given to her by her abusive care-givers, drawing an analogy with how one might have a perfectly good computer (i.e. her brain) that has been programmed with faulty software that prevents it functioning as it should, the problem being not that the computer is rubbish but that it requires improved software. Pursuing this analogy further, I explained that it may not be possible to modify the "faulty software" but what can be done is to introduce new information. The point of this analogy was that negative self-images, arising from repeated abusive experiences in childhood, may never be directly modified, but that what may be possible is for new, more appropriate self-images to be introduced as an alternative. I pointed out that if she looks to see whether her self-image as "a worthless piece of shit" had changed she might conclude there was no progress because this self-image will not change, but instead she could look to see what was emerging in her mind that was new. All this, which in EMDR terms would be viewed as a "cognitive interweave", introducing new ideas and information, seemed to make much sense to her.

Day eleven

Janet reported continuing anger towards her uncle. She said she had punched the wall and had hurt her hand, but she felt this was a positive development in that her anger was expressed outwards—i.e. the aggression was towards the wall, even though she had inadvertently hurt her hand. She also reported having had a "proper cry", and said she had never sobbed like that before. We processed her feelings of anger, located in her chest (difficulty breathing), in her stomach (wanting to vomit), then in her hands (wanting to punch), and we looked at how she had originally "swallowed" her anger because it would have seemed too dangerous to be angry with her uncle.

Day twelve

Janet reported that she had cut herself over the weekend. In addition to feelings of anger about childhood abuse, she had been very distressed by a theft of her purse. Her perception of the failure of the authorities to protect her from this crime resonated with childhood feelings of being unprotected from her uncle's crimes against her. She talked of nightmares and memories, and referred to her fifth birthday party when some of her uncle's friends had joined him in abusing her. She spoke of having cried a lot and how this had helped her to sleep. Janet's rage was considerable; she said she had "never felt this angry with anyone before". She revealed powerful impulses to cut her body. This level of anger did not diminish with further attempts at processing, using various forms of EMDR and tapping. However, later in the day, when we met again and engaged in further processing, she reported a shift from anger to sadness. It then became apparent that the mounting sadness and urge to cry was creating great tension within her because of strong inhibitions against crying, especially in front of others. This tension functioned to maintain her anger, which she tended to use defensively against the underlying sadness.

Day thirteen

The next day Janet reported that she had punched the wall and cried the previous night. She said she was now feeling less angry but more sad, feeling "hurt and let down" by her uncle. Later in the day she described feelings of hopelessness and helplessness, with thoughts of killing herself or cutting, and said her internal voice had been "banging on again". With further long, slow eye movements and tapping, she described a feeling of being "lost and consumed", with moments of panic, which gradually lessened. She then spoke of a "lost swimming feeling, like there is nothing solid", which alarmed her. This "swimming" feeling was probably a positive indication of changes in the emotional energy within her body.

Day fourteen

Janet reported that she continued to feel sad as well as angry. She spoke of further dreams of being abused by her uncle and other men. However, she mentioned a specific dream from the previous night, which had been a recurrent dream of childhood. In this dream, her uncle is locked in a special building, like a prison, because he is a werewolf and he takes her away with him in a big white van. Janet's thoughts about a werewolf were that it was someone who could appear quite normal at times, but then turn into something terrifying, a theme which reflected very vividly her experience of her uncle. Janet said that sometimes she and her uncle would get along very well, especially when in public. With further processing, mainly using eye movements, she focused on feelings of deep sadness and feelings of hopelessness. However, we also identified again her fear of becoming relaxed and letting down her guard. I linked this with what she had told me of how her uncle could appear friendly and normal at times but then become terrifying later, and how she may have learned that it was not safe to feel lulled into a sense of safety and security because her uncle, in his friendly state, might later turn into the werewolf. She spoke of a feeling of anxiety, as if she was going to be punished for having done something wrong. This led us to look at her continuing fear of her uncle's retaliation and punishment for having talked about the abuse, and she seemed to perceive this as a real danger, just as, in her dream, no one could protect her from her uncle, who escaped from his prison and took her away.

Day fifteen

Janet spoke of anxiety regarding her changing perceptions of herself and of her uncle. She felt very angry with her uncle, but felt she should love him because he was her uncle and had brought her up. I explored the distorting role of positive affective experiences with her uncle, including some of the sexual experiences, which had been associated with her perception that he loved her. It was possible to see that she had needed to cling to a perception of herself as "bad" in order to preserve a sense of having been loved by her uncle. If she were to view her uncle as not loving her, then it would be as if no love existed in her world. As an alternative to this bleak perception, I drew her attention to her own capacity to love, that she knew that she had loved her uncle even if she now doubted that he had loved her. She was able to agree that her own capacity to love, even when not being loved in return, was enormous. We were also able to explore her hopes and fears regarding future relationships. She articulated the kind of relationship with a man that she would like, but expressed her fears that she might continue to be attracted to men who would abuse her. We looked at how a previous abusive relationship had followed a pattern that turned out to be closely modelled on her experiences with her uncle.

Day sixteen

Janet mentioned that she had dreamt again about her uncle turning into a werewolf, but this time, as she was referring to the building from where her uncle had escaped, she described it as like a hospital (rather than a prison). This seemed to reflect her changing view of her uncle, now perceiving him as possibly ill rather than essentially bad. We reviewed the work done over the three weeks in hospital. Janet felt that we had covered a great deal of ground and that she had managed to talk about many issues that she had not expected to be able to. She felt that both EMDR and EFT had been helpful, but mentioned that she noticed more changes in physical sensations when using EFT.

Components and structure of Janet's disturbance as revealed in the three weeks of EMDR/EFT processing

Janet's self-image was organized around having been abandoned by her mother. This formed a core of belief that she was unlovable. Subsequent mistreatment by her uncle and aunt confirmed this view of herself. Her aunt appears to have regarded her with unrelenting hostility, with an almost delusional belief that Janet was responsible for all that was wrong in the household—a belief that Janet came to share. Janet treasured episodes of seemingly positive emotional experience with her uncle, including some sexual

activities, as evidence that he did love her, despite their incongru-
ence with other overtly abusive behaviour towards her. She could
not relinquish her view of herself as "a worthless piece of shit"
without abandoning any pretence that her uncle loved her. In addition, she was faced with the dilemma that in pleasing her uncle
sexually she was incurring her aunt's disapproval, while if she
rejected her uncle's sexual advances she feared she would lose his
love and be subject to his wrath. Her uncle apparently instilled in
her mind a deep programme forbidding her to talk about his sexual
abuse of her. As a result, talking about her childhood experiences
evoked intense anxiety. Another conflict concerned crying. While
crying is a natural and relieving human response to distress, Janet
had apparently been consistently punished for crying, and so had
developed strong inhibitions against this. One of her usual strategies when she felt an impulse to cry was to cut herself. In this way
she felt she was re-establishing some control over her own emotions, as well as discharging her rage against her own body. Over
the three weeks, Janet became more able to cry. She also was able to
express intense rage against her uncle. Behind this, deep feelings of
sadness emerged. She feared that without the belief that her uncle
loved her (supported by her denigrated view of herself as deserving abuse), all hope of love would be lost from her world. By the
end of the three weeks, she was at least able to articulate her hope
of a loving relationship in the future.

Janet's negative self-image and her recurrent impulses to harm
herself were maintained partly by her hallucinatory internal voice.
This phenomenology is typical of people who have experienced
extensive abuse in childhood. It represented the internalization of
critical and abusive messages from her uncle and aunt, as well as
expressing her own rage channelled against herself. Thus, in terms
of classical Freudian metapsychology, it can be regarded as a primitive and dissociated superego, albeit a perverse one. However, such
trauma-derived internal hallucinatory voices seem to acquire a
malignant autonomy, perhaps analogous to tumours in the physical
body.

Janet's anxieties were concerned particularly with the potential
emergence of unmanageable affect (rage), with fears of retaliation
by her uncle. However, it can be seen that she suffered all four levels
of anxiety outlined by Freud (1926d): fear of loss of the care-giver

(threats of abandonment, following the original abandonment by her mother, and threats of losing her uncle if she told about the abuse); fear of loss of the care-giver's love (the continual message that she was unlovable and therefore any love she did receive was extremely tenuous); fear of the superego (the persecutory internal voice); fear of "castration" or other physical mutilation (as continually threatened and enacted by both her uncle and her aunt).

The bedrock resistance to the therapeutic process, which we encountered in various forms, was disintegration anxiety—the terror of loss of structure if the familiar organization of experience and meaning is surrendered. There were two main components to this, cognitive and physiological. Janet became very anxious at the prospect of her fundamental views of self and other changing. She had organized her self around the information imparted to her by abusive care-givers. Taking in more realistic information threatened the fundamental structure of her psyche. The physiological component was apparent in her fear of becoming relaxed. She used her muscular tension and physiological arousal as a means of holding herself together and maintaining a guard against a potentially hostile world. The relaxation that is a natural result of processing, using EMDR and EFT, gave rise to a paradoxical increase of anxiety.[4] This resistance formed a core aspect of what is termed in energy psychology "psychological reversal".

A note on transference

As is usual in work based on EMDR and EFT, transference was not prominent since the traumatic experiences, psychodynamic conflicts, and Janet's internal representational world, were located in their original developmental context and were explored intrapsychically rather than externalized and re-enacted in the present. Some transference issues could be discerned in Janet's relationship to the wider system of hospital and mental health team care: for example, in expectations of abandonment, neglect, and hatred, as well as anger at failures to protect her. There was the barest hint of an impression that Janet may have experienced the therapy sessions as somewhat like the secret sexual activities with her uncle, and may have viewed the nursing staff as like her aunt, but such dynamics were subtle. The careful building of an alliance with the consultant psychiatrist, so that she could participate as an equal partner in planning her care and treatment, was crucial.

A further elective admission

Some months later, Janet felt that a further planned admission for psychological therapy would be helpful and after careful discussion this was arranged. The work focused on her changing perceptions of her uncle, and her rage at his abuse of her. Using EmoTrance (Hartmann, 2003b) she became more confident of her ability to handle strong emotions without resorting to cutting herself. It was also possible for her to review her relationship with her destructive hallucinatory voice and increasingly to resist its entreaties for her to kill herself.

When to use EMDR and when to use an energy method

There is much overlap in the areas of application of EMDR and energy methods. Clients vary in terms of which method they are most comfortable with, for both intellectual and experiential reasons. For example, those who require a firm research evidence base will be likely to prefer EMDR. Similarly, for some, EMDR has a greater face validity and plausibility than energy methods. Some find eye movements unpleasant, while others are uncomfortable with tapping.

There are some clinical bases for choosing one method over the other. Energy methods are less likely than EMDR to induce overwhelming abreactions. Therefore an energy method may be more appropriate for vulnerable clients who have been severely and repeatedly traumatized. Similarly, an energy method may be less likely to destabilize a client with a dissociative disorder. On the other hand, EMDR seems better able to reveal and process the overall narrative of a trauma, probably because of its inherent free-associative and flowing nature. Similarly, EMDR is often more useful than an energy method with clients who present a poverty of emotional material, sometimes due not to resistance but simply to an incapacity to free associate. A set of eye movements may result in the emergence of important emotional and psychodynamic content, in place of what otherwise might have been a desultory and unproductive exchange between client and therapist. One way of combining the two methods is to use EMDR to reveal the spectrum of emotions and cognitions associated with a situation or issue, and then to use an energy method to process these various specific emotions and cognitions.

EMDR and energy methods do seem to combine and interact synergistically. Abbreviated versions of each may be incorporated into a hybrid method. Thus, tapping seems to enhance the processing using EMDR, while more extensive eye movements can often be effectively included in the "9 gamut" procedure of EFT and TFT.

Notes

1. Leeds and Shapiro (2000) outline fourteen steps in this process of resource development and installation. These are, in summary, as follows.

    1. The client focuses on the problematic situation or maladaptive belief.
    2. The client identifies what personal quality is needed in order to cope better with this situation. The therapist helps the client identify a memory of having experienced such a quality. If the client does not have such a memory, he or she is asked to think of another person who displays this quality. Alternatively, a symbolic representation of the desired quality may be created.
    3. The client is asked to focus on this personal quality/resource, allowing a relevant image or memory to arise.
    4. The client is asked to describe the image or memory, including sensory details.
    5. The client is asked to notice positive emotions or sensations associated with this image or quality, noting where these are experienced in the body.
    6. The experience of the resource is enhanced by the therapist's repeating the client's description, including its sensory and affective details.

7. The client is asked to produce a cue word or phrase that is associated with the desired resource.

8. The client is asked to imagine physically connecting with the resource, perhaps by stepping into the body image of a person, or an animal, with this quality, or by feeling it dissolve into his or her body.

9. As the client focuses on this image and associated feelings, bilateral stimulation is added (using brief sets, e.g. 6–14 movements).

10. If the bilateral stimulation enhances the client's experience of the resource, more sets are used. This is discontinued if the client associates to negative material. A different resource may then be considered.

11. This process is repeated for each quality the client wishes to strengthen.

12. The client may be asked to practise using the resource in imagination between sessions.

13. The installation of the resource is checked in subsequent sessions. When the client is ready to begin processing trauma, the installed resources may be accessed and reinforced.

14. During the subsequent processing of trauma, the installed resources may be used as cognitive interweaves.

2. I have noticed this effect with a number of clients. In addition, I once had a subtle but startlingly persuasive personal experience. Many years ago I attended an early morning psychoanalytic session with a mild hangover. I was not aware of any impairment in my mental functioning until I lay on the couch and discovered with surprise that I was completely unable to think free-associatively in my usual way.

3. The deepest and most comprehensive approach to psychological energy healing, which is also grounded in psychoanalytic understanding, is probably that of Clinton (2002). She outlines sixty-five matrices of core beliefs, relating, for example, to self-esteem, physical attractiveness, expectations of abandonment or abuse, expectations of admiration, feelings of alienation, the value and health of the body, compassion for self and others, need for control, safety, despair and helplessness, devastation, beliefs about emotions in general, and many others.

4. This is essentially the phenomenon described by Wilhelm Reich (1949), in his account of the use of the musculature to contain anger and other biological energies, resulting in the fantasy of the body as a taut bladder in danger of exploding. Reich described the bodily tensions that accompany "character defences".

CHAPTER TEN

A comprehensive model of the psychosomatic matrix: towards quantum energy therapy

I n the twenty-first century we now know quite a lot about the psyche-soma and the impact upon it of emotional trauma. As well as the psychodynamic processes identified originally by Freud (from his 1895 "Project" onwards), we also (since the mid-1980s) understand much about the neurobiology and physiology of trauma: cognitive therapists in the last decade or so have identified the core cognitions that stem from childhood interpersonal trauma; and, in the last few years, the field of energy psychology has shown how patterns of trauma are encoded within the meridian energy fields of the psychosomatic organization. All these areas of enquiry have something to contribute to the understanding and treatment of psychological trauma. Moreover, for many clinicians, the trauma paradigm, with its associated neurobiological and physiological ramifications, has become the predominant framework for making sense of psychopathology and psychological distress. It is time to attempt some kind of integration of these various perspectives and conceptual levels. The following is offered as the beginning of such a model, although I fear it may present more questions than answers.

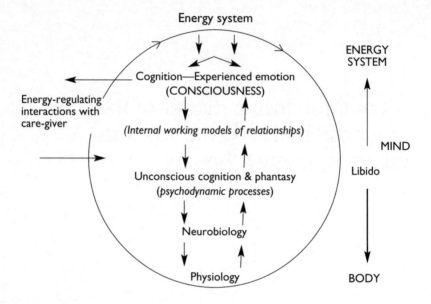

Figure 1. The psychosomatic energy matrix

Levels of the psychosomatic system and levels of intervention

The mind, body, and energy system are different interacting components of one psychosomatic system (Damasio, 1994). To some extent these are organized hierarchically. Certainly the brain functions in this way, with the higher cortex exercising an inhibiting and modulating influence over lower impulses, reactions and emotions, and Freud, the neurologist, also constructed his psychoanalytic model of the mind on this principle. However, these different components of the psychosomatic system probably interact and interface also in ways other than hierarchically, so the following is offered only as a partial and tentative model.

The highest level in the hierarchy is that of the energy system, where significant experiences are encoded, probably holographically as interference patterns (Talbot, 1996; Walther, 1988). The energy system follows quantum rather than Newtonian principles (Goswami, 1997, 2001). This level may have some similarity with the morphic fields postulated by the biologist Rupert Sheldrake (1985, 1988, 1999), and may include the meridian system, the *chakras*, (as well as various other layers and organizations frequently described in metaphysical texts (e.g. Stone, 1999). It acts, in effect, as a semi-permanent blueprint for the body's physiology, for experienced emotion, recurrent cognition, and resulting behaviour. Gallo (1999) states this hypothesis very clearly:

> . . . while psychological disturbance manifests behaviourally, systemically, cognitively, neurologically, and chemically, at the most fundamental level there exists a structured or codified energy component that provides the instructions that catalyze the entire process. [Gallo, 1999, p. 15]

Like the lowest levels of the system, the energy body is not normally available to consciousness (but may be so in the case of certain sensitive people). Consciousness is thus not the apex of the system but a midway feature (at the level of conscious cognition and experienced emotion).

The energy system is influenced by the lower levels, but its information patterning is *relatively* immune to change from below, particularly from the cognitive level, although the energy pattern does seem to change when the pathogenic traumas are *fully* processed through all their sensory, cognitive, neurobiological, and physiological aspects (as occurs with EMDR). Thus, altering a person's thoughts, or introducing greater intellectual understanding, may leave the energy pattern intact, resulting in a tendency for the problematic psychosomatic and behavioural pattern to recur. Such an intervention would be a form of "top-down" processing, essentially functioning to inhibit but not resolve the persisting lower psychosomatic residues of traumatic experience (van der Kolk, 2002), but, in addition, would also leave the upper energy pattern unmodified. This may go some way to explain the tendency for cognitive therapy to show impressive but not necessarily lasting effects (Westen & Morrison, 2001). Similarly, this postulate suggests that those forms of psychoanalytic work that identify, but do not process, the fundamental pathogenic experiences may be of limited effect, and also that exclusively "here-and-now" interpretation of "transference", without an appropriate engagement with the original traumas, will lead to change only at a relatively superficial (grafted on) level.

Underneath the energy system are the conscious levels of cognition and emotion, and then the unconscious levels of these (including unconscious phantasy). Some cognitive–emotional contents are relatively transient (and can be processed easily, using EMDR or an energy method), while others are deeper, core structures. The latter would include the "internal working models" of self in relation to other. For extensive personality change, these core structures must be processed (Clinton, 2002). Beneath the levels of cognition and emotion, lies the neurobiology that underpins perception—thought and feeling—and below that is the wider physiology of the body.

The lower levels of the system are interactive, mutually influencing each other through feedback. Cognition—a person's perception of a situation and the meaning he or she attributes to it—will affect experienced emotions and the physiological substrate of emotions; these in turn will affect cognition. Such a spiralling feedback process forms the cognitive therapy understanding of many states of psychopathology, particularly to do with anxiety and panic. However, therapeutic interventions at only one of these levels below the energy patterns may be relatively ineffective, whether it be cognitive therapy, pharmacological modification of physiology, or desensitization of experienced anxiety (through exposure therapy). On the other hand, EMDR may be particularly effective because it does address the various sub-energy levels simultaneously (Lazarus & Lazarus, 2002); thus, it evokes the traumatic experience in full sensory detail, focuses attention upon bodily sensations, and evokes trauma-related thoughts through free association. Moreover, EMDR does seem, at least in some cases, to bring about a more or less complete resolution of the patterns of trauma. It may be that, in tracking back through the layers of thematically associated trauma, and processing these systematically and comprehensively, the information patterning in the energy body is modified. The eye movements and other bilateral activities of EMDR are similar to the brain balancing methods employed within kinesiology and energy psychology (Hannaford, 1995; Krebs, 1998). Thus, it seems possible that EMDR may directly influence the energy system, bringing about a correction in disturbed meridian paths. Indeed, EMDR does seem to clear the energetic, mental, and physiological residues of traumatic memories, emotions, and beliefs.

Freud's original psychoanalysis also addressed various levels of the system. His concept of libido (1923a)—the energy flowing from bodily pleasure zones and existing on the boundary of the psyche and the soma—places his theory within the genre of energy psychologies. In tracking the complex shifts of direction and transformations of the libido through the method of free association, identifying the developmental layers of conflict and trauma that have given rise to these vicissitudes, and, in engaging the intellect with emotion by means of carefully timed interpretations, Freud would link body, mind, and energy in the process of healing.

Although Freud's psychoanalytic therapy aimed to release the energy of the libido, with its bodily roots, and to enable it to flow more freely along appropriate channels, or to be transformed into more useful qualities (sublimation), much contemporary psychoanalysis seems instead to focus on the mid levels of the system in the areas of conscious and unconscious cognition, phantasy, and internal working models of relationships. These mid levels contain the realm of "transference" (as currently understood, but not as Freud intended the concept), the "here-and-now" patterns of interaction with the analyst. Rather than considering transference as a "false connection" in which a repressed content of the psyche-soma is displaced onto an external figure or onto a preconscious element (as Freud viewed it),[1] the modern tendency is to view transference simply as the playing out in the consulting room of the patient's internal working models (or phantasies or templates) of relationships.

The place of psychodynamics within the psychosomatic system

In order to clarify the place of psychodynamics within the overall psychosomatic system, it is useful to review Freud's original formulations on the workings of the psyche.

Freud's most fundamental accounts of the nature of psychodynamic processes are found in his "Project" (1895) and his paper "Formulations on two principles of mental functioning" (1911b). He described neurotic phenomena as attempts to avoid pain inherent in reality:

We have long observed that every neurosis has as its result, and probably therefore as its purpose, a forcing of the patient out of real life, an alienating of him from reality. . . . Neurotics turn away from reality because they find it unbearable—either the whole or parts of it. [Freud, 1911b, p. 218]

He considered the unconscious mental processes at work in neurosis as

the older, primary processes, the residues of a phase of development in which they were the only kind of mental process . . . [which] . . . strive towards gaining pleasure; psychical activity draws back from any event which might arouse unpleasure. (Here we have repression.) [*ibid.*, p. 219]

Thus, the neurotic primary processes follow the "pleasure principle", contrasting with the later "momentous step" (*ibid.*, p. 219) of the development of the "reality principle", which meant that "what was presented in the mind was no longer what was agreeable but what was real, even if it happened to be disagreeable" (*ibid.*).

Freud described basically two related ways in which the pleasure principle and its primary processes contributed to neurosis. One was the simple turning away from recognition of sources of pain. The other way was through hallucinatory satisfaction: ". . . whatever was thought of (wished for) was simply presented in a hallucinatory manner, just as still happens to-day with our dream-thoughts every night" (Freud, 1911b, p. 219). He hypothesized that, with the introduction of the reality principle, one area of mental activity was kept free from reality-testing and continued to function in accord with the pleasure principle: "This activity is phantasying, which begins already in children's play, and later, continued as day-dreaming, abandons dependence on real objects" (*ibid.*, p. 222). Freud postulated that repression and phantasy are closely related:

In the realm of phantasy, repression remains all-powerful; it brings about the inhibition of ideas in statu nascendi before they can be noticed by consciousness, if their cathexis is likely to occasion a release of unpleasure. [Freud, 1911b, p. 223]

Thus, the realm of psychodynamics can be considered to consist of the use of phantasy (both conscious and unconscious), combined with repression and regression, as a means of avoiding pain and sustaining pleasure, at the expense of recognition of reality. The compromise between the reality and pleasure principles would result in neurotic symptoms, expressing repressed libidinal desires in disguised form. With regard to the psychodynamics of relationships of dependence, explored by later psychoanalysts, the narcissistic, manic, projective, and splitting defences can all be viewed as based on the use of "believed in" unconscious phantasy regarding self in relation to other (actually not essentially dissimilar to the alternative "realities" induced by hypnotic processes).

The majority of psychodynamic phenomena, therefore, can be viewed as taking place at the level of unconscious cognition and phantasy. However, some defensive strategies, particularly those in the realm of dissociation, draw upon more fundamental neurobiological substrates of reactions to trauma (Allen, 2001; Mollon, 2002a). The traumatized person learns to create actively, and elaborate upon, the dissociative reactions originally experienced passively and automatically.

Impact of trauma

Psychological trauma introduces representations of experience that cannot easily be processed and assimilated into the wider web of memory. One reason for this is that the natural movement of the representations into consciousness is resisted because it evokes intense mental pain and anxiety, very much as Freud described in his "Project" (1895). A second reason may be that the neuro-hormones released during states of trauma cause an increase in signal to noise ratio so that assimilation along the more direct associative paths is strongly privileged over the less direct associative paths (Foote, Bloom, & Ashton-Jones 1983). This means that traumatic experience remains "undigested" within the psyche-soma, forever pressing towards consciousness (as if it were a wish—see discussion of Freud's "Project" in Chapter Two) where it meets resistance to processing, and provokes dissociative and other strategies of defensive avoidance. Thus results the characteristic biphasic phenomena of numbing and intrusive images found in states of PTSD. EMDR seems to help foster the assimilation of traumatic experience along less direct associative paths so that it does not remain encapsulated and "undigested" (Shapiro, 2001). A further reason for the blocked processing is that the experience may be incoherent from the beginning. The very high levels of arousal, and the large quantities of neuro-hormones released under the impact of trauma, mean that although the amygdala (fear centre) will be increasingly active, the hippocampus (concerned with the integration of the different sensory modalities before passing to Broca's area for processing into language) will shut down (Yovell, 2001). Under such conditions the person will experience terror or dread, but will be unable to make linguistic sense of their experience and will be unable to communicate it to others in words. The person suffering from severe PTSD becomes, in effect, "subcortical", and "at the mercy of their sensations, physical reactions and emotions" (van der Kolk, 2002, p. 69), and in the grip of the Freudian "primary processes" (Freud, 1895, 1911b).

Given the beneficial EMDR effect of bilateral stimulation whereby the two cerebral hemispheres are activated alternately, it seems likely that another result of trauma is to block communication across the corpus collosum. This would mean a loss of integration of linguistic and emotion-processing functions. EMDR presumably enhances interhemispheric communication. Other forms of neurological disorganization, brain confusion, or loss of brain integration, may also occur (Krebs, 1998), and could play a role in some instances of schizophrenia (Goodheart, 1970; Walther, 1988; Whatmore & Ellis, 1964). In order to correct this level of disruption, either EMDR or procedures from kinesiology or energy psychology are required. Both EMDR and EFT contain brain balancing procedures (eye movements) and methods of correcting "massive reversal", as does Callahan's Thought Field Therapy.

Childhood interpersonal trauma affects later development. It is not that an optimum personal environment is essential for healthy development, since the psyche-soma will normally make use of whatever psychological nutrients are available. The problem is that trauma-based "internal working models" of relationships will tend to prevent psychological nutrients being used, because trust and healthy dependence will be feared as resulting in betrayal and pain, and therefore will be prohibited by the internal defensive organization. This also means that psychotherapeutic treatment that focuses on the relationship between therapist and patient will be highly problematic in the case of those traumatized in childhood. The advantage of EMDR and energy methods is that the focus is upon the client's internal, or intrapsychic, system rather than upon a rela- tionship (van der Kolk, 2002). They rest essentially upon a "one body" framework (as did Freud's original approach), a point noted by Wachtel (2002). However, although a primary focus on the trans- ference relationship may be contraindicated in the case of those severely interpersonally traumatized in childhood, the provision of a therapeutic space conducive to feelings of safety and trust is essential.

One aspect of the trauma-derived internal working models is the core cognitions and metacognitions, identified by cognitive therapists (e.g. Wells, 2000). These are similar to the "negative cognitions" targeted during EMDR, and tend to involve beliefs in the inevitability of personal failure, of being unlovable, worthless, etc. For thorough therapeutic work these deep core beliefs must be addressed, using EMDR (Young, Zangwill, & Behary, 2002) or a comprehensive energy method (e.g. Clinton, 2002).

Early interpersonal development

Studies of the neurobiology of early attachment (summarized by Schore 1994, 2003a,b,c) show the intricate, rapid, and subtle inter- actions between baby and mother, and how these organize not only the internal working models of the infant, but the patterning of the infant's brain at the neurobiological level. The orbitofrontal system processes the emotional information provided by the mother's face and voice, directing this down through the limbic system and into the physiology of the body. Thus, the mother's smile, scowl, or blank face has an immediate response in the baby's neurobiology and physiology. The mother's moods, her joy or despair, or her postnatal depression, powerfully influence the mental and bodily state of her infant. It seems plausible to consider that these neuro- biological transfers also involve energy exchanges between mother and infant, and that the mother's moods and emotional responses to her infant leave lasting imprints on the child's energy informa- tion system.[2]

Kohut's (1971, 1977) psychoeconomic theory of development describes how the child forms an energy-regulating system with the mother or other care-giver. The child seeks energy from the mother, and, if this is not forthcoming, may slip into a state of energy depletion or may seek the mother's help in discharging excessive energy. In general, according to Kohut's theory, the mother's provision of empathy has an energy-regulating function for the child and the absence of empathy leads to states of energy imbalance and psychological disorganization. It is not difficult to construe much of human relationships in terms of energy transactions and energy-regulating interactions (Hartmann, 2003b).

If the energy systems of mother and baby combine at times to form one system, this seems a possible means by which (dysfunctional) emotional information may be transmitted through the generations, as postulated by Callahan (1994, reported in Gallo, 1999). A related process may occur whenever human beings are in intimate physical and emotional contact, such that each begin to experience and be troubled by the dysfunctional emotional information encoded in the other's energy system. This may not reflect an active defensive process of projective identification, but rather may simply be an outcome of the intercourse of energy systems. Related processes may also partly explain the susceptibility of psychotherapists to "infection" by their patients' emotional illnesses.

Psychological reversal, polarity reversal, and "resistance"

Most forms of psychological therapy describe ways in which a person may consciously wish to recover or bring about constructive change but unconsciously act to resist or sabotage this. There may be various levels to this. Deep beliefs that structure the psyche may be clung to because their modification threatens "disintegration anxiety" (Chapter Five). Similarly, concerns for the preservation of autonomy may result in resistance to the therapist's endeavours. Unconscious needs for suffering may play a part, as Freud (1920g) described in his account of the "negative therapeutic reaction". The body's physiology or the brain's neurobiology may have an inherent resistance to change, perhaps particularly in states of entrenched

depression or in post-viral fatigue. However, kinesiologists and
energy psychologists have identified resistances or "reversals" also
in the energy system (Callahan, 1981). Sometimes this is called
"polarity reversal" and is regarded as a literal reversal of electro-
magnetic direction. The energy therapist, Donna Eden, who, like
other clairvoyants, claims to be able to see subtle energy, has
described its vicissitudes as follows:

> Meridian energy sometimes literally reverses its direction, and that
> is exactly how it looks. When a meridian is flowing normally, the
> lines are crisp, the pathway is smooth and clear, the movement has
> vigour. When a meridian's flow is disturbed, it appears murky, the
> pathway is no longer smooth, the movement is sluggish. Some-
> times the energies appear to be forming stagnant puddles along the
> meridian pathway. Sometimes they begin to slowly flow back-
> wards. [Eden, 2001, quoted in Hitlin, 2002, p. 213]

The problem of "personality disorder"

Traumatic experience always evokes attempts to avoid the pain
associated with it, giving rise to a variety of defensive strategies. In
most cases[3] it is still quite possible to work collaboratively with the
person in a therapeutic context to overcome their "resistance" and
enable processing of the trauma to take place. However, there are
people who develop a more malignant defensive organization,
dedicated to avoiding rather than processing mental pain, and it
may be that this is often what is implied by the currently much-
used term "personality disorder". Such people, if they seek therapy,
will attempt to misuse it (albeit unconsciously), and will endeavour
to incorporate it into their malignant defensive organization. They
will attempt to focus excessively on the relationship with the therapist as a means (unconsciously) of avoiding the pains and traumas
of the past, and in an attempt to seek gratification in the present.
Current trends in psychoanalytic technique, towards a particular
emphasis upon the here-and-now "transference" relationship and a
relative avoidance of exploring childhood experience (discussed in
Chapter Four) may tend, in effect, to collude with this defensive
endeavour. Such people may not initially benefit from EMDR or

energy psychology, since their personalities may be essentially
organized against processing the traumas of the past. For them,
extensive conventional psychoanalytic work may be necessary
before they are able to begin the more fundamental therapy of
processing trauma.

Schematic summary of the therapeutic process

It is not assumed that the following is necessarily a linear process.
Psychoanalytically inspired work tends to be relatively unstructured, free-associative, non-directive, and characterized by an openness to the emergence of new meanings and avenues of enquiry.
Nevertheless, it is possible to point to inherent patterns and components of the therapeutic work when it is guided by the principles
deriving from EMDR and energy psychology. These seem to me to
be as follows.

1. Rapport with the client/patient is established. This may require
    both empathy and energy attunement.
2. Through free-associative discourse, areas of emotional and
    psychological distress and conflict are explored.
3. An initial target problem is identified, i.e. a disturbing experi-
    ence, an anxiety, or a problematic behaviour. Basically this is
    something that the client would like to be different.
4. The various emotional aspects of this problem are clarified,
    including the associated thoughts and phantasies.
5. Thematically associated childhood experiences are identified,
    perhaps elicited through the simple question "When have you
    felt like this before?"
6. The deep cognitive schemas associated with the target problem
    are clarified, i.e. the person's persisting core beliefs about self
    in relation to others (derived particularly from early attach-
    ment experiences).
7. Psychological reversals are identified, either through simply
    listening and observing psychoanalytically, or through energy
    muscle testing. In these ways, a person's unconscious wish to
    retain symptoms or illness can be addressed.

8. Neurological disorganization, if present, is noted. The eye movements of EMDR may help to correct this, especially if "figure of eight" movements are used. Other methods from kinesiology and energy psychology may be considered.
9. The core recurrent psychodynamic conflicts are identified— Luborsky's "Core Conflictual Relationship Theme" (e.g. Luborsky & Crits-Christoph, 1997). While these may be observed in the transference, the transference is not the vehicle of the therapy.
10. EMDR or an energy method is then used to process painful experiences. This involves both desensitization and associative assimilation of the experience and its various emotional and cognitive aspects. The processing continues until the previously troubling experience no longer evokes distress.
11. During the processing, the client is asked to observe bodily sensations. Areas of tension experienced within the body are released, using EMDR or an energy method.
12. Dysfunctional core beliefs about self in relation to others are processed using EMDR or an energy method. The psyche then naturally moves in a positive direction, without cognitive intervention from the therapist.
13. Core psychodynamic conflicts are processed using EMDR or an energy method. The use of these facilitating methods enables the client to evolve creative and maturational solutions to recurrent conflicts.
14. The target problem is tested following therapeutic work. If difficulties remain, further work is done.
15. In the case of complex psychopathology, multiple targets are selected over a period of time.
16. Some problematic experiences and psychodynamic conflicts are relatively accessible to consciousness from the beginning, while others may emerge only gradually after significant therapeutic work has been done.
17. The client's free-associative discourse is scrutinized for unconscious feedback on the therapeutic process.
18. The overall approach avoids excessive structure that would impede the emergence of psychodynamic material, while containing sufficient inherent structure to allow the core psychodynamic issues to be identified and processed.

Notes

1. Kohut & Rubovitz-Seitz (1963) note the following:

    The influence of the primary process on the secondary process (the penetration of unconscious psychic contents and forces into preconscious thoughts, feelings, or wishes) was originally designated by the term "transference" by Freud (1900). It is important to note that transference, in the original meaning of the term, referred essentially to an endopsychic, not an interpersonal process. [Kohut & Rubovitz-Seitz, 1963, p. 347]

2. Neither the energy system nor the mind and its thoughts are confined within an individual body or skull. There is considerable evidence that thoughts, subtle energy, and intention travel outside the individual—and instantly so, following quantum rather than Newtonian principles (Lorimer, 2001; Powell, 2003; Radin, 1997;Tiller, 1997). This clearly has many implications in relation to the role of the therapist's attitude and intention in the healing process.

3. By "in most cases", I am thinking of patients seen within an NHS mental health service, rather than those electing to seek long-term psychotherapy on a private basis. It seems to me possible that the latter tend to be amongst those who have developed an entrenched defensive organization dedicated to avoiding rather than resolving early childhood trauma. I hypothesize that those who choose to train to become psychotherapists may also tend to be amongst this group (while not necessarily having "personality disorders" in the generally accepted sense!).

CHAPTER ELEVEN

Research conclusions

Research on EMDR

The research literature on EMDR is very extensive. An excellent overview can be found in Shapiro (2002a, Appendix A) and Maxfield (2002). The following is a summary of the main overall conclusions.

Is EMDR effective?

EMDR is the most researched treatment for post traumatic stress disorder. Its effectiveness has been clearly demonstrated. At the time of writing, at least twenty controlled studies have investigated the efficacy of EMDR in the treatment of PTSD. All found EMDR to be effective and, in most cases, more effective, or more efficient (i.e. involving fewer number of sessions), than other methods. These studies are: Boudewyns & Hyer (1996); Carlson, Chemtob, Rusnak, Hedlund, & Maraoka (1998); Chemtob, Nakashima, Hamada, & Carlson (2002); Edmond, Rubin, & Wambach (1999); Ironson, Freund, Strauss, & Williams (2002); Lee, Gavriel, Drummond,

Richards, & Greenwald (2002); Marcus, Marquis, & Sakai (1997); McFarlane (1999); Power *et al.* (2002); Rogers *et al.* (1999); Rothbaum (1997; 2001); Scheck, Schaeffer, & Gillette (1998); Shapiro (1989); Sprang (2001); Taylor *et al.* (2001); Vaughan *et al.* (1994); Wilson, Silver, Covi, & Foster (1996); Wilson, Becker, & Tinker (1997); Wilson, Becker, Tinker, & Logan (2001).

One exception to the trend favouring EMDR is Devilly & Spence (1999). This reported that a CBT protocol was superior to EMDR. However, the description of EMDR in this study deviated in various ways from standard practice, and thus cannot be considered a fair trial of EMDR.

Meta-analyses

Three meta-analyses, examining outcome across a number of studies, have evaluated EMDR.

Van Etten and Taylor (1998) found that EMDR and exposure therapies achieved similar outcomes and were superior to other psychotherapeutic treatments, but EMDR required fewer sessions to achieve the same effect. The authors comment, "The results of the present study suggest that EMDR is effective for PTSD, and that it is more efficient than other treatments" (p. 140).

Davidson and Parker (2001) evaluated thirty-four EMDR studies, finding that EMDR was effective and equivalent in outcome to exposure therapies.

Maxfield and Hyer (2002) found that the studies with more rigorous methodology (including fidelity to the treatment method) reported a larger effect of EMDR than those with less rigour. Thus, it appeared that greater methodological rigour allowed the true effect of EMDR to be revealed more clearly.

EMDR is officially recognized as an effective and appropriate treatment for PTSD

As a result of extensive clinical trials, EMDR is officially recognized as an effective treatment for PTSD (Chambless *et al.*, 1998; Chemtob, Tolin, van der Kolk, & Pitman, 2000; United Kingdom Department of Health, 2001).

There is no other psychological therapy that is more established than EMDR as a treatment for PTSD. When the first controlled study of EMDR (Shapiro, 1989) was undertaken, there had been no previously published controlled trials of treatment of PTSD.

The only other form of psychological treatment that has become recognized as an appropriate treatment for PTSD is "exposure" (Rothbaum, Meadows, Resnick, & Foy, 2000), essentially any form of behaviour therapy involving exposure to the feared situation or traumatic memory until the anxiety is extinguished.

Application to other disorders

The original application of EMDR was to PTSD, and this has been the area of most extensive research involving many controlled randomized studies. There have been many other clinical applications of EMDR, but these are less well established through research. However, the reality is that extensively researched (using randomized control studies) methods of treatment have not been established yet for most psychological disorders. Moreover, psychopathology is often more complicated than is suggested by a single diagnostic designation, and its exploration and resolution may not always be adequately accommodated by a standardized therapeutic protocol.

Despite these caveats, there are an enormous number of published studies and clinical reports illustrating the use of EMDR in relation to a wide variety of clinical problems.[1] Some examples are as follows:

Phobias and panic: De Jongh & Ten Broeke (1998); Goldstein & Feske (1994).
Complicated grief reactions: Lazrove, Kite, Triffleman, McGlashan, & Rounsaville (1998); Shapiro & Solomon (1995).
Severe burns trauma: McCann (1992).
Sexual dysfunction: Levin, 1993; Wernik (1993).
Addiction: Henry (1996); Shapiro & Forrest (1997).
Shame: Leeds (1998).
Post partum depression: Parnell (1998).
Dissociative disorders: Fine & Berkowitz (2001); Lazrove & Fine (1996); Twombly (2000).

Performance anxiety: Crabbe (1996); Maxfield & Melnyk (2000).
Body dysmorphic disorder: Brown, McGoldrick, & Buchanan (1997).
Personality disorders: Fensterheim (1996); Manfield (1998).

Are the eye movements (or other bilateral stimulation) an important component of EMDR?

Studies have shown that eye movements contribute significantly to the relaxing and emotion-processing action of EMDR (Cerone, 2000; Lohr, Tolin, & Kleinknecht, 1995, 1996; Montgomery & Ayllon, 1994). In one of these studies, Montgomery and Ayllon (1994) state, "The data indicate that with PTSD subjects the use of short duration repeated exposure and cognitive restructuring alone were insufficient for positive treatment gain" (p. 228) and that the addition of eye movements "resulted in the significant decreases in self-reports of distress previously addressed. These findings are reflected by decreases in psychophysiological arousal" (p. 228).

Studies of eye movements in isolation from the rest of the EMDR format show that these decrease the vividness of memory images and their associated affect (Andrade, Kavanagh, & Baddeley, 1997; Kavanaugh, Freese, Andrade, & May, 2001; van den Hout, Muris, Salemink, & Kindt, 2001). Barrowcliff, Gray, Freeman, and MacCulloch (2004) compared the effect of recalling memories while making eye movements with recalling memories without the eye movements; significant reductions in emotional valence and vividness, as well as physiological arousal, were found only in the eye movements condition.

Brain changes after EMDR

Levin, Lazrove, and van der Kolk (1999) report a study of brain changes following treatment of a patient with PTSD. Following treatment with three ninety-minute sessions of EMDR, neuroimaging showed increased activity in the anterior cingulated gyrus and the left frontal lobe. The authors suggest this may indicate that the patient had learned to differentiate real from imagined threat. These brain function changes were accompanied by positive changes on psychological testing. In an outline of further work along these lines, van der Kolk (2002) reports that several of their subjects showed increased frontal lobe activation following EMDR, suggesting an enhanced capacity to make sense of incoming sensory stimulation. These changes were linked with alterations in the quality of the patients' narratives of trauma, which became more coherent and manageable. Van der Kolk comments, "These sorts of changes in personal narratives suggest that EMDR is capable of helping people generate associations between previously dissociated, fragmented sensory impressions" (2002, p. 73).

Brain changes were also reported by Lansing and Amen (2003). In a study of cumulatively traumatized police officers, they found changes following EMDR in the level of activity in the following areas: cingulated gyrus; basal ganglia; deep limbic system; cerebellum. Prior to treatment, all these areas had shown overactivity. This dropped following EMDR. In addition, reduced activity was found in the prefrontal cortex after treatment. These changes accompanied a marked reduction in symptoms of PTSD.

Theories regarding the mechanism of action of bilateral stimulation

There have been many interesting neurobiological speculations regarding the possible mode of action of eye movements and other bilateral stimulation used in EMDR. Shapiro (2002a Appendix A) lists seven hypotheses, proposed by various authors. In summary, these are as follows:

1. Interference with working memory (Andrade, Kavanagh, & Baddeley, 1998; Kavanaugh, Freese, Andrade, & May, 2001.)
2. Elicitation of an orientating or investigatory response that provokes an instinctive reaction of interest, excitement, or a sense of safety (Armstrong & Vaughan, 1996; Lipke, 2000; MacCulloch & Feldman, 1996)
3. Evocation of a relaxation or inhibitory response (Shapiro, 1989; Wilson, Silver, Covi, & Foster, 1996)[2]
4. Facilitation of neurological processes linked to REM sleep (Bergmann, 2000; Stickgold, 2002)

5. Distraction, acting as extinction of classical conditioning (Dyck, 1993)
6. Reduction of the experience or emotional intensity, thereby allowing processing to take place (van den Hout, Muris, Salemink, & Kindt, 2001)
7. Inhibition of the avoidance process (Becker, Todd-Overmann, Stoothoff, & Lawson, 1998).

Misrepresentations of EMDR

Despite its robust research support, EMDR has always attracted a peculiar amount of rather intense hostility, often taking the form of scorn and mockery. Disparaging terms such as "junk science" or "pseudoscience" are frequently used in reference to EMDR. A typical example of a dismissive comment is "what is effective in EMDR is not new, and what is new is not effective" (McNally, 1999, p. 619). At times, scientific debate has been replaced by bizarre *ad hominen* attacks, explored and refuted in an important paper by Perkins and Rouanzoin (2002), which clarifies many areas of confusion and responds to a "global attempt to malign the reputations of respected scientists and clinicians who support EMDR". One aspect of the distortion of genuine scientific enquiry is that, in a number of instances, inaccurate statements have been made in journal papers (opposing EMDR) regarding the contents of previous papers (supportive of EMDR), detailed carefully by Perkins and Rouanzoin (2002).

A clear example of the trend of misrepresentation is a press release from the University of Arkansas, dated 11 January 2001.[3] It is headed: "UA Psychologist Labels Popular Trauma Therapy 'Pseudoscience'." The press release goes on to quote their psychologist as follows:

> The creators of EMDR developed the therapy based on research that showed that rapid eye movement aided in the processing of memories during sleep. They theorized, therefore, that inducing rapid eye movements while a patient remembered a traumatic event would help the subject more quickly process and come to grips with that memory. . . . This effort to appear scientific is what qualifies EMDR as pseudoscience . . .

This Arkansas psychologist, who has "dedicated his expertise to identifying and debunking pseudosciences", furthermore argues that the eye movement component of EMDR makes no difference to the outcome and that whatever is effective in the method is therefore merely due to the familiar effect of exposure to the anxiety-evoking stimulus. He concludes:

> The fact that some psychologists—who are supposedly trained in scientific methodology—are disregarding scientific evidence and continuing to offer an ineffective treatment does not bode well for the integrity of our profession or for the public's perception of psychology as a science.

In the light of the evidence summarized above, such arguments and claims are clearly incongruent with reality. Unfortunately they are repeated (Lilienfeld, Lynn, & Lohr, 2003) in a recently published book on pseudoscience! The facts are clear and public. EMDR is an effective treatment. It was *not* developed out of a theory of the role of eye movements in REM sleep. The desensitization potential of eye movements was observed by Francine Shapiro and explored for its therapeutic potential. Theorizing regarding the nature of this effect followed later. Research has demonstrated that the eye movements *do* have a definite measurable effect. The desensitization effect of EMDR cannot be due to exposure, as normally understood, since that effect is thought to depend on continuous rather than intermittent stimulation; on that principle, the brief intermittent exposure employed during EMDR would be likely to sensitize rather than desensitize (Eysenck, 1979; Lyons & Scotti, 1995; Marks, Lovell, Noshirvant, Livanou, & Thrasher, 1998). Francine Shapiro's account of EMDR (Shapiro, 2001) appears to me to be the most cautious, balanced, carefully reasoned, clinically informed, professionally responsible, scientifically grounded, and scholarly piece of work that we could hope to encounter. Really, we might wonder who are the real "pseudoscientists" among these gunslingers of the American academy.

Research in relation to energy psychology

Research in energy psychology is relatively limited at present, although more studies are in preparation.

The study by Wells and colleagues (2003)

The best paper, reporting a controlled study of EFT, is that by Wells, Polglase, Andrews, Carrington, and Baker (2003). Participants with phobias of small animals, such as spiders, rodents, or cockroaches, were randomly assigned to two groups. One group received a thirty-minute treatment with EFT. The other received training in a procedure called diaphragmatic breathing, which has been shown to produce physiological changes consistent with deep relaxation (Lehrer, Sasoki, & Saito, 1999). Thus, the control group treatment did contain active ingredients likely to induce relaxation and therefore likely to facilitate desensitization. Moreover, the deep-breathing condition was designed to parallel as closely as possible the EFT condition. While the EFT group tapped on the meridian points, repeating the reminder phrase (e.g. "this fear of spiders") at each point, the deep-breathing group were asked to repeat this phrase between each breath. Each emotional aspect of the problem was addressed with "rounds" of deep breathing, paralleling the rounds of meridian tapping with EFT. Levels of fear were assessed by taking SUDs at different stages of a Behavioural Approach Task (BAT). The BAT involved eight points at distances progressively nearer to the feared animal. A further measure was how far the participant could tolerate approaching the animal on the BAT. Follow-up measures were taken six months or more later. The results were that the EFT treatment produced significantly greater improvement than did the deep-breathing condition, as measured behaviourally and on self-report measures. The improvement was found to be largely sustained at follow-up.

The significance of this study is that it contained a control condition for comparison and it was randomized, thus meeting the highest research standards. The choice of a control condition that mimicked the procedure of EFT in all details except for (a) the use of a self-acceptance statement, and (b) tapping on the meridian points, suggests that the effective factors did have something to do with the ingredients specific to EFT. Since deep-breathing does induce relaxation, the superiority of the EFT condition must be due to more than induction of an ordinary relaxation response.

Dr Patricia Carrington reports on a series of studies planned or in progress, building upon this study, by one of the co-authors,

Dr Harvey Baker and colleagues (www.eftupdate.com/ ResearchonEFT.html):

1. a replication of the Wells et al. procedures, but using two different forms of control group—a form of non-directive counselling, and a no treatment group;
2. a controlled study in a clinical setting, comparing EFT with two control groups;
3. a comparison of EFT and a sham variant (no true acupoints being tapped) examining the effect on maths anxiety;
4. a study of the effect of EFT versus two control conditions on basketball skill;
5. a study of the effect of EFT on alcohol addiction in a small village in India;
6. a comparison of EFT using the standard tapping points with a version using tapping on other body locations; a study of the effect of EFT on fears of public speaking, using a virtual reality programme to test this.

The study by Joaquin Andrade MD and colleagues from Uruguay

Preliminary data has been reported (Andrade & Feinstein, 2001; Feinstein, 2001), of a variety of randomized double-blind pilot studies, involving more than 29,000 patients, conducted at eleven centres in South America during a fourteen-year period. In one of these, approximately 5000 patients, diagnosed as suffering from an anxiety disorder, were randomly assigned to a group that received an energy tapping method and a control group that received cognitive behaviour therapy and/or medication. At the close of therapy, 90% of the tapping group were rated as improved, while 63% of the control group were rated as improved. Seventy-six per cent of the tapping group were rated as symptom free, while 51% of the control group were rated as symptom free. At one year follow-up, the patients in the tapping treatment were substantially less prone to relapse than those in the control group.

These findings are dramatic. As the authors comment, "No reasonable clinician, regardless of school of practice, can disregard the clinical responses that tapping elicits in anxiety disorders (over 70% improvement in a large sample in 11 centers involving 36 therapists over 14 years)" (Feinstein, 2004, p. 201).

However, these pilot studies were conducted for the purpose of internal validation of procedures and protocols for the clinical team:

> These were pilot studies, viewed as possible precursors for future research, but were not themselves designed with publication in mind. Specifically, not all the variables that need to be controlled in robust research were tracked, not all criteria were defined with rigorous precision, the record-keeping was relatively informal, and source data were not always maintained. Nevertheless, the studies all used randomized samples, control groups, and double blind assessment. The findings were so striking that the research team decided to make them more widely available. [Feinstein, 2004, p. 201]

There were some interesting findings regarding the effectiveness of tapping methods for different clinical groups. The best results of tapping methods were with various kinds of anxiety disorders. Also, various other emotional problems responded well, including grief, guilt, anger, shame, jealousy, rejection, painful memories, loneliness, love pain, and procrastination. Good results were also obtained in relation to adjustment disorders, ADHD, impulse control disorders, and problems stemming from abuse or neglect. Responding slightly less well, but still better than with other methods, were OCD, generalized anxiety disorder, anxiety related to medical conditions, social phobias, and certain specific phobias. Energy interventions fared as well but no better than other methods in relation to mild to moderate reactive depression, substance abuse disorders, and eating disorders. Results that were inferior to those obtained with other methods were found in relation to major endogenous depression, personality disorders, and dissociative disorders. No improvement was found using energy methods in relation to psychotic disorders, bipolar disorders, delirium, dementia, and chronic fatigue.

Brain scan images from this study, showing results before and after energy tapping, can be found at www.innersource.net/energy_psych/epi_neuro_foundations.htm

Descriptions of a number of other pilot studies and work in progress researching energy psychology methods can be found at www.energypsych.org

Two studies on EFT by Swingle and colleagues

One study looked at the effects of EFT treatment on road traffic victims suffering from PTSD. The subjects were taught EFT tapping in two sessions. Follow-up at three months showed significant positive changes in brain-waves and in self-reported symptoms of stress. This study (Swingle, Pulos, & Swingle, 2001) was reported at a scientific meeting and has been submitted for publication.

In another study (Swingle, 2001), EFT was used as a treatment for children diagnosed with epilepsy. The children were given EFT every night by their parents each day when the parents suspected a seizure might occur. After two weeks of home EFT treatment, significant reductions in seizure frequency were reported, as well as improvement in EEG readings. This study has not yet been published.

Research on thought field therapy

A number of studies have been published relating to Callahan's thought field therapy (TFT).

Figley and Carbonell (1999) report a preliminary investigation, without a control group, into the clinical effectiveness of TFT, EMDR, and two other new treatments for PTSD. They found that all the new therapies accelerated treatment for trauma in contrast to lengthy traditional therapies. Meaningful comparisons between the treatments could not be made with certainty, for methodological reasons, but TFT was the most rapid treatment. Figley (1999) comments: "Our investigation showed that this method worked dramatically and permanently to eliminate psychologically based distress in a substantial number of people" (p. viii).

Some papers have presented data on heart rate variability (HRV) as an outcome measure of TFT (Callahan, 2001b,c; Pignotti & Steinberg, 2001), arguing that both very high and very low HRV are a sign of ill-health, and that TFT helps restore a healthy HRV. While this seems an interesting area to explore further, the combination of a novel treatment process and a novel outcome measure tends to strain the credulity of readers and reviewers; moreover, there are methodological problems in these studies, such as a failure to control for the statistical tendency of extreme measures to regress to the mean (Kline, 2001; Herbert & Gaudiano, 2001).

Some preliminary data on changes in level of self-reported distress with 714 patients with a variety of psychological disorders are described by Sakai and colleagues (Sakai *et al.*, 2001). The methodology of this study is criticized by Lohr (2001), but some of his arguments seem a little odd, based apparently on his perception of TFT and its rationale as implausible. He appears to argue that regardless of results, a study of the *effectiveness* of TFT is invalid because the *efficacy* of this treatment method has not been established: "Effectiveness is a valuable research tool, but only when there is prior efficacy research to support its validity in more restrictive controlled experiments" (*ibid.*, p. 1230). He further argues that since there have been no controlled studies of TFT and since the claims for evidence of the existence of energy meridians are "unconvincing", the report by Sakai and colleagues is "scientifically premature and beside the point" (*ibid.*, p. 1233).[4] Lohr's argument that, without prior establishment of efficacy, there can be no meaning to a study of efficacy, seems puzzling. Speaking personally, if I hear that a new treatment gives rise to a statistically significant lessening of self-reported distress in a sample of 714 patients, then I would conclude that some positive effect is taking place, even if I am puzzled by the nature and rationale for the treatment, and even if there are as yet no methodologically sound demonstrations of its efficacy in comparison to a control group. A study of effectiveness surely *implies* efficacy, even if it is not itself a sound demonstration of efficacy (because the experimental conditions have not been adequately controlled).[5] Lohr's complete dismissal of the study seems a little harsh, especially in view of the authors' own comment in the abstract: "These . . . are preliminary data that call for controlled studies to examine validity, reliability, and maintenance of effects over time" (*ibid.*, p. 1215).

Another report (Johnson, Shala, Sejdijai, Odell, & Dabishevci, 2001) described the use of TFT with people suffering war trauma in remote villages in Kosovo; 105 patients were treated and self-reported complete relief was reported by 103 of these, and follow-up data revealed that these improvements had been sustained. This report was criticized by Rosner (2001), on the grounds that (a) only superficial information about the sample was provided, (b) diagnostic information was absent, (c) the self-report measure of distress was rather crude, (d) the description of TFT was rather short. However, the reviewer does note that "doing research in a post war society is more than difficult" and that "it is only to be expected that methodological standards should be of lesser importance than in a review of laboratory research performed in safety in a rich country" (*ibid.*, pp. 1241–1242). By contrast, Hartung and Galvin (2003) comment:

> Scientists can criticise this study's lack of randomization of subjects, use of nonstandardized measures, failure to account for competing hypotheses, and the like. Practicing psychotherapists, on the other hand, . . . will more likely feel exhilarated when reading about this work. A report of 98% recovery from trauma, even if informal, is likely to encourage a clinician who is dedicated to alleviating the suffering of trauma victims. [Hartung & Galvin, 2003, p. 60]

Two studies (Callahan, 1987, 2001a; Leonoff, 1996) have reported the results of radio phone-in programmes, where callers were treated over the phone for various problems, such as phobias, anxieties, addictions, guilt, and marital problems. Callahan reported a success rate of 97% and Leonoff reported 100%. While many questions can be raised regarding the reliability and accuracy of the data, these studies may still have some merit. As Hartung and Galvin (2003) comment, the clinicians deserve some credit for having the courage to expose their method so publicly: "After all, it might have turned out the other way: ninety per cent of the callers could have announced to thousands of listeners that they did not feel any better and that TFT is a hoax" (p. 61).

Darby (2001) conducted a study of TFT with twenty people with severe needle phobias that prevented them getting appropriate medical treatment. They were treated with just one hour of TFT. Statistically significant improvements were shown at one month follow-up. (Reported in Hartung & Galvin, 2003.)

Schoninger (2001) treated with TFT forty-eight people with public speaking anxiety. Various questionnaire measures were used, as well as the SUDs, relating to actual (*in vivo*) public speaking exercises. Substantial lowering of anxiety was revealed following treatment. (Reported in Hartung & Galvin 2003.)

One study by Carbonell and colleagues conducted a randomized double-blind study, comparing TFT with a placebo treatment in which the subjects tapped points not used in true TFT. The subjects in the true TFT condition showed significantly greater improvement than the placebo group. This is not yet published in full, but a summary is available at www.tftrx.com/ref_articles/6heights.html

Research on the validity of muscle testing as a means of energy checks

Although muscle testing inherently contains subjective elements and may be open to a variety of influences, including suggestion, there are quite a number of studies providing support for its essential validity. Monti, Sinnott, Marchese, Kunkel, and Greeson (1999) used computerized dynamometer to demonstrate that, in a group of eighty-nine subjects, there were highly significant differences in muscle strength according to whether the person made a semantically congruent (i.e. true) statement as opposed to an incongruent statement. Two studies demonstrated significant interexaminer reliability for muscle testing (Caruso & Leisman, 2000; Lawson & Calderon, 1997). Several studies have shown differences in the electrical activity of muscles which test weak as opposed to those which test strong, and that this cannot be attributed simply to fatigue (e.g. Leisman, 1995; Leisman, Shambaugh, & Ferentz, 1989; Perot, Meldener, & Gouble, 1991). Schmitt and Leisman (1998) found a high degree of correlation between muscle testing for allergies and the presence of antibodies (serum immunoglobulins) for foods identified as allergenic by this procedure. Nevertheless, muscle testing should clearly only be used as a guide rather than a foolproof technique.

Research relating to meridians and subtle energy

Acupuncture, from which energy psychology methods is partly derived, has been extensively studied (Stux & Pomeranx, 1995) and is widely accepted as a useful and effective treatment for many conditions—approved, for example, by the US National Institute of Health, who list more than a hundred conditions that may be helped with acupuncture (NIH, 1997).

The specific points on the skin that are stimulated during acupressure and energy tapping show differences in electrical resistance compared to other points (Becker, 1990; Bergsmann & Woolley-Hart, 1973; Cho, 1998; Cho & Chung, 1994; Liboff, 1997; Syldona & Rein, 1999), and the meridian lines that connect the acupressure points have a different electrical resistance compared to other parts of the skin.[6] Various studies, using brain scanning techniques, have shown that changes in function in various parts of the brain are associated with stimulation of specific acupressure points (Cho, 1998; Darras, 1993; Hui, 2000; Omura, 1989, 1990). Stimulation of the acupressure points provokes release of opioid peptides (Swack, 2001). Further evidence for the existence of the meridians was demonstrated by the French researcher, Pierre de Vernejoul, who injected radioactive isotopes into the acupoints and found that the movement of the isotopes corresponded to the meridians; there was no significant flow when the isotopes were injected at other randomly chosen points (de Vernejoul, 1985), although some have suggested that de Vernejoul was actually detecting the lymphatic system rather than the meridians (Stux & Pomeranx, 1995). A Russian scientist, Vladimir Zagriadskii, found that soft laser light was conducted along pathways corresponding to the meridians; concluding that the meridians are superconductors, he constructed a sensitive electrical device to detect and optimize the activity within the meridians and this was then used successfully to sustain the health of cosmonauts to the Mir Space Station (Narvaez, Rohsmann, & Stegenda, 2002). Support for the existence of the *chakra* system is provided by Pert (1999, 2000), who reports finding high concentrations of neuropeptides at the sites of the first six of the seven main *chakras*.

Evidence that body tissues polarize and interconnect through subtle bioelectric currents is provided by radiologist Bjorn Nordenstrom (1983), while research suggesting a bodily energy system responsible for the organization and healing of the body is reported by Becker and Selden (1985). Similarly, the writings of biologist Rupert Sheldrake (1985, 1988, 1999) present much evidence for the existence of an organizing morphogenetic field, carrying a blueprint for the body, but also capable of learning and of transmitting information down the generations. This idea of an organizing bioelectric field—or "L-field"—was also explored in earlier research by Burr (1972), who concludes:

> Until modern instruments revealed the existence of the controlling L-fields, biologists were at a loss to explain how our bodies "kept in shape" through ceaseless metabolism and changes of material. Now the mystery has been solved, the electro-dynamic field of the body serves as a matrix, which preserves the "shape" or arrangement of any material poured into it, however often the material be changed. [Burr, 1972, p. 13]

The whole area of research on biological energy, particularly the photon emissions of biological systems and their regulatory role, is discussed extensively by Marco Bischof (1995)—unfortunately not yet available in English.[7]

The detection and measurement of the subtle energy fields of the body are discussed in depth by Stanford physicist, William Tiller (Tiller, 1997). These energies seem to have some similarity with conventional magnetic fields, but in other ways appear different. For example, Dr Justa Smith of Rosary Hill College in New York, found that both conventional high intensity magnetic fields and the subtle magnetic fields of healers consistently accelerated the activity of enzymes, but no significant magnetic activity could be detected around the healers' hands using a standard magnetometer (reported in Gerber, 2000, p. 326).

Notes

1. http://advancement.uark.edu/news/NEWS_ARCHIVES/jan01/ Pseudoscience.html
2. Gallo aptly observes, "Although caution is certainly indicated to advance and protect the integrity of any field, extremes of caution have been observed repeatedly when the established paradigm is "challenged" by unexplainable anomalous facts" (1999, p. 46).
3. A distinction between "effectiveness" and "efficacy" is rather subtle, possibly bordering on spurious, since dictionary definitions equate the two meanings.

4. Becker (1990) comments, "We found that these meridians had the electrical characteristics of transmission lines, while the nonmeridian skin did not. We concluded that the acupuncture system was really there, and that it most likely operated electrically" (p. 46).

5. Although Marco Bischof's book *Biophotons—The Light in our Cells* is not yet published in English, there is a summary on his website. This includes the following:

> According to the biphoton theory . . . the biophoton light is stored in the cells of the organism—more precisely, in the DNA molecules of their nuclei—and a dynamic web of light constantly released and stored by the DNA may connect cell organelles, cells, tissues, and organs within the body and serve as the organism's main communication network and as the principal regulating instance for all life processes. The process of morphogenesis, growth, differentiation and regeneration are also explained by the structuring and regulating activity of the coherent biophoton field. The holographic biophoton field of the brain and the nervous system, and maybe even that of the whole organism, may also be the basis of memory and other phenomena of consciousness, as postulated by neurophysiologist Karl Pribram and others. The consciousness-like coherence properties of the biophoton field are closely related to its base in the properties of the physical vacuum and indicate its possible role as an interface to the non-physical realms of mind, psyche and consciousness. [www.transpersonal-de/mbischof/englisch/webbookend.htm]

CHAPTER TWELVE

Two therapists' personal experiences

1. Mind the gap: an analytic psychotherapist's experience of conventional therapy and EMDR therapy

T he author of this book has asked me to provide a case history of my own experiences of analytic therapy and how this contrasts with EMDR therapy. I will provide an overview of the issues explored in analytic therapy and how interpretation impacted on these presenting problems, along with the difference in approach in EMDR therapy.

My introduction to EMDR therapy was through working with Dr Mollon within an NHS setting. I had sat in on several EMDR sessions and had been astonished at the speed with which EMDR appeared to process and ameliorate profound presenting problems such as obsessive compulsive disorder. At the time of writing I have undertaken the Level 1 and intermediate level EMDR trainings. However, I felt that if I was going to integrate EMDR into my analytic practice, I should experience this psychological therapy myself. There was also an element that having gained considerable self-awareness through conventional therapy the "acid test" would be whether EMDR worked on areas of my inner world that I felt required further processing.

Background history

I have, until recently, been in analytic therapy for the past seven years, with the majority of this time in twice and three times weekly work. The major issues explored have been an insecure maternal relationship involving compliance during early childhood, compounded by a peripheral paternal figure. At the age of five these issues reached a crisis point when I began to attend infant school. At the point of attending school, I had had little experience of being with other children or away from my home environment. In part, this was due to my older sister (eight years my senior) suffering from serious and life threatening childhood illnesses. I suspect that my mother was traumatized by this experience and wanted to keep me close to her and safe from danger. Inevitably I introjected my mother's anxiety towards her perceived dangerous external world. My own anxiety was somatized and I began for a period of around eighteen months to vomit at night following a recurring dream.

I would suggest that my issues could be viewed from the Winnicottian perspective of compliance. My mother took pride that I would respond to her raised eyebrow, whereby verbal communication was not needed. I also recall being told that as a child I could be dressed in white clothes at the start of a day and that these would remain in pristine condition until night-time.

The issue of insecure relationships and compliance have inevitably been a feature of my adult relationships.

Conventional therapy

Much of my early work in analytic therapy, related to the therapist gently interpreting using object relations theory to highlight the splitting of good and bad that was occurring in contemporary relationships. I began to understand how external relationships were influenced and skewed by my inner world. The recurring dream from childhood, for example, was explored and viewed symbolically as a way in which bad feelings were physically expelled from my body through vomiting. Anger and feelings of shame were also explored. While I gained much insight into my inner world, I also recognized that key relationships in my life had not been changed by this insight. My feelings, principally of anger, the reverse affect of compliance as suggested by Winnicott, remained as powerful as ever. None the less, I had been able to understand and experience the emotional pain as would be expected when undergoing conventional therapy.

EMDR therapy

When the EMDR processing commenced I was asked to provide a target memory. I chose an occasion from childhood at the age of eight, when my mother became very angry with me for scuffing a pair of new shoes and threatened to send me away to boarding school. Once the EMDR processing had begun with bilateral stimulation (eye movements and sound) I was struck by how the bilateral stimulation allowed a different and more powerful form of free association. It was as though my feelings were immediately liberated through pictures in my mind, rather than the more structured words in conventional therapy. My EMDR therapist was also more of a facilitator in the process than an interpreter of the stream of material. I was encouraged to experience whatever mental images or bodily sensations entered my consciousness. This is what I would describe as an *EMDR self-state*. For the sake of brevity I will condense a number of sessions where the scuffed shoe theme was followed. I initially began to experience the sense of helplessness and distress of the eight-year-old. This gradually changed, when as an adult I appeared in the imagery alongside me as a child. It was as though my adult self was comforting and protecting the child me. In many ways this struck me as being a self-state where I began to nurture the inner child. Through following body sensations such as a pain in the chest, my mental images developed to a point where the adult me became active in the imagery and brought the child me to live in my current home. I can recall an image during the session where I led the child me out of a place of quite profound misery in my childhood environment.

During a subsequent session, there was a period of time where no imagery occurred and I experienced a sharp pain in my neck covering a number of sets of eye movements. I knew intellectually through analytic theory that profound anger existed within me. While conventional therapy had explored that anger, the intensity of what I began to experience on this occasion shocked me. I then visualized the anger as the emergence of a Mr Hyde self-state similar to that in the Spencer Tracy film. I had located a part of me consumed with rage but also tortured with physical pain.

My work currently in EMDR therapy is with this anger and establishing a dialogue with this self-state and integrating it into the whole. What I have also begun to understand is that aspects of my masculinity and consequently self-esteem have been locked in with this repressed anger.

Richard H J Reeves, FiP, UKCP
Analytic Psychotherapist

2. Baya's journey to lose weight using EFT

As she walked away from the reception desk, one of the secretaries shouted, "My God, you've lost weight! What have you been eating?" "It's not about food", she replied, walking away. She stopped dead, inside somewhere, jubilation started. That's right, it's nothing to do with food . . .

Eleven years of therapies, amphetamines, gym, diets . . . nothing worked. She had bashed cushions, blamed her mother, been on training courses, thought about losing weight, danced it, sung it, cried it, prayed for it . . . nothing. She'd eaten less and less and nothing happened. A million voices in her head: "it's a question of will power"; "it's hereditary"; "you're allergic to wheat"; "your set point was destroyed for ever"; "your appetite regulator was messed up"; "childhood traumas"; "emotional abuse"; "you must be cheating"; "it's impossible".

Two years previously, she'd gone on to yet another diet, because the title of the book was amusing. This one she had stuck to, more or less—pitiful results, but still, had managed to keep some weight off. People who invited her out to dinner would ask the list of what she could eat because it would be faster than asking what she could not.

Then EFT turns up. What a lot of nonsense, she thought, clinging to her story, clinging to old rancours, old angers she did not even know were lurking in her deepest unconscious. After all, she'd "worked it out in therapy". She'd remembered the childhood bits and understood why she was like that. She had "accepted" that was her. She had been messed up and there was nothing she could do about it. On the whole, give or take, a size twenty was better than a size thirty and that was all she could aspire to. She'd dealt with it. Closed the door.

Curiosity, then, took over. There were articles about boosting the metabolism using EFT, also information about psychological reversals, and about "Choices". She knew it would not work—nothing ever had. In the secure knowledge that tapping on parts of one's body was idiotic, she asked her friend to tap on her.

It took twenty minutes to journey through eleven years of therapy. The feelings of anger, sadness, and fear were still there, still as powerful as ever. From being fed on schedule and left to cry out in despair, to being force fed at a later date, to eating secretly with her beloved dad of the forbidden fruits, via her fury with her weight obsessed mother, to the message that her destiny was to be fat, that she was lazy and just a slob, to the fact that she was never fat in the first place, and to the horrifying realization that maybe her refusal to lose weight was her unconscious desire to punish her mother . . . All these factors firmly linked together, a succession of events, decisions at cross roads. Finally, she came to the most important thing: accepting that she had been actually refusing to lose weight, that her mind and her body just would not do it. Somewhere inside of her, wires that had been crossed for forty-seven years slowly started to unravel. Energy currents started flowing again all over her body. Inside her brain, neuropathways reconnected. No tears, no hysterics, the pain went, the memories, devoid of their emotional content, became just that . . . memories, photo albums in the cupboards of her past . . .

The next day, she sat down to breakfast. The previous day's session forgotten, she ate an egg. Period. Could not eat anymore, thought "I wonder", then dismissed the thought. Then the rest of the day, ate bits, nothing much. Appetite reconnected to what she had been like as a baby, "fussy" they'd called it, but in fact "choosy", well aware of what her body and soul needed. That sense of knowing returned, mysteriously.

She waited for it to fade. Colleagues started to comment on her change of appearance. People at the gym noticed. She was still waiting for it to fade . . . it did.

By that time, however, she had had such a good time, being in charge for a change, that she returned to EFT and worked out that "it" had faded because she wanted it to, deep down, she had not been ready to let go of all of the memories, the emotions, that were so much part of her self. So she owned up to that. She never found out exactly what these other memories were—no need. What mattered was that her body breathed a sigh of relief and started choosing again.

She is still waiting for it to stop. Work in progress she calls it. Still she taps and comes to some amazing realizations. Like the day she, on a whim, decided to tap on "I choose to be sixty kilos" only to understand, a few days later, having lost her sense of knowing, that it was her mother's ideal weight for her that she was tapping on . . . toxic. She worked on that and it came back.

She forgets, gets side-tracked, and it fades and yet another bit has to be tapped on. She still gets obsessed with not eating from time to time, or with which food she should or should not eat, how much she should eat, how much and what she ate yesterday, but each time, so far, has managed to return to the beginning . . . it's not about food . . .

Baya Salmon-Hawk

REFERENCES

Allen, J. G. (2001). *Traumatic Relationships and Serious Mental Disorders*. Chichester: Wiley.

Andrade, J., & Feinstein, D. (2001). Energy psychology. Theory, indications, evidence. Available from: www.innersource.net. A report is also available at www.energypsych.org. Also published in D. Feinstein. (2004) *Energy Psychology Interactive. Rapid Interventions for Lasting Change*. Ashland, OR: Innersource.

Andrade, J., Kavanagh, D., & Baddeley, A. (1997) Eye-movements and visual imagery: a working memory approach to the treatment of post-traumatic stress disorder. *British Journal of Clinical Psychology*, 36: 209–223.

Antrobus, J. S., Antrobus, J. S., & Singer, J. L. (1964). Eye movements accompanying daydreaming, visual imagery, and thought suppression. *Journal of Abnormal and Social Psychology*, 69: 244–252.

Apostolopoulos, A., & Karavi, M. (1996). Overeating: treatment of obesity and anxiety by auricular acupuncture. An analysis of 800 cases. *Acupuncture in Medicine, 14*: Abstract. Available: http://www.medical-acupuncture.co.uk/journal/nov1996/eleven/shtml

Arlow, J. S. (2002). Transference as defense. *Journal of the American Psychoanalytic Association, 50*(4): 1139–1150.

Armstrong, M. S., & Vaughan, K. (1996). An orienting response model of eye movement desensitization. *Journal of Behavior Therapy and Experimental Psychiatry, 27*: 21–32.

Balint, M. (1968). *The Basic Fault.* London: Tavistock.

Barrowcliff, A. L., MacCulloch, M. J., & Gray, N. S. (2001). The de-arousal model of eye movement desensitisation and reprocessing (EMDR), Part III: Psychophysiological and psychological concomitants of change in the treatment of post-traumatic stress disorder (PTSD) and their relation to the EMDR protocol. Paper presented at the second annual meeting of the EMDR Europe, London.

Barrowcliff, A. L., Gray, N. S., Freeman, T. C. A., & MacCulloch, M. J. (2004). Eye movements reduce the vividness, emotional valence and electrodermal arousal associated with negative autobiographical memories. Submitted for publication. Available from: Alastair Barrocliff, School of Psychiatry and Behavioural Sciences, Dept. of Clinical Psychology, Wythenshawe Hospital, Manchester, M23 9LT.

Becker, L. A., Todd-Overmann, A., Stoothoff, W., & Lawson, T. (1998). Ironic memory, PTSD and EMDR: do eye movements hinder the avoidance process leading to greater accessibility of traumatic memories? Paper presented at the annual meeting of the EMDR International Association, July, Baltimore.

Becker, R. O. (1990). *Cross Currents.* New York: Plenum.

Becker, R. O., & Selden, G. (1985). *The Body Electric.* New York: Morrow.

Benor, D. (2002). Self-healing: meridian-based therapies and EMDR. In: W. Lammers & B. Kirchner (Eds.), *The Energy Odyssey: New Directions in Energy Psychology.* Eastbourne: DragonRising.

Bergmann, U. (2000). Further thoughts on the neurobiology of EMDR: the role of the cerebellum in accelerated information processing. *Traumatology, VI*(3): October, Article 4. http://www.fsu.edu/~trauma/v6i3a4.html

Bergsman, O., & Woolley-Hart, A. (1973). Differences in electrical skin conductivity between acupuncture points and adjacent areas. *American Journal of Acupuncture, 1*: 27–32.

Bion, W. R. (1970). *Attention and Interpretation.* London: Tavistock [reprinted as *Seven Servants,* New York: Aronson, 1977].

Bischof, M. (1995). *Biophotonon- das Licht in unseren Zellen (Biphotons— the Light in our Cells).* Frankfurt: Zweitausendeins.

Blum, H. P. (2003). Repression, transference and reconstruction. *International Journal of Psychoanalysis, 84*(3): 497–503).

Bohm, D., & Sheldrake, R. (1985). Morphogenetic fields and the implicate order. In: R. Sheldrake (Ed.), *New Science of Life* (2nd edn). London: Blond.

Bollas, C. (1989). *Forces of Destiny. Psychoanalysis and Human Idiom.* London: Free Association Books.

Bollas, C. (2000). *Hysteria.* London: Routledge.

Bordin, E. S. (1979). The generalisability of the concept of the working alliance. *Psychotherapy, Research and Practice, 16*: 252–260.

Boudewyns, P. A., & Hyer, L. A. (1996). Eye movement desensitisation and reprocessing (EMDR) as a treatment for post-traumatic stress disorder (PTSD). *Clinical Psychology and Psychotherapy, 3*: 185–195.

Breuer, J., & Freud, S. (1895d). Studies on hysteria. *Standard Edition of the Complete Psychological Works of Sigmund Freud. II.* London: Hogarth Press.

Brewin, C. R. (2001). A cognitive neuroscience account of posttraumatic stress disorder and its treatment. *Behaviour Research and Therapy, 39*: 372–393.

Brewin, C. R. (2003). *Posttraumatic Stress Disorder.* New Haven, CT: Yale University Press.

Brown, K. W., McGoldrick, T., & Buchanan, R. (1997). Body dysmorphic disorder. Seven cases treated with eye movement desensitisation and reprocessing. *Behavioral and Cognitive Psychotherapy, 25*: 203–207.

Burr, H. S. (1972). *Blueprint for Immortality. The Electric Patterns of Life.* Saffron Walden, Essex: C. W. Daniel.

Callahan, R. J. (1981). Psychological reversal. Paper presented at the proceedings of the International College of Applied Kinesiology, Winter Meeting, Acapulco, Mexico.

Callahan, R. J. (1987). Successful treatment of phobias and anxiety by telephone and radio. *Collected Papers of the International College of Applied Kinesiology.* Shawnee Mission, KS: ICAK.

Callahan, R. J. (1994). The five minute phobia cure: a reproducible revolutionary experiment in psychology based upon the language of negative emotions. Paper presented at the International Association for New Science, Fort Collins, Colorado.

Callahan, R. J. (with Trubo, R.) (2001). *Tapping the Healer Within.* Chicago: Contemporary Books.

Callahan, R. J. (2001b). The impact of thought field therapy on heart rate variability. *Journal of Clinical Psychology, 57*(10): 1153–1170.

Callahan, R. J. (2001c). Raising and lowering of heart rate variability. Some clinical findings of thought field therapy. *Journal of Clinical Psychology, 57*(10): 1175–1186.

Callahan, R. J., & Callahan, J. (1996). *Thought Field Therapy and Trauma. Treatment and Theory*. Indian Wells, CA: published by the author.

Carbonell, J. (1997). An experimental study of TFT and acrophobia. *The Thought Field*, 2: 1–6.

Carlson, J. G., Chemtob, C., Rusnak, K., Hedlund, N. L., & Maraoka, M. Y. (1998). Eye movement desensitisation and reprocessing for combat-related post traumatic stress disorder. *Journal of Traumatic Stress*, 11: 3–24.

Carrington, P. (2001). *How to Create Positive Choices in Energy Psychology: The Choices Training Manual*. Pace Educational Systems, www. eftsuport.com

Carrington, P., & Craig, G. (2000). A meridian-based intervention for the treatment of trauma. *Journal of the International Society for the Study of Subtle Energies and Energy Medicine*, August: 148–151.

Carroll, R. (2003). "At the border between chaos and order": what psychotherapy and neuroscience have in common. In: J. Corrigall & H. Wilkinson (Eds.), *Revolutionary Connections. Psychotherapy and Neuroscience*. London: Karnac.

Caruso, B., & Leisman, G. (2000). A forced/displacement analysis of muscle testing. *Perceptual and Motor Skills*, 91: 683–692.

Casement, P. (1985). *On Learning from the Patient*. London: Tavistock.

Cerone, M. R. (2000). EMDR treatment of combat-related guilt: a study of the effects of eye movements. Presented at the annual meeting of the International Society for Traumatic Stress Studies, San Antonio, Texas, November.

Chambless, D. L., Baker, M. J., Baucom, D. H., Beutler, L. E., Calhoun, K. S., & Crits-Christoph, P. (1998). Update on empirically validated therapies, II. *The Clinical Psychologist*, 51: 3–16.

Chemtob, C. M., Tolin, D. F., van der Kolk, B. A., & Pitman, R. K. (2000). Eye movement desensitisation and reprocessing. In: E. A. Foa, T. M. Keane, & M. J. Friedman (Eds.), *Effective Treatments for PTSD: Practice Guidelines from the International Society for Traumatic Stress Studies* (pp. 139–155, pp. 333–335), *Literature Review*, 139–155; Treatment guidelines, 333–335.

Chemtob, C. M., Nakashima, J., Hamada, R. S., & Carlson, J. G. (2002). Brief treatment for elementary school children with disaster-related posttraumatic stress disorders. A field study. *Journal of Clinical Psychology*, 58: 99–112.

Chiarello, C., & Richards, L. (1992). Another look at categorical priming in the cerebral hemisphere. *Neuropsychologia*, 30: 381–392.

Cho, S., & Chung, S. (1994). The basal electrical skin resistance of acupuncture points in normal subjects. *Yonsei Medical Journal*, 35: 464–474.

Cho, Z. H. (1998). New findings of the correlation between acupoints and corresponding brain cortices using functional MRI. *Proceedings of the National Academy of Sciences*, 95: 2670–2673.

Clinton, A. N. (2002). *Seemorg Matrix Work. Basic Manual (3rd edn)*. Princetown, NJ: Energy Revolution, Inc.

Connolly, M. B., Crits-Christoph, P., Shappell, S., Barber, J. P., Luborsky, L., & Shaffer, C. (1999). Relation of transference interpretations to outcome in the early sessions of brief supportive-expressive psychotherapy. *Psychotherapy Research*, 9(4): 485–495.

Cortina, M., & Marrone, M. (2003). *Attachment Theory and the Psychoanalytic Process*. London: Whurr.

Couch, A. S. (2002). Extra-transference interpretation: a defence of classical technique. *The Psychoanalytic Study of the Child*, 57: 63–92.

Courtois, C. A., & Bloom, S. L. (2000). Inpatient treatment. In: E. B. Foa, T. M. Keane, & M. J. Friedman (Eds.), *Effective Treatments for PTSD. Practice Guidelines from the International Society for Traumatic Stress Studies*. New York: Guilford.

Crabbe, B. (1996). Can eye movement therapy improve your riding? *Dressage Today*, November: 28–33.

Damasio, A. R. (1994). *Descartes' Error. Emotion, Reason and the Human Brain*. New York. Putnam.

Damasio, A. R. (1999). *The Feeling of What Happens*. New York: Harcourt Brace.

Darby, D. (2001). The efficacy of thought field therapy as a treatment modality for individuals diagnosed with blood-injection-injury phobia. Unpublished doctoral dissertation. Minneapolis, MN: Walden University.

Darras, J. C. (1993). Nuclear medicine investigation of transmission of acupuncture information. *Acupuncture in Medicine: Journal of the British Medical Acupuncture Society*, 11(1): 22–28.

Davidson, P. R., & Parker, K. C. H. (2001). Eye movement desensitisation and reprocessing (EMDR): a meta-analysis. *Journal of Consulting and Clinical Psychology*, 69: 305–316.

De Jongh, A., & Ten Broeke, E. (1998). Treatment of choking phobia by targeting traumatic memories with EMDR: a case study. *Clinical Psychology and Psychotherapy*, 5: 264–269.

De Masi, F. (2003). On the nature of intuitive and delusional thought. *International Journal of Psychoanalysis*, 84(5): 1149–1169.

De Vernejoul, P. (1985). Etudes des meridians d'acupuncture par les traceurs radioactifs. *Bulletin de L'Academie Nationale de Medicine,* 169(7): 1071–1075.

Dennison, P. & Dennison, G. E. (1994). *Brain Gym. Teachers Edition.* Ventura, CA: Edu-Kinesthetics Inc.

Devilly, G. J., & Spence, S. H. (1999). The relative efficacy and treatment distress of EMDR and a cognitive behavioural trauma treatment protocol in the amelioration of post traumatic stress disorder. *Journal of Anxiety Disorders, 13*: 131–157.

Diamond, J. (1979). *Your Body Doesn't Lie. BK—Behavioral Kinesiology.* New York: Harper & Row.

Diamond, J. (1985). *Life Energy.* New York: Dodd, Mead & Co.

Diamond, J. (1988). *Life Energy Analysis. A Way to Cantillation.* New York: Archaeus.

Diepold, J. (2002). Touch and breathe. In: W. Lammers & B. Kircher (Eds.),*The Energy Odyssey: New Directions in Energy Psychology.* Eastbourne: DragonRising.

Durlacher, J. V. (1995). *Freedom from Fear Forever.* Mesa, AZ: Van Ness Publishing.

Dyck, M. J. (1993). A proposal for a conditioning model of eye movement desensitisation treatment for posttraumatic stress disorder. *Journal of Behavior Therapy and Experimental Psychiatry, 24*: 201–210.

Eden, D. (1998). *Energy Medicine.* London: Piatkus.

Edmond, T., Rubin, A., & Wambach, K. G. (1999). The effectiveness of EMDR with adult female survivors of childhood sexual abuse. *Social Work Research, 23*: 103–116.

Eysenck, H. (1979). The conditioning model of neurosis. *Behavioral and Brain Sciences, 2*: 155–199.

Fairbairn, W. R. D. (1952). *Psychoanalytic Studies of the Personality.* London: Routledge.

Feinstein, D. (2004). *Energy Psychology Interactive. Rapid Interventions for Lasting Change.* Ashland, OR: Innersource.

Fensterheim, H. (1996). Eye movement desensitisation and reprocessing with complex personality pathology. An integrative therapy. *Journal of Psychotherapy Integration, 6*: 27–38.

Figley, C. R. (Ed.) (1978). *Stress Disorders Among Vietnam Veterans: Theory, Research and Treatment.* New York: Brunner/Mazel.

Figley, C. R. (1999). Editorial note by the series editor. In: F. P. Gallo (Ed.), *Energy Psychology. Explorations at the Interface of Energy, Cognition, Behavior and Health.* Boca Raton, FL: CRC.

Figley, C. R., & Carbonell, J. L. (1995). Active ingredients project: the systematic clinical demonstration of the most efficient treatments of PTSD. Florida State University Psychosocial Research Program and Clinical Laboratory. Reported in F. P. Gallo (1999), *Energy Psychology* (pp. 18–25). New York: CRC Press.

Figley, C. R., & Carbonell, J. L. (1999). Promising PTSD treatment approaches. A systematic clinical demonstration. *TRAUMA-TOLOGYe*, 5(1). Article 4. www.fsu.edu/~trauma/promising.html

Fine, C. G., & Berkowitz, A. S. (2001). The wreathing protocol. The imbrication of hypnosis and EMDR in the treatment of dissociative identity disorder and other maladaptive dissociative responses. *American Journal of Clinical Hypnosis*, 43: 275–290.

Fleming, T. (1999). *You Can Heal Now: The Tapas Acupressure Technique (TAT)*. Redondo Beach, CA: TAT International.

Foa, E. B., & McNally, R. J. (1996). Mechanisms of change in exposure therapy. In: R. M. Rapee (Ed.), *Current Controversies in the Anxiety Disorders* (pp. 329–343). New York: Guilford.

Fonagy, P. (1999). The process of change and the change of processes. What can change in a "good" analysis. Keynote address to the Spring Meeting of Division 39 of the American Psychological Association, 16 April, New York.

Fonagy, P., Gergely, G., Jurist, E. L., & Target, M. (2002). *Affect Regulation, Mentalization, and the Development of the Self*. New York. Other Press.

Foote, S. L., Bloom, F. E., & Ashton-Jones, G. (1983). Nucleus locus ceruleus: new evidence of anatomical and physiological specificity. *Physiological Reviews*, 63: 844–914.

Freud, S. (1894a). The neuropsychoses of defence. *S.E., III*: London: Hogarth Press.

Freud, S. (1895/1950a). Project for a scientific psychology. *S.E., I*: 283–397. London: Hogarth Press.

Freud, S. (1896b). Further remarks on the neuropsychoses of defence. *S.E., III*: 159–185. London: Hogarth.

Freud, S. (1896c). The aetiology of hysteria. *S.E., III*: 189–221. London: Hogarth

Freud, S. (1900a). The interpretation of dreams. *S.E., V*. London: Hogarth.

Freud, S. (1905d). Three essays on the theory of sexuality. *S.E., VII*: 135–243. London: Hogarth.

Freud, S. (1910a). Five lectures on psychoanalysis. *S.E., XI*: 3–55. London: Hogarth.

Freud, S. (1911b). Formulations on the two principles of mental functioning. *S.E., XII*: 213–226. London: Hogarth.

Freud, S. (1912b). The dynamics of transference. *S.E., XII*: 97–108. London: Hogarth.

Freud, S. (1914g). Remembering, repeating and working through (Further recommendations on the technique of psychoanalysis II). *S.E., XII*: 145–156. London: Hogarth Press.

Freud, S. (1915a). Observations on transference love. *S.E., XII*: 157–171. London: Hogarth Press.

Freud, S. (1920g). Beyond the pleasure principle. *S.E., XVIII*: 1–64. London: Hogarth.

Freud, S. (1923a). Two encyclopaedia articles. B. The libido theory. *S.E., XVIII*: 255–259. London: Hogarth.

Freud, S. (1923b). The ego and the id. *S.E., XIX*: 1–66. London: Hogarth.

Freud, S. (1926d). Inhibitions, symptoms and anxiety. *S.E., XX*: 77–174. London: Hogarth.

Freud, S. (1933a). New introductory lectures on psychoanalysis. *S.E., XX11*: 1–182. London: Hogarth.

Freud, S. (1940a). An outline of psychoanalysis. *S.E., XXIII*: 139–207. London: Hogarth.

Freud, S. (1940e). Splitting of the ego in the process of defence. *S.E., XXIII*: 271–278. London: Hogarth.

Furman, M., & Gallo, F. P. (2000). *The Neurophysics of Human Behavior*. Boca Raton, FL: CRC Press.

Gallo, F. P. (1999). *Energy Psychology. Explorations at the Interface of Energy, Cognition, Behavior and Health*. Boca Raton, FL: CRC Press.

Gallo, F. P. (2000). *Energy Diagnostic and Treatment Methods*. New York: Norton.

Gallo, F. P. (2002). Foreword to J. G. Hartung & M. D. Galvin (2003). *Energy Psychology and EMDR*. New York: Norton.

Garfield, S. L. (1995). *Psychotherapy: An Eclective–Integrative Approach* (2nd edn). New York: Wiley.

Gaston, L. (1990). The concept of the alliance and its role in psychotherapy. Theoretical and empirical considerations. *Psychotherapy, 27*: 143–153.

Gerber, R. (2000). *Vibrational Medicine for the 21st Century*. London: Piatkus.

Goldstein, A., & Feske, U. (1994). Eye movement desensitisation and reprocessing for panic disorder. A case series. *Journal of Anxiety Disorders, 8*: 351–362.

Goodheart, G. J. (1970). The schizophrenic pattern. *Chiropractic Economics*, *13*(1): July/August 5–8.

Goswami, A. (1997). Consciousness and biological order: toward a quantum theory of life and its evolution. *Integrative Physiological and Behavioral Science*, *32*: 86–100.

Goswami, A. (2001). *Physics of the Soul*. Charlottesville, VA: Hampton Roads.

Grand, D. (1998). Emerging from the coffin. Treatment of a masochistic personality disorder. In: P. Manfield (Ed.), *Extending EMDR. A Casebook of Innovative Applications*. New York: Norton.

Grand, D. (2001). *Emotional Healing at Warp Speed. The Power of EMDR*. New York: Harmony Books.

Greenson, R. R. (1974). *The Technique and Practice of Psycho-Analysis*. London: Hogarth.

Grotstein, J. S. (1997). Why Oedipus and not Christ? A psychoanalytic inquiry into innocence, human sacrifice, and the sacred—part 1: innocence, spirituality and human sacrifice. *American Journal of Psychoanalysis*, *57*(3): 193–220.

Grudermeyer, D. (2002). Getting on the same page. How all the different energy psychology approaches fit together. In: W. Lammers & B. Kirchner (Eds.), *The Energy Odyssey. New Directions in Energy Psychology* (pp. 123–126). Eastbourne: DragonRising.

Grudermeyer, D. (2003). *The Energy Psychology Desktop* Companion (2nd edn). Del Mar, CA: Willingness Works.

Hannaford, C. (1995). *Smart Moves. Why Learning is Not All In Your Head*. Arlington, VA: Great Ocean.

Hartmann, E. (1996). Who develops PTSD nightmares and who doesn't. In: D. Barrett (Ed.), *Trauma and Dreams*. Cambridge, MA: Harvard University Press.

Hartmann, S. (2002). *The Advanced Patterns of EFT*. Eastbourne: DragonRising.

Hartmann, S. (2003a). *Adventures in EFT. 6th Edition*. Eastbourne: DragonRising.

✳ Hartmann, S. (2003b). *Oceans of Energy. The Patterns and Techniques of EmoTrance*. Eastbourne: DragonRising.

Hartmann, S. (2004). *Living Energy. The Patterns and Techniques of EmoTrance*, Volume 2. Eastbourne: RisingDragon.

Hartung, J. G. & Galvin, M. D. (2003). *Energy Psychology and EMDR.* ✳ *Combining Forces to Optimize Treatment*. New York: Norton.

Hawkins, D. R. (1995). *Power vs Force: The Hidden Determinants of Life*. Sedona, AZ: Veritas.

Hebb, D. O. (1949)[1961]. *The Organisation of Behavior. A Neurophysiological Theory.* New York: Wiley.

Henry, S. L. (1996). Pathological gambling. Etiological considerations and treatment efficacy of eye movement desensitisation/reprocessing. *Journal of Gambling Studies, 12:* 395–405.

Herbert, J. D., & Gaudiano, B. A. (2001). The search for the holy grail: heart rate variability and thought field therapy. *Journal of Clinical Psychology, 57*(10): 1207–1214.

Hitlin, J. (2002). Penelope's shroud. In: W. Lammers & B. Kircher (Eds.), *The Energy Odyssey. New Directions in Energy Psychology* (pp. 211–216). Eastbourne: DragonRising.

Høglend, P. (1993). Transference interpretations and long-term change after dynamic psychotherapy of brief to moderate length. *American Journal of Psychotherapy, 47*(4): 494–507.

Hover-Kramer, D. (2002). *Creative Energies. Integrative Energy Psychotherapy for Self-Expression and Healing.* New York: Norton.

Hui, K. S. (2000). Acupuncture modulates the limbic system and subcortical gray structures of the human brain: evidence from MRI studies in normal subjects. *Human Brain Mapping, 13:* 13–25.

Ironson, G. I., Freund, B., Strauss, J. L., & Williams, J. (2002). A comparison of two treatments for traumatic stress: a pilot study of EMDR and prolonged exposure. *Journal of Clinical Psychology, 58:* 113–128.

Johnson, C., Shala, M., Sejdijai, X., Odell, R., & Dabishevci, K. (2001). Thought field therapy—soothing the bad moments of Kosovo. *Journal of Clinical Psychology, 57*(10): 1237–1240.

Joseph, B. (1985). Transference: the total situation. *International Journal of Psycho-Analysis, 66:* 447–454. Reprinted in E. Spillius (Ed.), *Psychic Equilibrium and Psychic Change. Selected Papers of Betty Joseph.* London: Routledge, 1989.

Kavanaugh, D. J., Freese, S., Andrade, J., & May, J. (2001). Effects of visuospatial tasks on desensitisation to emotive memories. *British Journal of Clinical Psychology, 40:* 267–280.

King, P., & Steiner, R. (1991). *The Freud–Klein Controversies. 1941–45.* London: Routledge.

Kinowski, K. (2003). "Put your best foot forward": a somatosensory anchoring of confidence using modified EMDR. Presented at the European EMDR conference. 17-18 May, Rome. (CD available from the EMDR UK & Ireland Association.)

Kinsbourne, M. (1972). Eye and head turning indicates cerebral lateralization. *Science, 176:* 539–541.

Kinsbourne, M. (1974). Direction of gaze and distribution of cerebral thought processes. *Neuropsychologia*, 12(2): 279–281.

Kline, J. P. (2001). Heart rate variability does not tap putative efficacy of thought field therapy. *Journal of Clinical Psychology*, 57(10): 1187–1192.

Kohut, H. (1971). *The Analysis of the Self*. New York: International Universities Press.

Kohut, H. (1972). Thoughts on narcissism and narcissistic rage. In: P. Ornstein (Ed.), *The Search for the Self. Selected Writings of Heinz Kohut. Volume 2* (pp. 615–658). New York: International Universities Press.

Kohut, H. (1977). *The Restoration of the Self*. New York: International Universities Press.

Kohut, H. (1979) The two analyses of Mr. Z. *International Journal of Psychoanalysis*, 60: 3–27 [reprinted in P. Ornstein (Ed.), *The Search for the Self. Selected Writings of Heinz Kohut. Volume 4*, Madison, CT: International Universities Press, 1991].

Kohut, H. (1984). *How Does Analysis Cure?* Chicago: University of Chicago Press.

Kohut, H., & Rubovitz-Seitz. P. F. D. (1963). Concepts and theories of psychoanalysis. In: J. M. Wepman & R. W. Heine (Eds.), *Concepts of Personality*. Chicago: Aldine. Republished in P. Ornstein (Ed.), *The Search for the Self. Selected Writings of Heinz Kohut 1950–1978. Volume 1* (pp. 337–374). New York: International Universities Press, 1978.

Korn, D. L., & Leeds, A. M. (2002). Preliminary evidence of efficacy for EMDR resource development and installation in the stabilization phase of treatment of complex posttraumatic stress disorder. *Journal of Clinical Psychology*, 58(12): 1465–1487.

Krebs, C. (1998). *A Revolutionary Way of Thinking*. Melbourne: Hill of Content.

Lacan, J. (1948). Aggressivity in psychoanalysis. Paper presented to the 11th Congrès des Psychoanalystes de langue français, Brussels, May. In: *Écrits*, A. Sheridan (Trans.). London: Tavistock, 1977.

Lacan, J. (1949). The mirror stage as formative of the function of the I as revealed in psychoanalytic experience. Paper given to the 16th International Congress of Psychoanalysis, Zürich, 17 July. In: *Écrits*, A. Sheridan (Trans.). London: Tavistock, 1977.

Lane, J. (2002). Energy meridian tapping and EMDR. In: W. Lammers & B. Kircher (Eds.), *The Energy Odyssey. New Directions in Energy Psychology*. Eastbourne: DragonRising.

Lansing, K., & Amen, D. (2003). Portraits in healing. A clinical study in neurological outcomes of EMDR in treatment for cumulative PTSD in police officers. Presented at the EMDR European Conference, 17–18 May, Rome. (CD available from the EMDR UK & Ireland Association.)

Lawson, A., & Calderon, L. (1997). Interexaminer agreement for applied kinesiology manual muscle testing. *Perceptual and Motor Skills, 84*: 539–546.

Lazarus, C. N., & Lazarus, A. A. (2002). EMDR: an elegantly concentrated multimodal procedure? In: F. Shapiro (Ed.), *EMDR as an Integrative Psychotherapy Approach. Experts of Diverse Orientations Explore the Paradigm Prism* (pp. 209–223). Washington: American Psychological Association.

Lazrove, S., & Fine, C. G. (1996). The use of EMDR in patients with dissociative identity disorder. *Dissociation*, 9: 289–299.

Lazrove, S., Kite, L., Triffleman, E., McGlashan, T., & Rounsaville, B. (1998), The use of EMDR as treatment for chronic PTSD—encouraging results of an open trial. *American Journal of Orthopsychiatry*, 69: 601–608.

LeDoux, J. (1996). *The Emotional Brain*. New York: Simon & Schuster.

Lee, C., Gavriel, H., Drummond, P., Richards, J., & Greenwald, R. (2002). Treatment of post-traumatic stress disorder: a comparison of stress-inoculation training with prolonged exposure and eye movement desensitisation and reprocessing. *Journal of Clinical Psychology*, 58: 1071–1089

Leeds, A. M. (1998). Lifting the burden of shame. Using EMDR resource installation to resolve a therapeutic impasse. In: P. Manfield (Ed.), *Extending EMDR. A Casebook of Innovative Applications* (pp. 256–281). New York: Norton.

Leeds, A. M., & Shapiro, F. (2000). EMDR and resource installation: principles and procedures for enhancing current functioning and resolving traumatic experiences. In: J. Carlson & L. Sperry (Eds.), *Brief Therapy with Individuals and Couples* (pp. 469–534). Zeig, Phoenix, AZ: Tucker & Theison.

Lehrer, P. M., Sasoki, Y., & Saito, Y. (1999). Zazen and cardiac variability. *Psychosomatic Medicine, 61*: 812–821.

Leisman, G. (1995). Electromyographic effects of fatigue and task repetition on the validity of estimates of strong and weak muscles in applied kinesiology muscle testing procedures. *Perceptual and Motor Skills, 80*: 963–977.

Leisman, G., Shambaugh, P., & Ferentz, A. (1989). Somatosensory evoked potential changes during muscle testing. *International Journal of Neuroscience*, 45: 143–151.

Leonoff, G. (1996). Successful treatment of phobias and anxiety by telephone and radio: a preliminary report on a replication of Callahan's 1987 study. *The Thought Field*, 2(1): 3–4.

Leuzinger-Bohleber, M., & Target, M. (2002). *Outcomes of Psychoanalytic Treatment*. London: Whurr.

Levin, C. (1993) The enigma of EMDR. *Family Therapy Networker*, July/August: 75–83.

Levin, P., Lazrove, S., & van der Kolk, B. (1999). What psychological testing and neuroimaging tell us about the treatment of post-traumatic stress disorder by eye movement desensitisation and reprocessing. *Journal of Anxiety Disorders*, 13: 159–172.

Liboff, A. R. (1997). Bioelectrical fields and acupuncture. *Journal of Alternative and Complementary Medicine*, 3: 577–587.

Lilienfeld, S. O., Lynn, S. J., & Lohr, J. M. (Eds.) (2003). *Science and Pseudoscience in Clinical Psychology*. New York: Guilford Press.

Linehan, M. M. (1993). *Cognitive-behavioral Treatment of Borderline Personality Disorder*. New York: Guilford Press.

Lipke, H. (2000). *EMDR and Psychotherapy Integration: Theoretical and Clinical Suggestions with Focus on Traumatic Stress*. New York: CRC Press.

Llewellyn-Edwards, T., & Butterell, V. (2003). *Success Unlimited with Energy Therapy*. Tickhill: Llewellyn & Butterell.

Loden, S. (2003). The fate of the dream in contemporary psychoanalysis. *Journal of the American Psychoanalytic Association*, 51(1): 43–70.

Lohr, J. M. (2001). Sakai et al. is not an adequate demonstration of TFT effectiveness. *Journal of Clinical Psychology*, 57(10): 1229–1236.

Lohr, J. M., Tolin, D. F., & Kleinknecht, R. A. (1995). An intensive investigation of eye movement desensitisation of medical phobias. *Journal of Behavior Therapy and Experimental Psychiatry*, 26: 141–151.

Lohr, J. M., Tolin, D. F., & Kleinknecht, R. A. (1996). An intensive investigation of eye movement desensitisation of claustrophobia. *Journal of Anxiety Disorders*, 10: 73–88.

Lohr, J. M., Lilienfield, S. O., Tolin, D. F., & Herbert, J. D. (1999). Eye movement desensitisation and reprocessing: an analysis of specific versus non-specific factors. *Journal of Anxiety Disorders*, 13: 185–207.

Lorimer, D. (Ed.) (2001). *Thinking Beyond the Brain. A Wider Science of Consciousness*. New York: Floris Books.

Luborsky, L. & Crits-Christoph, P. (1997). *Understanding Transference: Core Conflictual Relationship Theme Method*. Washington, DC: American Psychological Association.

Lynch, V., & Lynch, P. (2001). *Emotional Healing in Minutes*. London: Thorsons.

Lyons, J. A., & Keane, T. M. (1989). Implosive therapy for the treatment of combat-related PTSD. *Journal of Traumatic Stress*, 2: 137–152.

Lyons, J. A., & Scotti, J. R. (1995). Behavioral treatment of a motor vehicle accident survivor: an illustrative case of direct therapeutic exposure. *Cognitive and Behavioral Practice*, 2: 343–364.

MacCulloch, M. J., & Feldman, P. (1996). Eye movement desensitisation treatment utilises the positive visceral element of the investigatory reflex to inhibit the memories of post-traumatic stress disorder. A theoretical analysis. *British Journal of Psychiatry,169*: 571–579.

Magliano, L. (2003). EMDR. An extremely flexible therapeutic tool. Presented at the European EMDR conference, 17–18 May, Rome. (CD available from the EMDR UK & Ireland Association.)

Manfield, P. (Ed.) (1998). *Extending EMDR: a Casebook of Innovative Applications*. New York: Norton.

Marcus, S. V., Marquis, P., & Sakai, C. (1997). Controlled study of treatment of PTSD using EMDR in an HMO setting. *Psychotherapy*, *34*: 307–315.

Marks, I. M., Lovell, K., Noshirvant, H., Livanou, M., & Thrasher, S. (1998). Treatment of posttraumatic stress disorder by exposure and/or cognitive restructuring. A controlled study. *Archives of General Psychiatry*, *55*: 317–325.

Martin, R. J. (Ed.) (1977). *Dynamics of Correction of Abnormal Function—Terence J. Bennett Lectures*. Sierra Madre, CA. Privately published.

Maxfield, L. (2002). Commonly asked questions about EMDR and suggestions for research parameters. In: F. Shapiro (Ed.), *EMDR as an Integrative Psychotherapy Approach* (pp. 393–418). Washington, DC: American Psychological Press.

Maxfield, L., & Hyer, L. A. (2002). The relationship between efficacy and methodology in studies investigating EMDR treatment of PTSD. *Journal of Clinical Psychology*, *58*: 23–41.

Maxfield, L., & Melnyk, W. T. (2000). Single session treatment of test anxiety with eye movement desensitisation and reprocessing (EMDR). *International Journal of Stress Management*, 7: 87–101.

McCann, D. L. (1992). Post-traumatic stress disorder due to devastating burns overcome by a single session eye movement desensitisation. *Journal of Behavior Therapy and Experimental Psychiatry*. 23: 319–323.

McDermott, V. A. (2003). Is free association still fundamental? Panel report. *Journal of the American Psychoanalytic Association, 51*(4): 1349–1356.

McFarlane, A. (1999). Comparison of EMDR with CBT in PTSD patients. Paper presented at the annual meeting of the International Society for Traumatic Stress Studies, November, Miami, Florida.

McNally, R. (1999). On eye movements and animal magnetism: a reply to Greenwald's defence of EMDR. *Journal of Anxiety Disorders, 13:* 617–620.

Melbeck, H. H. (2003). Trauma-therapy with in-patients—a ward concept. Presented at the European EMDR Conference. 17–18 May, Rome. (CD available from EMDR UK & Ireland.)

Millet, M. G. (2001). Elevated energy therapy Kundalini Protocol. www.elevatedtherapy.com

Mollon, P. (1993). *The Fragile Self. The Structure of Narcissistic Disturbance.* London: Whurr.

Mollon, P. (1996). *Multiple Selves, Multiple Voices. Working with Trauma, Violation, and Dissociation.* Chichester: Wiley.

Mollon, P. (2001). *Releasing the Self. The Healing Legacy of Heinz Kohut.* London: Whurr.

Mollon, P. (2002a). *Remembering Trauma. A Psychotherapist's Guide to Memory and Illusion* (2nd edn). London: Whurr.

Mollon, P. (2002b). *Shame and Jealousy. The Hidden Turmoils.* London: Karnac.

Montgomery, R. W., & Ayllon, T. (1994). Eye movement desensitisation across subjects. Subjective and physiological measures of treatment efficacy. *Journal of Behavior Therapy and Experimental Psychiatry, 25:* 217–230

Monti, D., Sinnott, J., Marchese, M., Kunkel, E., & Greeson, J. (1999). Muscle test comparisons of congruent and incongruent self-referential statements. *Perceptual and Motor Skills, 88:* 1019–1028.

Nakagawa, A. (1991) Role of anterior and posterior attention networks in hemispheric asymmetries during lexical decisions. *Journal of Cognitive Neuroscience, 3:* 313–321.

Narvaez, T., Rohsmann, P., & Stegenda, J. (2002). Evaluating the effects of energy psychology on acupuncture meridians using Prognos analysis. In: W. Lammers & B. Kircher (Eds.) *The Energy Odyssey. New Directions in Energy Psychology* (pp. 241–247). Eastbourne: DragonRising.

NIH (1997). *Acupuncture NIH Consensus Statement Online, 1997.* 3–5 November. *15*(5): 1–34.

Nims, L. (2001). *Be Set Free Fast. Training Manual*. Orange, CA: L. Nims.

Nordenstrom, B. (1983). *Biologically Closed Electric Circuits: Clinical, Experimental and Theoretical Evidence for an Additional Circulatory System*. Stockholm: Nordic.

Omaha, J. (2004). *Psychotherapeutic Interventions for Emotion Regulation. EMDR and Bilateral Stimulation for Affect Management*. New York: Norton.

Omura, Y. (1989). Connections found between each meridian (heart, stomach, triple burner, etc.) and organ representation area of corresponding internal organs in each side of the cerebral cortex; release of common neurotransmitters and hormones unique to each meridian and a corresponding acupuncture point and internal organ after acupuncture, electrical stimulation, mechanical stimulation (including Shiatsu), soft laser stimulation of Qi Gong. *Acupuncture and Electro-Therapeutics Research International Journal, 14*: 155–186.

Omura, Y. (1990). Meridian-like networks of internal organs, corresponding to traditional Chinese 12 main meridians and their acupuncture points as detected by the Bi-Digital O-Ring Test Imaging Method. Search for corresponding internal organs of western medicine for each meridian—part 1. *Acupuncture and Electro-Therapeutics Research International Journal, 12*: 53–70.

Orlinsky, D. E., Grawe, K., & Parks, B. K. (1994). Process and outcome in psychotherapy. In: A. E. Bergin & S. L. Garfield (Eds.), *Handbook of Psychotherapy and Behavior Change* (4th edn) (pp. 270–376). New York: Wiley.

Parnell, L. (1998). Postpartum depression. Helping a new mother to bond. In: P. Manfield (Ed.), *Extending EMDR. A Casebook of Innovative Applications* (pp. 37–64). New York: Norton.

Perkins, B. R., & Rouanzoin, C. C. (2002). A critical evaluation of current views regarding eye movement desensitisation and reprocessing (EMDR); clarifying points of confusion. *Journal of Clinical Psychology, 58*(1): 77–97.

Perot, C., Meldener, R., & Gouble, F. (1991). Objective measurement of proprioceptive technique consequences on muscular maximal voluntary contraction during manual muscle testing. *Agressologie, 32*(10): 471–474.

Pert, C. (1999). *Molecules of Emotion*. New York: Simon & Schuster.

Pert, C. (2000). *Study Guide to "Your Body is Your Subconscious Mind"* (two audiocassettes). Boulder, CO: Sounds True.

Phillips, M. (2000). *Finding the Energy to Heal. How EMDR, Hypnosis, TFT, Imagery, and Body-Focused Therapy Can Help Restore Mindbody Health.* New York: Norton.

Pignotti, M., & Steinberg, M. (2001). Heart rate variability as an outcome measure for thought field therapy in clinical practice. *Journal of Clinical Psychology, 57*(10): 1193–1206.

Piper, W. E., Hassan, Azim, H. F. A., Joyce, A. S., McCallum, M. (1990). Transference interpretations, therapeutic alliance, and outcome in short-term individual psychotherapy. *Archives of General Psychiatry,* 48: 946–953.

Ponomareva, N. (2003). Do we marry our parents? Unpublished MA dissertation. School of Psychotherapy and Counselling, London, Regents College.

Powell, A. (2003). Consciousness that transcends spacetime: its significance for the therapeutic process. *Self & Society, 31*(4): 27–44.

Power, K., McGoldrick, T., Brown, K., Buchanan, R., Sharp, D., Swanson, V., & Karatzias, A. (2002). A controlled comparison of eye movement desensitisation and reprocessing versus exposure plus cognitive restructuring versus waiting list in the treatment of post-traumatic stress disorder. *Clinical Psychology and Psychotherapy, 9*: 299–318.

Pribram, K. & Gill, M. (1976). *Freud's Project Reassessed.* London: Hutchinson.

Quinn, N., & Hartmann, S. (2002). *Using Tachyon and the EmoTrance Healing System.* Eastbourne: DragonRising.

Radin, D. (1997). *The Conscious Universe. The Scientific Truth of Psychic Phenomena.* San Francisco: Harper Collins.

Radomski, S. (2000). *Allergy Antidotes.* Available as an e-book from www.theamt.com

Radomski, S. (2002). Energy psychology treatment of allergy-like reactions. In: W. Lammers & B. Kircher (Eds.), *The Energy Odyssey. New Directions in Energy Psychology* (2nd edn). Eastbourne: DragonRising.

Rauch, S. L., van der Kolk, B. A., Fisler, R. E. A., Nathaniel, M., Orr, S. P., & Savage, C. R. (1996). A symptom provocation study of post-traumatic stress disorder using positron emission tomography and script-driven imagery. *Archives of General Psychiatry, 53*: 380–387.

Reich, W. R. (1942). *The Function of the Orgasm. Sex-Economic Problems of Biological Energy.* New York: Orgone Institute Press, [reprinted London: Panther Books, 1968].

Reich, W. R. (1949). *Character Analysis*. New York: Orgone Institute Press [reprinted New York: Farrar, Straus and Giroux, 1980].

Rogers, S., Silver, S., Goss, J., Obenchain, J., Willis, A., & Whitney, R. (1999). A single session, controlled group study of flooding and eye movement desensitisation and reprocessing in treating posttraumatic stress disorder among Vietnam War veterans. Preliminary data. *Journal of Anxiety Disorders, 13*: 119–130.

Rosner, R. (2001). Between search and research: how to find your way around? Review of the article "Thought field therapy—soothing the bad moments of Kosovo". *Journal of Clinical Psychology, 57*(10): 1241–1244.

Roth, A., & Fonagy, P. (1996). *What Works for Whom? A Critical Review of Psychotherapy Research*. New York: Guilford Press.

Rothbaum, B. O. (1997). A controlled study of eye movement desensitisation and reprocessing for posttraumatic stress disordered sexual assault victims. *Bulletin of the Menninger Clinic*. 61. 317–334.

Rothbaum, B. O. (2001). Prolonged exposure versus EMDR for PTSD rape victims. Paper presented at the annual meeting of the Association for the Advancement of Behavior Therapy, November, Philadelphia.

Rothbaum, B. O., Meadows, E. A. Resnick, P., & Foy, D. W. (2000). Cognitive behavioural therapy. In: E. B. Foa, T. M. Keane, & M. J. Friedman (Eds.), *Effective Treatments for PTSD. Practice Guidelines from the International Society for Traumatic Stress Studies* (pp. 320–325). New York: Guilford Press.

Rubovits-Seitz, P. F. D. (1999). *Kohut's Freudian Vision*. Hillsdale, NJ: The Analytic Press.

Sakai, C., Paperny, D., Mathews, M., Tanida, G., Boyd, G., Simons, A., Yamamoto, C., Man, C., & Nutter, L. (2001). Thought field therapy clinical applications: utilization in a HMO in Behavioral Medicine and Behavioral Health Services. *Journal of Clinical Psychology, 57*(10): 1215–1228.

Sandler, J., & Sandler, A.-M. (1983). The "second censorship", the "three box model" and some technical implications. *International Journal of Psychoanalysis, 64*: 413–425.

Sandler, J., & Sandler, A.-M. (1984). The past unconscious, the present unconscious and interpretation of the transference. *Psychoanalytic Inquiry, 4*: 367–399.

Sandler, J., & Sandler, A.-M. (1994). The past unconscious and the present unconscious. A contribution to a technical frame of reference. *Psychoanalytic Study of the Child, 49*: 278–292.

Scarfone, D. (2002). Panel report. "Controversial discussions". The issue of differences in method. *International Journal of Psychoanalysis, 83*: 453–456.

Scheck, M. M., Schaeffer, J. A., & Gillette, C. S. (1998). Brief psychological intervention with traumatized young women: the efficacy of eye movement desensitisation and reprocessing. *Journal of Traumatic Stress, 11*: 25–44.

Schmitt, W., & Leisman, G. (1998). Correlation of applied kinesiology muscle testing findings with serum immunoglobulin levels for food allergies. *International Journal of Neuroscience, 96*: 237–244.

Schoninger, B. (2001). TFT in the treatment of speaking anxiety. Unpublished Ph.D. dissertation. Cincinnati, OH, Union Institute.

Schore, A. N. (1994). *Affect Regulation and the Origin of the Self.* Hillsdale, NJ: Erlbaum.

Schore, A. N. (2003a). *Affect Regulation and Disorders of the Self.* New York: Norton.

Schore, A. N. (2003b). *Affect Regulation and the Repair of the Self.* New York: Norton.

Schore, A. N. (2003c). Minds in the making: attachment, the self-organising brain, and developmentally-oriented psychoanalytic psychotherapy. In: J. Corrigall & H. Wilkison (Eds.), *Revolutionary Connections. Psychotherapy and Neuroscience* (pp. 7–21). London: Karnac.

Scott, J., & Goss, K. (1988). *Clear Your Allergies in Minutes.* San Francisco, CA: Health Kinesiology Publishing.

Segal, Z. V., Williams, J. M. G., & Teasdale, J. D. (2002). *Mindfulness-based Cognitive Therapy for Depression.* New York. Guilford.

Shapiro, F. (1989a). Efficacy of the eye movement desensitisation procedure in the treatment of traumatic memories. *Journal of Traumatic Stress Studies, 2*: 199–223.

Shapiro, F. (1989b). Eye movement desensitization: a new treatment for post traumatic stress disorder. *Journal of Behavior Therapy and Experimental Psychiatry, 20*: 211–217.

Shapiro, F. (2001). *Eye Movement Desensitization and Reprocessing* (2nd edn). New York: Guilford Press.

Shapiro, F. (Ed.) (2002a). *EMDR as an Integrative Psychotherapy. Experts of Diverse Orientations Explore the Paradigm Prism.* Washington, DC: American Psychological Press.

Shapiro, F. (2002b). Introduction: paradigms, processing and personality development. In: F. Shapiro (Ed.) *EMDR as an Integrative*

Psychotherapy. Experts of Diverse Orientations Explore the Pradigm Prism (pp. 3–26). Washington, DC: American Psychological Press.

Shapiro, F. (2002c). EMDR treatment overview and integration. In: F. Shapiro (Ed.), *EMDR as an Integrative Psychotherapy. Experts of Diverse Orientations Explore the Paradigm Prism* (pp. 27–55). Washington, DC: American Psychological Press.

Shapiro, F., & Forrest, M. (1997). *EMDR.* New York: Basic Books.

Shapiro, F. & Solomon, R. (1995). Eye movement desensitisation and reprocessing: neurocognitive information processing. In: G. Everley (Ed.), *Innovations in Disaster and Trauma Psychology. Volume 1* (pp. 216–237. Elliot City, MD: Chevron Publishing.

Sharaf, M. (1983). *Fury on Earth. A Biography of Wilhelm Reich.* London: Andre Deutsch.

Sharpley, C. F., Montgomery, I. M., & Scalzo, L. A. (1996). Comparative efficacy of EMDR and alternative procedures in reducing the vividness of mental images. *Scandinavian Journal of Behavior Therapy, 25*: 37–42.

Sheldrake, R. (1985). *A New Science of Life. The Hypothesis of Formative Causation.* London: Blond and Briggs.

Sheldrake, R. (1988). *The Presence of the Past: Morphic Resonance and the Habits of Nature.* London: Collins.

Sheldrake, R. (1999). *Dogs That Know When Their Owners Are Coming Home and Other Unexplained Powers of Animals.* London: Hutchinson.

Sheldrake, R., McKenna, T., & Abraham, R. (1998). *The Evolutionary Mind.* Santa Cruz: Trialogue Press.

Siegel, D. J. (2002). The developing mind and the resolution of trauma: some ideas about information processing and an interpersonal neurobiology of psychotherapy. In: F. Shapiro (Ed.), *EMDR as an Integrative Psychotherapy Approach* (pp. 85–121). Washington, DC: American Psychological Association.

Smyth, N. J., & Poole, D. (2002). EMDR and cognitive-behavior therapy. Exploring convergence and divergence. In: F. Shapiro (Ed.), *EMDR as an Integrative Psychotherapy Approach* (pp. 151–180). Washington, DC: American Psychological Association.

Sprang, G. (2001). The use of eye movement desensitisation and reprocessing (EMDR) in the treatment of traumatic stress and complicated mourning. Psychological and behavioral outcomes. *Research on Social Work Practice, 11*: 300–320.

Stickgold, R. (2002). EMDR: A putative neurobiological mechanism of action. *Journal of Clinical Psychology, 58*: 61–75.

Stickgold, R., Scott, L., Rittenhouse, C., & Hobson, J. A. (1999). Sleep-induced changes in associative memory. *Journal of Cognitive Neuroscience*, 11(2): 182–193.

Stokes, G., & Whiteside, D. (1985). *Structural Neurology*. Burbank, CA: Three in One Concepts.

Stolorow, R., Brandchaft, B., & Atwood, G. (1987). *Psychoanalytic Treatment. An Intersubjective Approach*. Hillsdale, NJ: Analytic Press.

Stone, J. D. (1999). *Soul Psychology*. New York: Ballantine Wellspring.

Strachey, J. (1934). The nature of the therapeutic action of psycho-analysis. *International Journal of Psycho-Analysis*, 15: 127–159.

Strachey, J. (1962). The emergence of Freud's fundamental hypotheses. In: S. Freud, *Standard Edition of the Complete Psychological Works of Sigmund Freud*, III (pp. 62–68). London. Hogarth.

Stux, G., & Pomeranx, B. (1995). *Basics of Acupuncture* (3rd edn). New York: Springer.

Swack, J. A. (2001). The biochemistry of energy psychology. An immunologist's perspective on physiological mechanisms underlying energy psychology treatments. Plenary speech at the 2001 Energy Psychology Conference. Available from www.jaswack.com

Swingle, P. (2001). Effects of the Emotional Freedom Technique (EFT) method on seizure frequency in children diagnosed with epilepsy. Paper presented at the annual meeting of the Association for Comprehensive Energy Psychology, Las Vegas, Nevada.

Swingle, P., Pulos, L., & Swingle, M. (2001). Effects of a meridian-based therapy, (EFT), on symptoms of PTSD in auto accident victims. Paper presented at the annual meeting of the Association for Comprehensive Energy Psychology, Las Vegas, Nevada.

Syldona, M., & Rein, G. (1999). The use of DC electrodermal potential measurements and healer's felt sense to assess the energetic nature of Qi. *Journal of Alternative and Complementary Medicine*, 5: 329–347.

Talbot, M. (1996). *The Holgoraphic Universe*. London: HarperCollins.

Taylor, S., Thordarson, D., Maxfield, L., Wilensky, M. S., Ladd, W. G., & Lanius, U. F. (2001). EMDR, exposure therapy, and relaxation training for PTSD: a controlled outcome study. Paper presented at the World Congress meeting of the Association for the Advancement of Behavior Therapy, July,Vancouver, Canada.

Tenpenny, S. (2002). Treating ADHD through allergy elimination. In: W. Lammers & B. Kirchner (Eds.), *The Energy Odyssey: New Directions in Energy Psychology* (pp. 233–240). Eastbourne: DragonRising.

Thie, J. F. (1979). *Touch for Health*. Marina del Rey, CA: De Vorss & Company.

Tiller, W. A. (1997). *Science and Human Transformation. Subtle Energies, Intentionality and Consciousness*. Walnut Creek, CA: Pavior Publishing.

Twombly, J. H. (2000). Incorporating EMDR and EMDR adaptations into the treatment of clients with dissociative identity disorder. *Journal of Trauma and Dissociation*, 1: 61–81.

United Kingdom Department of Health (2001). *Treatment Choice in Psychological Therapies and Counselling*. London: HMSO.

van den Hout, M., Muris, P., Salemink, E., & Kindt, M. (2001). Autobiographical memories become less vivid and emotional after eye movements. *British Journal of Clinical Psychology*. 40: 121–130.

Van der Kolk, B. A. (2002). Beyond the talking cure. Somatic experience and subcortical imprints in the treatment of trauma. In: F. Shapiro (Ed.), *EMDR as an Integrative Psychotherapy Approach* (pp. 57–83). Washington: American Psychological Association.

Van Etten, M. J., & Taylor, S. (1998). Comparative efficacy of treatments for posttraumatic stress disorder: a meta-analysis. *Clinical Psychology and Psychotherapy*, 5: 126–144.

Vaughan, K., Armstrong, M., Gold, R., O'Connor, N., Jenneke, W., & Tannier, N. (1994). A trial of eye movement desensitisation compared to image habituation training and applied muscle relaxation in post-traumatic stress disorder. *Journal of Behavior Therapy and Experimental Psychiatry*, 25: 283–291.

Wachtel, P. L. (2002). EMDR and psychoanalysis. In: F. Shapiro (Ed.), *EMDR as an Integrative Psychotherapy* (pp. 123–150). Washington, DC: American Psychological Press.

Wagner, D., & Cousens, G. (1999). *Tachyon Energy. A New Paradigm in Holistic Healing*. Berkeley, CA: North Atlantic Books.

Walther, D. S. (1988). *Applied Kinesiology. Synopsis*. Pueblo, CO: Systems DC.

Weil, T. (2002). Relationship-oriented meridian-based psychotherapy and counselling. In: W. Lammers & B. Kirchner (Eds.), *The Energy Odyssey: New Directions in Energy Psychology* (pp. 165–176). Eastbourne: DragonRising.

Wells, A. (2000). *Emotional Disorders and Metacognition: Innovative Cognitive Therapy*. Chichester: Wiley,

Wells, S., Polglase, K., Andrews, H.B., Carrington, P., & Baker, A. H. (2003). Evaluation of a meridian-based intervention, Emotional

Freedom Techniques (EFT), for reducing specific phobias of small animals. *Journal of Clinical Psychology*, *59*(9): 943–966.

Wernik, U. (1993). The role of the traumatic component in the etiology of sexual dysfunctions and its treatment with eye movement desensitisation procedure. *Journal of Sex Education and Therapy*, *19*: 212–222.

Westen, D., & Morrison, K. (2001). A multidimensional meta-analysis of treatments for depression, panic, and generalized anxiety disorder: an empirical examination of the status of empirically supported therapies. *Journal of Consulting and Clinical Psychology*, *69*: 875–899.

Whatmore, G. B., & Ellis, R. M. (1964). Some neurophysiologic aspects of schizophrenia: an electromyographic study. *American Journal of Psychiatry*, *120*: June.

Wilson, D., Silver, S. M., Covi, W., & Foster, S. (1996). Eye movement desensitisation and reprocessing: effectiveness and autonomic correlates. *Journal of Behavior Therapy and Experimental Psychiatry*, *27*: 219–229.

Wilson, S. A., Becker, L. A., & Tinker, R. H. (1997). Fifteen-month follow-up of eye movement desensitisation and reprocessing (EMDR) treatment for PTSD and psychological trauma. *Journal of Consulting and Clinical Psychology*, *65*: 1047–1056.

Wilson, S. A., Becker, L. A., Tinker, R. H., & Logan, C. R. (2001). Stress management with law enforcement personnel. A controlled outcome study of EMDR versus a traditional stress management program. *International Journal of Stress Management*, *8*: 179–200.

Winnicott, D. W. (1958) The capacity to be alone. In: J. D. Sutherland (Ed.), *The Maturational Processes and the Facilitating Environment* (pp. 29–36). London: Hogarth.

Winnicott, D. W. (1960)[1965]. Ego distortion in terms of true and false self. In: J. D. Sutherland (Ed.), *The Maturational Processes and the Facilitating Environment* (pp. 140–152). London: Hogarth.

Wolpe, J. (1990). *The Practice of Behavior Therapy* (4th edn). New York: Pergamon Press.

Wolpe, J., & Abrams, J. (1991). Post-traumatic stress disorder overcome by eye movement desensitisation: a case report. *Journal of Behavior Therapy and Experimental Psychiatry*, *22*: 39–43.

Young, J. E., Zangwill, W. M., & Behary, W. E. (2002). Combining EMDR and schema-focused therapy: the whole may be greater than the sum of the parts. In: F. Shapiro (Ed.) *EMDR as an Integrative Psychotherapy Approach: Experts of Diverse Orientations Explore the Paradigm Prism* (pp. 181–208). Washington: American Psychological Press.

Yovell, Y. (2001). From hysteria to posttraumatic stress disorder: psychoanalysis and the neurobiology of traumatic memories. *Neuro-Psychoanalysis, 2*(2): 171–181.

Appendix 1

Useful websites for further information

EMDR

www.emdr-europe.net	The European EMDR association.
www.emdr.org.uk	Useful information on training and research.
www.emdria.org	The EMDR Internation Organization.
www.emdrportal.com	Information and discussion regarding EMDR.

Energy psychology

www.energypsych.org	The Association for Comprehensive Energy Psychology.
www.theamt.com	The Association for Meridian Energy Therapies.
www.meridiantherapy.org	The Association for the Advancement of Meridian Energy Therapy

www.emofree.com	Gary Craig's Emotional Freedom Techniques.
www.innersource.net	For training materials in energy psychology.
www.passionforhealth.com	For UK trainings in energy psychology.
www.emotrance.com	Silvia Hartmann's EmoTrance.
www.nicolaquinn.com	For information on Tachyon Energy.
www.besetfreefast.com	Larry Nims' Be Set Free Fast.
www.unstressforsuccess.com	Tapas Acupressure Technique (TAT).
www.tftworldwide.com	Evolving Thought Field Therapy.
www.tftrx.com	Callahan's Thought Field Therapy.
www.diamondcenter.net	Dr John Diamond.
www.allergyantidotes.com	Sandra Radomski's Allergy Antidotes.
www.seemorgmatrix.org	Seemorg Matrix energy therapy.

INDEX

Wells, A., 247, 298
Wells, S., 17, 260–261, 298
Wernik, U., 255, 299
Westen, D., 241, 299
Whatmore, G. B., 246, 299
Whiteside, D., 19, 297
Whitney, R., 254, 294
Wilensky, M. S., 254, 297
Williams, J., 253, 286
Williams, J. M. G., 3, 19, 200, 295
Willis, A., 254, 294

Wilson, D., 6, 254, 257, 299
Wilson, S. A., 254, 299
Winnicott, D. W., 80, 104, 109, 273, 299
Wolpe, J., 2, 49, 299
Woolley-Hart, A., 267, 278

Yamanoto, C., 17, 264, 294
Young, J. E., 247, 299
Yovell, Y, 246, 300

Zangwill, W. M., 247, 299